# THE
# Whole Golf Book

### Little-Known Facts,
### Top Flight Tips,
### and Fascinating Lore
### for the Golf Addict

## JOHN MACINTYRE

SOURCEBOOKS, INC.
NAPERVILLE, ILLINOIS

Published by Sourcebooks, Inc.
P.O. Box 4410, Naperville, Illinois 60567-4410
(630) 961-3900
FAX: (630) 961-2168
www.sourcebooks.com

Library of Congress Cataloging-in-Publication Data

MacIntyre, John
  The whole golf book : little-known facts, top flight tips, and fascinating
lore for the golf addict / John MacIntyre.
      p. cm.
ISBN 1-4022-0354-3 (alk. paper)
1. Golf--Miscellanea. I. Title.

GV967.M227 2005
796.352--dc22

                                        2004029936

Printed and bound in Canada
WC 10 9 8 7 6 5 4 3 2 1

*Get well soon*

*2013*

## DEDICATION

*There are certain people*
*who help get you where you are going.*
*They are wives, family, friends, and agents.*
*To all of them who pitched in along*
*the road, this is for you.*

*Lots of Love*

*always*

*Garth*

# TABLE OF CONTENTS

# ACKNOWLEDGMENTS

I owe a large debt to my dedicated researcher, Nick Hatt. To call him a researcher is, perhaps, inadequate, because I see his handiwork all over the final manuscript. I would like to thank all of the people, tours, organizations, and corporations that took our phone calls and supplied us with data. I would also like to thank my agent, John Willig, for staying the course; my editor at Sourcebooks, Deb Werksman, for her invaluable guidance; and my family, for always being there. Cheers.

# INTRODUCTION

Just over a century ago, golf was largely unknown outside the borders of the United Kingdom. Today, the globe is dotted with more than 32,000 courses being played by upwards of 57 million players. From Greenland to Australia, from China to the U.S. and South America, people are slapping a little dimpled ball across the countryside.

This book is meant to celebrate the game of golf and those who helped make it what it is today. We celebrate it with profiles not only of great players like Nicklaus and Hagen, but also caddies like Bruce Edwards, and course designers like Donald Ross and Robert Trent Jones.

The greats of the game usually get their due, and they do here, as well. There are sections on the majors and on the great courses, but also there are intriguing sections about hackers like you and me. From presidents to golf and the business deal, from holes-in-one to America's love affair with the game, there is no other book with all of the disparate elements of golf brought together in one tribute.

Our objective with this book is to deliver to you an entertaining portrait of a game in all its dimensions. We had a lot of fun writing it. We hope you have a lot of fun reading it.

# Origin of a Game

The truth is that nobody knows the precise origin of the game of golf. Before it was a game, it was most certainly an activity engaged in by fisherman or shepherds to while away the hours. Countries as diverse as China, Ireland, the Netherlands, France, and of course, Scotland, all claim to be inventors of the game.

Most experts believe that golf is a combination of the elements of two sports that were played in continental Europe. It combined the implements used in the game "chole" and the rules of "jeu de mail," both games imported into Holland from France and Belgium.

The origin of the name "golf" can be traced to be the Dutch word "kolf," which means "club." The Scots of the late fourteenth or early fifteenth century corrupted the term to become "goff' or "gouff." It was only in the sixteenth century it became what we know today as "golf."

Why the relationship between the Dutch and the Scots? Economics, of course. There was a very vibrant trade between the two, especially from the fourteenth through seventeenth centuries. Many scholars believe it was the Dutch game of "kolf," played as it was with a stick and ball on frozen canals, that was brought to Scotland by Dutch sailors, where it was eventually adapted to the linksland and became the game we know today.

The game of golf in Scotland is at least six hundred years old and there is evidence that golf was played at St. Andrews in Scotland before the founding of the university there in 1411.

Fishermen, shepherds, and later royalty found Scotland's abundant linksland with its crisp turf and natural hazards perfectly suited to this new game. When King James IV took up the new game in the mid-1400s, he gave it the royal stamp of approval. The game did not spread to England until 1864 and not to North America until 1873. Today the game is played by 57 million people on more than 32,000 golf courses worldwide.

## More, More, More

GOLFERS WILL FOREVER be looking for secrets to getting more distance out of their shots. One of the tricks of the trade some professionals use is to keep their right knee (opposite for lefties) pointed slightly inward on the backswing. It gives you greater coil and leg drive.

# Timeline: First Four Centuries

**1353** First recorded reference to "chole," the probable antecedent of golf. It is a derivative of hockey played in Flanders (Belgium).

**1457** First of three references to the game of "gouf" are found in the Acts of Parliament. Golf and football are banned because they are taking too much time away from archery practice and military training.

**1502** Ban on golf is lifted. King James IV becomes the first recorded golfer to buy clubs and balls.

**1553** Archbishop of St. Andrews issues a decree giving the local populace the right to play golf on the St. Andrews links.

**1567** Mary, Queen of Scots, accused of playing golf just two days after the murder of her husband.

**1592** Golf at Leith, Scotland, is forbidden because it interferes with Sunday worship.

**1589** Golf is banned in the Blackfriars Yard, Glasgow. Earliest reference to golf in the west of Scotland.

**1603** James I becomes the English king. He appoints a royal club-maker.

**1618** James I approves Sunday play…after worship, of course.

**1618** Invention of the feathery ball.

**1637** Boy is hanged in Banff, Scotland, for stealing golf balls.

**1641** King Charles I is playing golf at Leith when he learns of the Irish rebellion, marking the beginning of the English Civil War. He finishes his round.

**1642** John Dickson receives a license as ball-maker for Aberdeen, Scotland.

**1659** Golf is banned from the streets of Albany, New York—the first reference to golf in America.

**1682** In the first recorded international golf match, the Duke of York and John Paterstone of Scotland defeat two English noblemen in a match played on the links of Leith.

**1687** A book by Thomas Kincaid, *Thoughts on Golve*, contains the first references to how golf clubs are made.

**1691** St. Andrews is referred to in print as the "metropolis of golfing."

**1735** The Royal Burgess Golfing Society of Edinburgh is formed. It is still in existence today, making it the world's oldest golf club.

**1743** For the first time on record, golf equipment is shipped from Scotland to America.

**1744** John Rattray wins the first club competition for Honorable Company of Edinburgh Golfers' Silver Club.

## Taking Aim

WHEN PUTTING BEYOND 20 feet smart golfers are going for the putt, but they are going for it cautiously, and by that we mean they don't put themselves in danger of three-putting. The objective beyond 20 feet is to make, but if you miss you better be close.

# Old Tom Morris

Even those only remotely familiar with golf history may have heard of Old Tom Morris—such was the force of his personality. Old Tom grew up the son of a mail-delivery man, who later gave up delivering letters to begin caddying.

The decision didn't have much impact on the life of Tom's father, but it did have for the man who would eventually be called Old Tom Morris. He followed his father to the golf course at St. Andrews and began playing the game by the time he was ten.

He was originally slated to become a carpenter, but at sixteen an opportunity presented itself and he was apprenticed to feather-ball maker Allan Robertson, with whom he worked for twelve years until 1849, when the new gutta-percha ball (referred to as a "guttie") took away their livelihood.

Not only did Morris work with Robertson, but the two men also played in foursomes together (the main game at that time) and were never beaten from 1842 until Robertson's death in 1859. Rumor has it that the golfing public was desperate for a Robertson-Morris match to settle who was better, but Robertson declined probably with good reason.

After the introduction of the guttie, Morris went into business as a club and ball maker on his own, before moving to Prestwick to take up the job of greenkeeper there. In the first British Open he finished second, two strokes behind Willie Parks. He would compensate for the loss with victories in 1861 and 1862, and again in 1864 and 1867.

If all Old Tom Morris did was win the British Open four times, that would be enough to make the man a legend, but with Morris it didn't end there. In 1867, after repeated requests by the Royal and Ancient Golf Club of St. Andrews (R&A) to move back there as greenkeeper, he finally relented. From 1865 until his death in 1908, he was a fixture at St. Andrews. Golfers throughout the world would stop in and seek the understated Morris's opinions. Old Tom's clubmaking business was established in 1867 by the side of the 18th green of The Old Course and the business continued to run during his lifetime.

His skill as a greenkeeper led to work designing courses (for which he charged a pound a day, plus, he proudly said, expenses). Those courses are now some of the greatest courses in the British Isles. He is said to have spent more than thirty years making the green on the St. Andrews Old Course just perfect.

Old Tom Morris died in 1908 at age 86. He fractured his skull falling down the stairs in The New Club at St. Andrews. The funeral was one of the largest in St. Andrews' history, as people came to pay their respects to an extraordinary life.

## TIME CRUNCH

THIRTY MINUTES on the practice tee prior to your game may seem like a lot to ask, but not doing so may mean you spend more time in the woods looking for your ball. The practice tee not only warms up your muscles, it gives you the quiet time to go over your own personal checklist. Review your grip and stance and experiment with new things you are trying.

# 2

# Golf Equipment: Balls, Balls, Balls...

**N**early every change in the game of golf throughout the centuries has followed a change in the golf ball. Mind you, in the beginning folks weren't that imaginative; simply a piece of wood and a round rock batted around on an acre of farmland was sufficient. But as the game caught on, and especially as the nobility and gentry found it an acceptable and leisurely pastime, they demanded something a little more elaborate and fitting to knock about.

In 1618, the first manufactured ball was introduced to the game: the "feathery." It was simple, consisting of strips of leather stuffed with boiled goose or chicken feathers—only the finest materials. It didn't, of course, make much of a ball, never really being perfectly spherical and never really traveling in a straight line. But it made quite a scene after a few rounds when it either just fell apart or exploded. And if you're a rich squire out for an afternoon game, what does it matter? You can afford to have another ball handmade.

## The Guttie

Somehow the feathery lasted a good two and a half centuries, but the next incarnation for the golf ball would be hardened tree sap from the gutta-percha, a tree found mainly in Malaysia. Introduced to the game by British cleric Robert Adams Paterson in 1848, the "guttie" was made by heating the sap in hot water and molding it into a sphere by hand.

In time, manufacturers found they could pour the sap into

molds and produce a perfect guttie with standardized weights. Soon all manner of manufacturers entered the business, including most tire and rubber companies. Suddenly golf balls could be mass produced, and at a much reduced cost. Everyone, not just the rich, could now afford to buy balls. Golf became accessible to the masses.

## The Haskell

The guttie's reign came to an end at the turn of the century. A wealthy young American named Coburn Haskell, along with Goodrich Rubber company engineer Bertram Work, had the idea that a different kind of ball, made of rubber twine spun around a soft rubber core, and covered in gutta-percha, might give golfers distance and be more responsive, and thereby more controllable. The rubber core ball was patented in 1898 and commercially available by 1901.

In 1901 Walter Travis won the U.S. Amateur with a Haskell ball, and in the 1902 British Open Championship, Alexander Herd soundly trounced his opponents with one. Manufacturers went wild. A rubber ball could be manipulated in so many ways—different tensions of rubber twine, a core filled with water, you name it. One inventor even tried filling the core with tapioca to see what would happen. Players took advantage of the various balls, using different ones to counter the different hazards: a "floater" for courses with a lot of water traps, or a lighter ball on a longer course.

## Standardization

The R&A and the United States Golf Association (USGA) finally had to put their collective foot down and bring some standards to the game. Thus, in 1921 a conference was held and the weight of a standard golf ball was set to 1.62 ounces—a standard broken ten years later by the Americans. The British stuck to their guns for fifty-five years, but in 1987 they finally relented and adopted the heavier standard used in the U.S. The golf world had a universal standard at last.

## The Dimple

The next big advance for the golf ball was the applied use of aerodynamics and the manipulation of the dimple. Most golf balls today consist of two or three pieces: core and cover, or core, windings, and cover. Who knows where the golf ball is headed next? From rock to boiled goose feathers, hardened tree sap to rubber twine, one really can't predict what people will want to hit around a field with a stick in the future.

---

### Wind Tip

ALWAYS PLAY THE BALL against the wind no matter what the direction. How far against the wind? The answer to that you will only learn through practice and experience. Another factor to take into account is that a right-to-left wind puts a topspin on the ball, giving you an extra five to seven yards.

---

## Recipes for a Ball

### A Solid Beginning

In the 1400s, the first golf balls were made from solid wood.

### The Feathery

Stitch three or four pieces of leather together into a pouch, fill with boiled goose feathers, and allow to harden. Makes a solid pellet, good for a few rounds.

- A good worker could produce three or four featheries on a good day.
- Because of its intricate, handmade design, a feathery ball would cost $150 to $400 to produce today.
- The longest drive ever recorded with a feathery was 361 yards.

## The Guttie

Import sap from the gutta-percha tree in Malaysia, allow to harden, and cut into strips. Run under hot water and roll into sphere, or pour into molds and allow to harden again. Improves with age and abuse.
- Depending upon how much sap had been worn off, a guttie ball's weight ranged from 1.4 to 1.7 ounces.
- A dimple-patterned guttie in good condition today would have a value of $500.

## The Haskell

Wind rubber twine around a soft rubber ball. Cover with gutta-percha sap, and place in ball press to dimple surface.
- In 1900, the patent was filed on an automatic winding machine, allowing rubber balls to be mass-produced.

### THE SWING

THE FOCUS OF YOUR SWING is to strike the ball in a fluid arc that optimally uses as much club speed as is necessary to get to your target.

# *Oh, Balls*

- 144 million golf balls are sold annually in the U.S., according to Golf Datatech.
- 14 percent of golf course superintendents say that high-tech golf balls have played the biggest factor in improving scoring for touring professionals during the past ten years, according to a survey by the Golf Course Superintendents Association of America.

## ANOTHER FIRST

The first American-made golf ball, a guttie, was produced by A. G. Spalding and Bros. in 1898.

## We Need Standards

- 1.62 ounces is now the minimum allowed weight of a golf ball, according to the R&A and USGA.
- The minimum diameter required is 1.68 inches.
- It took the R&A and the USGA sixty-nine years to finally agree to the same standard, after the USGA broke ranks with the initial standards that were set in 1921.
- In 1983 the USGA required that a golf ball must fly the same distance and speed when it is hit, regardless of how it is placed on the tee.
- The maximum initial velocity at which a ball is allowed to travel when struck is 280 feet/second.

## A Revolution

- A golf ball will rotate at 3,600 revolutions per minute immediately after being struck by a wood or iron, according to the USGA.
- Immediately after being struck by a pitching wedge, a golf ball will rotate at 6,000 revolutions per minute.

## TWO-PIECE

- Spalding introduced the first solid-core (two-piece) ball, which has greater distance, in 1968.
- Titleist Pro VI, a solid-core ball, became the No. 1 non-wound golf ball in its first week on the PGA Tour in 2001.

## What Cute Dimples

When golfers found that a guttie that had been beaten up traveled straighter and farther than new, smooth ones, they began to wonder. The same held true for the rubber balls—hence, the beginning of bumps (and eventually dimples) on a golf ball to improve aerodynamics, which were eventually incorporated into the ball molds.

- The dimple pattern was first used in 1908.
- The most popular numbers of dimples found on golf balls, according to a Technical University of Budapest study, are 252, 286, and 332.
- A smooth golf ball will travel, on average, 130 yards.
- A dimpled golf ball will travel, on average, 270 yards.

## Guinness World Records

- On October 4, 1998, Don Athey of Bridgeport, Ohio, stacked nine golf balls vertically without the use of adhesives, setting the world record for the most golf balls ever stacked together.
- Ted Hoz of Baton Rouge, Louisiana, owns 69,384 golf balls, giving him the largest golf ball collection in the world. If laid out side by side, 69,384 golf balls would stretch for two miles.

## PATENT GRANTED

622834 is the patent number for the machine invented by Goodrich engineer John Gammeter. The machine replaced the

"Goodrich girls" who were initially hired to wind the rubber band around the Haskell ball. The 1899 invention has been called the single most important invention to revolutionize the game of golf.

## Boom

In 1906, Goodrich introduced a golf ball with a rubber core filled with compressed air. The "Pneu-matic" proved quite lively, but was also prone to explode in warm weather, often in a golfer's pocket.

## RUBBER HITS THE ROAD

A worldwide shortage of rubber during World War II created a shortage and huge price increase in golf balls. The U.S. government halted the manufacture of golf equipment for the duration of the war.

### Perfect Symmetry

IN 1980, THE USGA introduced the Symmetry Standard, banning balls such as the Polaris that correct themselves in flight.

## In The Drink

- 122,000 balls go into the water annually on the now famous 17th hole at Sawgrass in Ponte Vedra Beach, Florida.
- 3 balls per round played go into the "drink" on the 17th at Sawgrass.

## FLIGHT PATH

In 1976, the USGA instituted the Overall Distance Standard golf balls that fly more than 280 yards during a standard test are now banned.

## Iron Byron

The United States Golf Association keeps a close watch on ball manufacturers. Weight and size are all predetermined. No ball can go more than 250 feet per second and distance is measured by Iron Byron (named after the long-hitting Texan, Byron Nelson).

## More Balls

12,000 golf balls are used on the practice range at a U.S. Open.

## FEWER DIMPLES

- The solid-core Titleist Pro V1 took the pro tours by storm in 2000, becoming the first non-wound golf ball to gain wide acceptance among professional golfers. Wound balls all but disappeared from golf.
- The Pro V1X has 60 fewer dimples than the Pro V1.

## Nice Balls

$4,000 WILL BUY YOU a collection of golf balls signed by Masters' tournament champions, mounted in a shadow box with nameplates under each ball.

## The First Endorsement

In 1899, Harry Vardon, having just won his third British Open title, was offered an unprecedented 900 pounds (the British Open prize that year was 30 pounds) by Spalding to undertake a series of exhibition tours in America promoting Spalding's new gutta-percha ball, the Vardon Flyer. Exhibitions such as these by golf manufacturers served to introduce the game to masses of new players.

## Did You Know?

- Did you know that golf balls were first painted white in an attempt to cover up the dark-colored sap of the guttie balls?
- Did you know that Titleist golf equipment began in 1932 in a dentist's office? Dr. Phil Young, a good amateur golfer, was frustrated by the erratic performance of the golf balls he used. He x-rayed them in his office and found centers that were of varying size and not always round. He set out to remedy the problem.

## The Grip

How important is the grip? Professionals consistently agree that even if you have a beautiful swing that makes you the envy of your friends, your abilities will be severely hampered if you don't have the right grip. There are three grips: the Vardon grip, named after British legend Harry Vardon, the baseball grip, and the interlocking grip. Find out which one works best for you.

---

## Ely Callaway

When most golfers turn sixty-two, their thoughts turn to spending more time on the links, not to building a revolutionary new golf club. That wasn't the case with Ely Callaway.

After careers in the textile industry and later as head of his own winery, Ely Callaway decided to turn a lifelong passion for the game of golf into a business. In 1982, he sold Callaway Vineyard and Winery and bought Hickory Stick USA Inc., a small firm that manufactured and sold putters and wedges.

Hickory Stick became Callaway Golf, and the company, which Ely Callaway helped finance with $400,000 of his retirement money, became the world's largest golf equipment manufacturer. In a little less than a decade, he introduced to the world something it had never seen before: Big Bertha, the huge oversized driver that Callaway named after a World War I cannon.

By 1997, Callaway's Great Big Bertha Titanium Driver was the number one driver in use on each of the five major golf tours. Where pros go, hackers will follow, and they did—with a vengeance. They bought and they bought, first Big Bertha and then its offspring Great Big Bertha and Biggest Big Bertha. The Callaway Golf Company has now sold in excess of $5 billion in clubs worldwide.

Although he was careful not to promise the weekend duffers that using one of his clubs would save them strokes over the course of a round, the word was out to yardage-hungry golfers that they, too, could land one past the 250-yard marker.

The Callaway Golf Company wasn't as successful with Big Bertha's grandchildren, such as the ERC II, another driver with an even larger sweet spot. This time Callaway ended up in a fight with the United States Golf Association, which banned the use of the ERC II, saying it didn't comply with rules limiting a spring-like effect.

## DIFFERENT STROKES

Experienced golfers obviously have more options than their inexperienced counterparts. One of those options is choosing a different club from in close. The pitching wedge, 9-iron, and 8-iron may all get you there, but they do so in different ways. One will stop dead, others will run a bit more. Choose the one that works best for you.

# 3

# Golf Clubs

**W**ith so much energy expended to find the perfect ball, is it any surprise that equal amounts of energy should be spent finding the perfect stick? The first of the contrived clubs began arriving on the scene as early as the 1600s. The clubheads were made from tough woods like beech, holly, pear, and apple, and the shafts from ash or hazel. The cost to make the clubs was exorbitant even by today's standards, having the effect of reserving the sport largely for the gentry.

The introduction of the guttie ball in 1848 in many ways changed the way golf clubs were made. The ball was now made of hardened sap, and was much less supple than the feathery, which meant wooden clubs could and would break much more easily when hitting the ball.

Hickory, a supple and springy wood, had already replaced ash as the wood of choice for the shaft. Now persimmon would replace beech in the clubhead. The arrival of the guttie and later the Haskell ball excited such a revolution in club design that soon every manufacturer worth his salt was in on the act. Everything from spring-loaded to removable and adjustable clubheads began to arrive on the scene. In 1910, the R&A finally stepped in and banned any mechanical contrivances for the clubheads.

## Steel

The next revolution in the golf club design was triggered by the introduction of steel shafts. The first steel shaft was patented by blacksmith Thomas Horsburgh in 1893, but it wasn't until the 1930s that mass production became possible and with it matched sets of clubs, and clubs with numbers instead of names.

When Billy Burke won the 1931 U.S. Open using only steel-shafted golf clubs, the changeover quickly became complete. The USGA, after much deliberation, approved steel shafts in 1926 and was followed by the R&A in 1929.

## Onward and Upward

Steel is still in frequent use today in shafts, but since the end of World War II, new materials such as graphite and titanium have added yet more options for club manufacturers. In 1963, a new casting method for manufacturing clubheads was introduced, meaning that woods could now be mass-produced.

The graphite shaft was introduced in 1973. Taylor-Made was the first company to manufacture metal woods, but it was the competitor of Taylor-Made, Callaway, with its oversized driver, "Big Bertha," that stole the show, launching one of the most successful clubs in the history of the game. In keeping with the whole history of the golf club, all these modern modifications seek to give golfers one thing: an advantage, allowing them more distance, accuracy, and overall control—the perfect club.

## In The Beginning

- The first recorded purchase of golf equipment was made in 1502 by King James IV, from a bow-maker in Perth, Scotland.
- In 1603, William Mayne, also a bowmaker from Scotland, was commissioned as royal clubmaker (or cleekmaker, as they were then known) to James VI of Scotland shortly after his accession to the throne of England as James I.
- The first book of instructions on how to make golf clubs, *Thoughts on Golve* by Thomas Kincaid, appeared in 1687.

# Types of Clubs

## Clubs of the Feathery Period

Primarily clubs were wooden, with long, shallow heads resembling hockey sticks. Heads were made primarily at flat angles, from thorn, apple, pear, and beech wood, with ash or hazel shafts, both of which were glued and bound together with twine. Use of iron-headed clubs was rare, and they were only used to get the ball out of ruts and hazards.

### CLUBS (OFTEN CALLED LONGNOSES):

Long and Short Spoon
Baffy Spoon
Cleek of Iron
Track and Rut Irons (for getting out of just that)
Putter

## CLUBS OF THE GUTTIE PERIOD

Increasingly players made use of iron-headed clubs with hickory shafts. Wooden heads on clubs become thicker, giving rise to modern-shaped drivers, called "bulgers." There was also an increase in the use of angled lofts on both iron and wooden clubs.

| | | | |
|---|---|---|---|
| Bulger | 1-wood | Mashie Iron | 4-iron |
| Brassie | 2-wood | Mashie | 5-iron |
| Spoon | 3-wood | Spade Mashie | 6-iron |
| Cleek | 4-wood | Mashie Niblick | 7-iron |
| Driving Iron | 1-iron | Lofting Iron | 8-iron |
| Mid Iron | 2-iron | Niblick | 9-iron |
| Mid Mashie | 3-iron | Putter | Putter |

## Clubs of the Haskell Period

The 14-club rule was instituted by the USGA during this period, limiting the morass of clubs that a player could now have in his or her golf bag. Steel shafts were also increasingly used, opening up the golf market due to mass production. Grooves started being incorporated into the iron clubfaces, these were banned at first, but eventually adopted to give players more control and grip on the ball. Players began settling on the modern set of golf clubs, which were now, for the first time, matched sets.

## Modern Clubs

Graphite, titanium, aluminum, and thermoplastics are now used in golf shafts. Due to USGA and R&A golf-club standards, manufacturers now focus their energies on improving the materials and designs of existing types of clubs. Depending upon whether a player needs help gaining distance, accuracy, or overall control, different clubs can be suited to a player's needs.

## YA GOTTA HAVE STANDARDS

- 18 inches is the minimum length of all golf clubs required by the USGA.
- 48 inches is the maximum length of all clubs, except putters, that is allowed.

- 28.06 cubic inches is the maximum size of clubhead allowed.
- 0.02 inches is the maximum depth of a groove allowed on an iron clubhead.
- 0.035 inches is the maximum width of a groove allowed on an iron clubhead.

## Metal

- Johnny Farrell won the U.S. Open in 1928 using a metal-headed driver.
- Metal woods arrived on the scene in 1979.
- Mark Brooks won on the 1991 PGA Tour with Callaway's Big Bertha.
- Drivers with thin metal faces and a springlike effect were introduced in 1995. The Tour average driving distance improved 10 yards, to 270 yards.

## Buy or Rent

- The suggested cost for a set of golf clubs by the PGA to golf club manufacturers in 1922 was $3.00.
- Scotsman Robert Lockhart spent $2.00 to $2.50 per club when he ordered six clubs at the club shop at St. Andrew's golf course in Scotland to take with him to America, in the first recording of golf clubs to cross the Atlantic.
- Golfers spent $2.4 billion on equipment annually, according to U.S. Customs.
- 74,040 golf putters are sold in the U.S. each year, according to Golf Datatech.
- 355,740 irons are sold each year in the U.S.
- 159,730 woods are sold each year in the U.S.

## A Club in One Hand

*"We were all born with webbed feet
and a golf club in our hand here."*
—Old Tom Morris

## Are You Serious?

- 80 percent of golf equipment sales are by serious golfers—those who play an average of 67 rounds per year, according to a study by Golf Datatech.
- There are 7 to 8 million serious golfers in the U.S.
- 50 percent of serious golfers say they shop at an on- or off-course specialty shop more than once every two weeks.
- Golfsmith.com, eBay, tgw.com, and edwinwatts.com are ranked 1, 2, 3, and 4 as the websites most commonly used for golf equipment purchases by serious golfers.

### I'LL TAKE THE BABE

*"Give me golf clubs, fresh air, and a beautiful partner…
and you can keep the clubs and the fresh air."*
—Jack Benny

### Fits Like A Glove

- In 1963, the casting and mass production of clubheads was introduced, no longer making each club a custom fit.
- 99 percent of serious golfers surveyed by Golf Datatech are aware that golf clubs can be custom fit.
- 51 percent have had a custom fit at some time.

## Far and Wide

How far and wide your feet should be in your stance depends on two competing objectives. The wider they are apart, the more stability you have; the closer, the more control you have over your footwork. This is why your feet are widest apart when you strike your driver, and closest together when you use your wedges.

## PING

In 1969, ping inventor Karsten Solheim created perimeter-weighted irons (or cavity-backed irons), making them more forgiving.

## Wrong Club

*"In case of a thunderstorm, stand in the middle of the fairway and hold up a 1-iron. Not even God can hit a 1-iron."*
—Lee Trevino

## Sponsor Me

As golf became more and more a game for everyone, club makers began hiring prominent golfers to test and promote their materials. It was also an ideal way for early golfers to supplement their incomes from tournaments. Wilson Sporting Goods was the first to hire an advisory staff of prominent golfers, which included Babe Zaharias, Gene Sarazen, and Walter Hagen. It was the beginning of corporate sponsorships in golf.

## FAVORITE CLUBS

- 68 percent of golfers say the 8-iron is their favorite club, according to a survey by the InterContinental Hotels Group.
- 27 percent of golfers prefer a 3-wood most of all.

## I Missed Again, @!*?!@*!!

- 16 percent of golfers say they've broken a club in anger, according to the Golf Superintendents Association of America.

• 43 percent of golfers admit to having thrown a club at least once.

*"As a golf professional, I'll tell you the amount of flex you need in the shaft of your club. Remember, the more flex, the greater the strength you'll need to break it over your knee."*
*—David Wright*

• Countries in which golfers are most likely to have broken a club in anger, according to a survey by *Golf Digest*:
1. Australia
2. Canada
3. South Africa
4. Thailand
5. United States

## Not In the Same Round

*"Never break your putter and your driver in the same round or you're dead."*
*—Tommy Bolt*

## THE LOFT

The slope (or loft) of clubs has changed constantly over the years, but they tend to be:

| | | | |
|---|---|---|---|
| Putter | 0 degrees | 8-Iron | 39 degrees |
| Sand Wedge | 56 degrees | 7-Iron | 35 degrees |
| Pitching Wedge | 47 degrees | 6-Iron | 31 degrees |
| 9-Iron | 43 degrees | 5-Iron | 27 degrees |
| 4-Iron | 24 degrees | 5-Wood | 20 degrees |
| 3-Iron | 21 degrees | 3-Wood | 15 degrees |
| 7-Wood | 24 degrees | Driver (1-Wood) | 10 degrees |

## A Steel

- Steel-shafted clubs were first advertised in 1891.
- The Currie Metal Wood, a metal-headed driver, was patented in Britain in 1891.

## Teed Off

The golf tee was invented by George F. Grant, an African American, in 1899. The patent office gave him a trademark on his invention of the tee, but he never marketed it. He shared some with friends and playing partners, but most he kept at home. He died in 1910 without accumulating much wealth from the invention, leaving those who followed him to amass fortunes from the golf tee.

## PUTTER BAN

IN 1904, WALTER J. TRAVIS won the British Amateur at Royal St. George's, the first American ever to do so. He won using Schenectady center-shafted putter, later banned by the Royal and Ancient.

## Last of the Hickory

- In 1936, Johnny Fischer became the last golfer to win a major championship (the U.S. Amateur) with hickory-shafted clubs.
- In 1979, Taylor Made introduced the first commercially accepted metal woods.

## In the Groove

- The first grooved-faced irons were invented in 1902.
- Deep-grooved irons were banned by both the USGA and the R&A in 1925.

## Not in the Groove

Square-grooved clubs such as the PING Eye2 irons were banned in 1987 by the USGA, which claimed that tests show the clubs give an unfair competitive advantage. In 1989, the PGA Tour also banned the clubs.

Karsten Manufacturing, maker of the grooved clubs, launched a lawsuit against both the USGA and the PGA Tour to have the ban rescinded, eventually winning a temporary injunction. Both organizations dropped the ban, while Karsten acknowledged the right of the organizations to regulate equipment and pledged to make modifications to future designs.

## Graphite Arrival

The graphite shaft was invented in 1975.

## Location, Location

The PGA Merchandise Show is the single largest tenant of the Orange County Convention Center in Orlando. It was first held in 1954 in a parking lot in Dunedin, Florida. Salesmen worked the show out of the trunks of their cars. The show went on to become one of the main events of the golfing year, with:

- 500,000 square feet of exhibit space.
- 4 exhibit days.
- 45,000 attendees.

## Musical What?

- Dr. Yoshiro Nakamats patented 3,000 inventions, including a musical golf putter.
- Dr. Nakamats has won the grand prize at the International Exposition of Inventors in New York sixteen times.

## Made in China

Twenty-five percent annual growth is projected the golf-club market in India and China over the next five years, according to a survey by the research firm E-Composites.

## Ya Wanna Be In…

IN 1930, SPALDING ASSOCIATED itself with Grand Slam winner Bobby Jones to produce one of the first sets of matched clubs (hickory shafts).

## QUALITY ASSURANCE

In 1953, golfer Ben Hogan set out to make the finest golf clubs available. In 1954, just as his company was ready to make their first shipment of clubs, Hogan inspected them and, finding that they didn't meet his standards, ordered $100,000 worth of merchandise destroyed, and started again.

## The Slice

The most common error in ball striking by new golfers is the slice. The cause of the slice is obvious: cutting across the ball from outside in, instead of inside out. There are any number of possible causes, but the most common are your stance and grip. Check those first. Other possible causes can be swaying, overturning, or overswinging.

## Did You Know?

- Did you know that the sand wedge was developed by Gene Sarazen, who, while flying one day, noticed that lowering a plane's tail flaps made the nose rise? He applied the same principle to golf by lowering the tail of the club and bellowing the leading edge to help it cut through the sand and thrust the ball up into the air. He debuted the club at the 1932 British Open and won handily, playing superbly from the sand. In 1934 Wilson produced Sarazen's sand wedge, the R99.

- Did you know that the first American-made golf club was made in 1894, using a drop forge technique, by A. G. Spalding and Bros.?
- Did you know that before the invention of golf tees, golfers pinched together some sand to elevate their ball to tee for the next hole?
- Did you know that golfing great Harry Vardon (only person to win six British Opens) carried only ten clubs in his bag, two of which were drivers?
- Did you know that when Banc One Capital Partners' CEO John Farmer proposed taking a venture capital position in the Callaway Golf Company, he was almost laughed out of the investment committee? After all, would golfers really take to a club with the improbable name of Big Bertha? You bet they did—Callaway Golf became one of the best investments ever made by Banc One Capital Partners.
- Did you know that one of the first alternatives to teeing up on a piece of sand was to use a disposable teacup, bringing, of course, a whole new meaning to the area known as the tee box?
- Did you know that in 1942 the U.S. government halted the manufacture of all golf equipment—most notably golf balls—for the duration of the war due to a worldwide shortage of rubber, which was a vital military resource at the time?

## Spraying

If your shots are straying off-target but without any consistency, check your grip and stance. Try to make sure that your head stays behind the ball through impact and don't let your legs get too far ahead of your arms and hands in the downswing.

# Timeline: Golf Takes Root

**1744** The Gentleman Golfers of Leith (later renamed the Honorable Company of Edinburgh Golfers) produces the first known written rules of golf.

**1754** The St. Andrews Society of Golfers (later to become known as the Royal and Ancient Golf Club of St. Andrews) is formed.

**1754** St. Andrews men set up Silver Cup contest.

**1759** St. Andrews men change Silver Cup knockout from match play to stroke play.

**1764** St. Andrews converts its links from 22 holes in length to 18 holes in length.

**1766** Foundation of first club in England.

**1767** James Durham plays the St. Andrews's links in 94 strokes, a record that will stand for 86 years.

**1786** First known appearance of a golf club in the U.S.

**1786** The South Carolina Golf Club is founded in Charleston. (The club disbands twenty-five years later.)

**1810** First known women's tournament held at Musselburgh, Scotland.

**1819** Earliest known reference to a professional tournament. It's an event played, of course, at St. Andrews.

**1820** First golf course outside of Britain is opened in Bangalore, India.

**1826** Hickory imported from America is used to make golf shafts.

**1832** Mowers made specifically for trimming golf-course grass are manufactured, but many courses still use sheep to keep the grass from getting high.

**1834** "Royal and Ancient" title is bestowed on St. Andrews Club.

**1848** Gutta-percha ball is introduced.

**1856** Mainland Europe's first club is founded at Pau, France.

**1857** Inter-Club foursome's first Championship Meeting is suggested by Prestwick; won by Blackheath.

**1858** St. Andrews issues new rules for its members. Rule 1 states, "One round of the Links or 18 holes is reckoned a match unless otherwise stipulated." This encourages other courses to convert or be built to 18 holes in length.

**1858** Allan Robertson shoots 79 on the Old Course at St. Andrews, becoming the first person to break 80 on the course.

**1859** Death of Allan Robertson, leading professional of his time.

**1860** Willie Park wins the first British Open Golf Championship, played at Prestwick Golf Club.

**1861** Old Tom Morris wins second British Open as championship allows amateurs to compete.

**1870** Young Tom Morris wins his third British Open in a row and retains the championship belt for life.

**1872** Silver claret jug is offered by Prestwick, St. Andrews, and Honorable Company of Edinburgh Golfers as perpetual trophy for the British Open.

**1873** Royal Montreal is the first golf club formed in Canada (at present it is the oldest continuously operating golf club in North America).

**1888** Formation of St. Andrews Club, Yonkers, New York. Nicknamed the "Apple Tree Gang."

**1891** R&A rule hole width to be 4-1/2 inches, minimum 4 inches deep.

**1893** Ladies' Golf Union is founded in Britain. Lady Margaret Scott wins first championship.

**1894** J. H. Taylor is the first English pro to win the British Open. It is played in England for the first time, at Royal St. George's, Sandwich.

**1894** United States Golf Association (USGA) is formed.

**1895** USGA hosts its first Amateur Championship, which is won by Charles MacDonald. The U.S. Open is won by Horace Rawlins, an English pro, and the Women's Amateur is won by Mrs. Charles Brown.

**1896** Harry Vardon wins his first British Open.

**1897** The first NCAA golf championship is held.

**1898** Coburn Haskell patents a golf ball with gutta-percha cover over rubber bands, which are wound under tension around the core.

## ROUTINE

ALMOST ALL PROFESSIONALS TODAY have a checklist they go through before they take their swing. What you want out of your routine is repeatability, and the best way to do that is to have a series of checks you repeat until they become ingrained.

# Francis Ouimet

When Francis Ouimet beat two great British professionals, Harry Vardon and Ted Ray, in a play-off in 1913, it shocked the golf world. The Brookline, Massachusetts–born Ouimet only entered the tournament because the organizers were worried there were not enough competitors.

It was a three-way tie after regulation, and by all rights the 20-year-old Ouimet should have cracked under the pressure, but he beat both Ray and Vardon by five strokes. The victory was a signal of the changing of the guard. It was a shift in the balance of power from Britain to the U.S., but it was also a shift from the country club to the caddyshack.

Kids like Ouimet (and later Sarazen) were proof that money wasn't a necessary prerequisite to playing a fine game of golf. Ouimet had been a scavenger for balls at the Brookline club near his home. He practiced on a homemade three-hole course in his backyard, and sometimes sneaked onto the Country Club's fairways to practice in the early morning hours. At nine years old, Ouimet began caddying.

Rumor had it that when he did enter the U.S. Open it was as much to see the famous swing of Harry Vardon as anything else. When it looked as though Ouimet's prospects at the Open might be better than anticipated, he was offered an experienced member as his caddy. He turned it down, sticking with 10-year-old Eddie Lowery.

The year after his victory at the U.S. Open, Ouimet won the U.S. Amateur and won it again in 1931, when everyone had thought

Ouimet's skills on the golf course had left him. Ouimet's good nature and modesty made him a candidate for and then eventually the choice of the first American captain of the Royal and Ancient in St. Andrews.

## Easy Does It

MANY GOLFERS THINK they need the death grip to chip in and around the green. Wrong. This is a feel shot. Relax your grip. Loosen your wrists and arms and practice a rhythmic swing.

### 4

## Coming to America

Although there are references to golf in America as early as 1659, the American love affair with golf didn't begin until well into the twentieth century. The War of 1812 against Britain didn't exactly engender affection for any of its sports.

The first real stab at a golf course was taken in 1888 in Yonkers, New York. Shinnecock Hills on Eastern Long Island was the first 9-holer in 1891, but the honor of the first 18-hole course went to the Chicago Golf Club, built in 1893. It was a quiet beginning for golf in America, but in 1894 the United States Golf Association formed and held the first U.S. Open and U.S. Amateur.

From this small grab bag of courses, golf took off like a lightning bolt and by century's end there were upwards of a thousand courses. (In fact, there were more courses in the U.S. than there were in Britain.) This was conspicuous-consumption America, and there were few better places to show that one was a man of leisure and wealth than the golf course.

As the railroad shuffled passengers from east to west and north to south, they shuffled with them a demand for ever-more golf courses, from one thousand courses at the turn of the nineteenth century, jumping to five thousand at the beginning of 1940.

Still, golf was considered an elitist sport, and until 1962 there were more private than public clubs in America. Golfers like Sarazen, Hogan, Nelson, and later Palmer did much to introduce the sport to the common man. All had come from modest beginnings and were former caddies, who helped remove the snooty country-club label many associated with golf.

The arrival of television in the 1960s elevated golf to a new level, and by 1970 the U.S. had surpassed ten thousand golf courses with no end in sight. Although golf struggled with race issues well into the early 1990s, by the time Tiger Woods arrived on the professional scene in 1996, any bigoted residue from other eras had largely been put to bed.

America today has more than sixteen thousand golf courses, almost half of the world's total. One in twelve Americans has played the game. It may have taken America a little longer than other countries to warm to the sport, but it appears today that golf is now one of America's favorite pastimes.

## ≡ *Golf in America* ≡

### That Clothing

*"Although golf was originally restricted to wealthy, overweight protestants, today it's open to anybody who owns hideous clothing."*
—Dave Barry

# Golfers

- There are 36.7 million golfers in the U.S., according to the National Golf Foundation, and they play 500 million rounds annually.

## HOME ON THE RANGE

- 600 million range balls are hit in the U.S. annually, according to the Golf Research Group.

---

### Thou Shalt

*"I just hope I do not have to explain all the times
I have used his name in vain when I get up there."*
—Bob Hope

---

## Course Figures

- 22 percent of golfers regularly score better than 90 for 18 holes on a regulation length course, according to the National Golf Foundation.
- 97 is the average 18-hole score on a full-size course for men.
- 114 is the average score for women.
- 6 percent of men regularly break 80.
- 1 percent of women do.

## HANDICAP

- 20 percent of all golfers maintain a handicap, according to the National Golf Foundation.
- The average handicap is 19–20.

## 3,000 Hits

*"It took me seventeen years to get 3,000 hits in baseball.
I did it in one afternoon on the golf course."*
*—Hank Aaron*

## Cool

- 35 percent of golfers say that they will play golf in temperatures no lower than 40 degrees, according to a *Golf* poll.
- 28 percent say they will play golf in temperatures no lower than 30 degrees.
- 20 percent say they'd play even if hell froze over.

## Literary Golf

*"Golf is a good walk spoiled." —Mark Twain*

*"The game of golf would lose a great deal
if croquet mallets and billiard cues were allowed
on the putting green."*
*—Ernest Hemingway*

## Honey

- 4 percent of male golfers say their favorite golfing partner is their spouse, according to a survey conducted for *Golf Digest Women*.
- 24 percent of female golfers say their favorite golfing partner is their spouse.

## Yogi-ism

*"Ninety percent of putts that are short don't go in."*
*—Yogi Berra*

## Father's Day

- Birthdays are the number-one occasion for giving golf gifts, apart from the Christmas/Hanukkah holiday season, according to the National Golf Foundation.
- Father's Day is number two.

## Where's Dad?

*"The place of the father in the modern suburban family is a very small one, particularly if he plays golf."*
*—Bertrand Russell*

## Swingers

*"The golf swing is like a suitcase into which we are trying to pack one too many things." —John Updike*

## PLAYING TO WIN

- 19 percent of golfers say that their only concern when playing is how well they play, according to a National Golf Foundation/ *USA Today* survey.
- 67 percent say they are more concerned with how well they play than with winning.
- 39 percent say that they have thrown or slammed equipment, but do not anymore.
- 29 percent say they occasionally throw/slam equipment.
- 1 percent say they frequently throw or slam equipment when angry.

## Who's That On The Green?

*"Is my friend in the bunker or is the bastard on the green?"*
*—Anonymous*

## Avid

- 23 percent of golfers in the U.S. play more than 25-plus rounds annually, according to the National Golf Foundation. They account for 63 percent of total spending on golf in the country.

## Just a Nudge

*"He who has the fastest cart...never has a bad lie."*
*—Unknown*

## GETTING A ROUND

Thirty-six dollars is the average cost of a weekend round of golf at an 18-hole municipal golf course in the U.S., including cart and green fee, according to the National Golf Foundation.

## Hooking

The cause of the hook is the opposite to that of a slice. Now you are cutting across the ball from outside in versus inside out for the slice. Again the probable causes are your grip and your stance. Other possible causes can be rolling your right hand over, a loose left hand, or hitting too quickly.

## Golf Travel

- Florida, South Carolina, North Carolina, California, and Arizona are ranked 1, 2, 3, 4, and 5 respectively as the most popular travel destinations for golfers, according to the National Golf Foundation.
- Golfers spend $26.1 billion a year on golf travel.

## MAKING FRIENDS

*"If you think it's hard to meet new people, try picking up the wrong golf ball."—Jack Lemmon*

## Sunny Day

The weather and the economy are the two things most likely to lead to a decrease in the number of rounds played, according to the National Golf Foundation.

## Gimme

- 65 percent of golfers routinely concede short putts in stroke play, according to a National Golf Foundation/*USA Today* "Golf In America" online survey of 800 respondents.
- 37 percent say that they like to take mulligans on the first tee.
- 8 percent think that amateur golfers should be able to carry as many clubs as they want.
- 46 percent say that all should abide by the 14-club limit.

> ## MINISTERIAL GOLF
>
> *"Golf courses are the best place to observe ministers,*
> *but none of them are above cheating a bit."*
> *—John D. Rockefeller*

## Sneaky

- 14 percent of golfers say they've snuck onto a golf course at some point without paying.

## Minority Report

- 14.5 percent of white people living in the U.S. currently play golf, according to the "Minority Golf Participation in the U.S." report.
- 13.7 percent of Asian Americans play.
- 7 percent of African Americans play.
- 5.4 percent of Hispanic Americans play.

## TOUGH COURSE

*"Winged Foot has the toughest 18 finishing holes in golf."*
*—Dave Marr*

### Yippee!

- 20 percent of golfers admit to imbibing before a game in an attempt to prevent "yips," or small hand-jerking motions which can occur when a golfer swings, subsequently throwing off their swing.
- 22 percent of golfers who suffer from yips describe their symptoms in a way that indicates it is a psychological problem, according to a survey of seventy-two yipping golfers by the Mayo Clinic in Rochester, Minnesota.

### Golf, The Industry

- Golf contributes $13.4 billion to the hospitality/tourism industry annually, according to a report by SRI International.
- The game contributes $9.9 billion to the real-estate industry annually.

### Carts

- 66 percent of all 18-hole rounds are played with golf carts, according to the National Golf Foundation.

### Golf Crazy

Japan, the U.S., the U.K., South Korea, and Germany are ranked 1, 2, 3, 4, and 5 respectively as the countries with the highest number of active adults who intend to take up golf within the next year, according to a survey by Ipsos-Reid.

# Calorie Burn

- A 160-pound man burns an average of 2.8 calories per minute while playing golf using a golf cart to get around, according to the American Council on Exercise.
- A 160-pound man burns an average of 6.2 calories per minute playing golf walking around the course, pulling his clubs with him.
- 8.7 is the average number of calories that same man would burn per minute if just going for a walk.
- 1.5 is the average number of calories that same man would burn per minute if just sitting in one spot.

## THANK GOD

*"The only time my prayers are never answered*
*is on the golf course."*
—Billy Graham

---

## Head Down

WE KNOW THIS is close to being Rule Number One, but still many golfers refuse to pay attention to it. You keep your head down for a reason…to keep your eye on the ball. Surely you can wait that split second to see the splendor of your shot.

---

## Arnold Palmer

Arnold Palmer became the first jet-set golfer of the modern era. He was the first tour professional to win a million dollars in official prize money and the first to fly in his own private jet to tournaments and events. Throughout it all, however, this son of a Pennsylvania steel-mill worker (and later a club pro) remained true to his roots—and the crowds loved him for it.

During the late 1950s and early 1960s, Palmer was golf. Palmer fans began to accumulate in such large numbers that they became known simply as "Arnie's army." Palmer's rise also had the good fortune to coincide with television, and in particular with golf on television, making even armchair golfers part of Arnie's army.

Palmer's rise to fame began with his victory in the U.S. Amateur in 1954, after which he turned professional just a few months later. In 1955, he won his first professional tournament and the golf world was on notice.

In total, Palmer would go on to win 92 championships in his professional career, 61 of those victories coming on the U.S. PGA Tour. Seven of Palmer's victories came in what the golfing world considers the four major professional championships.

He won the Masters Tournament four times, the U.S. Open once (he placed second four other times), and the British Open twice. In the only other major he didn't capture, the PGA Championship, he finished second three times. In the 1960s, he was named Athlete of the Decade in an Associated Press poll.

Palmer's golf style was known for its daring. There wasn't a shot he wouldn't attempt, even when it meant possible danger. Often that meant even more spectacular recoveries. His ability to lay it on the line in the most important events meant every golfer of his era always looked for the name Palmer on the leaderboard.

His most spectacular comebacks not surprisingly came in the majors. In the 1960 Masters with Ken Venturi already in the clubhouse being interviewed as the winner, Palmer birdied out the last three holes to claim victory. In his U.S. Open victory, he was seven strokes behind entering the final round.

Palmer also single-handedly restored international luster to an ailing British Open. In 1960, he was hoping to follow in the footsteps of Ben Hogan, who until that time was the only player to capture the Masters and two Opens in a single season. It was not to be (although Palmer won the British Open in 1961 and 1962) however; Palmer came in second.

Besides the game of golf, Palmer is also known as one of the most astute businessmen ever to have played the sport. Even into the Tiger Woods era, Palmer was still giving current era players a run for the largest endorsements and other revenue.

It is a testimony to the man that after Palmer's time at the top of the golf game ended, Arnie's army just continued to grow. It grew because of the game, of course, but also because of the man behind it.

## Straight Shooter

To hit your ball straight, you must recognize the natural arc of your swing. The plane of your swing must be the same before and after impact. How steep or flat your plane determines how high your ball will fly.

# 5

# Black and White

The issue of race has plagued golf in America since the second U.S. Open at Shinnecock Hills in 1896. White golfers threatened to pull out of the tournament if two players from the club, one a black caddy named John Shippen and the other a full-blooded Shinnecock named Oscar Bunn, were allowed to play. To United States Golf Association (USGA) president Theodore Havemeyer's credit, he told the white golfers they could walk. The tournament was played anyway.

When the U.S. Professional Golf Association (PGA) formed in 1916, they dealt black golfers a blow that would not be remedied for half a century. They inserted a pernicious clause in their constitution stating that non-Caucasians could not be members. The likelihood of black golfers making it into the plush clubhouses of golf's early years was difficult enough, but this one-sentence clause was a death knell for black professional golf.

The saddest result is that much of black golfing history has been largely ignored, but thankfully some of it survives, such as players like John Dendy who made his own clubs and later went on to win the Southern Open three times. To give great black golfers some place to play, black golfers formed United Golfers Association (UGA) in 1925. If it was tough financially for the white PGA Tour, it was impossible for the UGA.

## The UGA

By the 1940s, the UGA had become a proving ground for top African American golfing talent such as Zeke Hartsfield, Bill Spiller, Teddy Rhodes, Charlie Sifford, and Lee Elder. Inevitably, great black golfers like Spiller, Rhodes, and Sifford developed great friendships with professional white players, some of whom, like the great Jimmy Demaret, argued forcibly for their inclusion on the white-only PGA Tour.

Three tournaments allowed black players to compete in 1948—they were the Canadian Open, the Tam O'Shanter All-American in Chicago, and the Los Angeles Open. There simply was no money to be made by black players. Even the great Billy Spiller had to make ends meet by caddying. The black golfing world can be glad that he did.

When the man he was caddying for asked him why he didn't play anymore, Spiller told him about the clause in the PGA constitution. The man told him to write California Attorney General Stanley Mosk, which he did. Mosk listened and quickly saw to it that California passed a statute making it illegal to stage PGA tournaments on public courses in California from which blacks were excluded.

## ≣ *Finally* ≣

Other states threatened to follow suit, and soon tournaments—and with them their large purses—were in very real jeopardy of being lost, so in 1961 the PGA of America took the only course available to it and abolished the almost 50-year-old clause. It was done quietly behind closed doors, but it was front-page news across the country.

This was not the end of discrimination, of course. Tournaments skirted the rules by changing tournaments previously known as "Opens" to "Invitationals" to exclude the black players. Even when golfers like Spiller, Pete Brown, and Charlie Sifford were free to enter and win tournaments on the tour, playing in the South was another matter. The heckling and abuse were so bad that Sifford had to withdraw from his first Greater Greensboro Open.

A big door was opened when Lee Elder became the first black golfer to play at the Masters in 1975. The door was kicked down completely at Shoal Creek Country Club in Alabama in 1990.

## ≋ *Shoal Creek* ≋

Shoal Creek founder Hall Thompson got called out in a local newspaper article, proclaiming that the club didn't discriminate in any area other than blacks. It was enough to have ABC threaten to pull its television coverage, forcing the PGA to threaten to pull the PGA Championship.

This time the U.S. Golf Association and PGA stepped up, issuing a warning to all other clubs that may have clung to the wink and a nod view that discrimination policies were acceptable. The PGA declaration stated that no club that discriminated on the basis of race, religion, sex, or national origin would be eligible to host PGA tournaments or events.

Two weeks before the event, the Shoal Creek Country Club named its first black member, Louis Willie, an Alabama businessman. Five years later Stanford University was in Shoal Creek to claim victory in the Jerry Pate National Intercollegiate tournament. Stanford was led by a young rookie by the name of Tiger Woods.

---

### THE ACTOR TIP

IT'S A MANTRA FOR ACTORS, and now golfers say it: "Stay in the moment." Don't think of your next shot, your last shot, or even your score. What counts for you is the here and now. As the great Bobby Jones said, the best games of golf are played between the ears.

# 6

# Golf-Course Architecture

*"The laying out of a golf course
is by no means a simple task."*
—Willie Park, Jr. (1896)

**A**ll we know about the original game of golf is that the game involved a player, a stick or club, and a pebble or something resembling what today we call a ball. It was played on barren land, land considered not good for much except grazing sheep, and even they found the grasses there a tough way to earn their keep.

Bunkers were created when the sheep would huddle together on the side of bumps and ridges and rub themselves into sandy soil to escape the wind. A hole was placed at some indeterminate distance from the previous one…and that, ladies and gentlemen, was the first golf course. The only reason golf courses came to have 18 holes was that the Royal and Ancient Golf Club at St. Andrew's shaved two holes off their 20-hole course and decreed in 1854 that 18 holes was to be considered a match. All other clubs followed suit.

From the fifteenth to the nineteenth century, golf was simply played on whatever land was available. It was merely a stroke of luck that some of the great courses, especially those in Scotland, were played on linksland, or land not suitable for anything else. That they just happened to hug the rugged coastline is one of the great good fortunes still enjoyed by golfers today.

# ⅀ *Rising Popularity* ⅀

Ironically enough, what changed golf and golf courses most was the introduction of a ball...the gutta-percha ball in the 1880s, to be precise. Until then, golfers had used a feathery, which consisted of a horse- or bull-hide cover stuffed with boiled goose feathers. They were expensive to make and easily damaged, and as a result very few people could afford them.

The guttie by contrast was made from rubber, which could be heated and formed into a ball. Not only was it more reliable, more accurate, and more durable, it was less expensive. In one technological leap, the game of golf became more accessible to the common man and woman.

New players meant a new demand for golf courses, and with that demand came questions that had largely been ignored by the golf industry until that point. Even questions like what shape golf courses should take were new. For answers to these questions, people turned, logically enough, to the great players. The problem was that skill at playing golf didn't always translate into skill at creating golf courses.

Scots like Old Tom Morris, Willie Park, and Willie and Tommy Dunn were the first golfers of note to make a mark in golf-course design. Most of their contributions though had to do with natural-shaped flat greens and the use of fairway bunkers taking rectangular form. More daring was Willie Park at Sunningdale outside London. The course he designed there included 103 bunkers, tree-lined fairways with pine, birch, and oak culminating in the famous 18th hole, and the final green below the famous Sunningdale Oak Tree.

# ⅀ *Golden Age* ⅀

The 1920s are largely considered the golden era of golf-course design. For the first time, golf-course architects designed their courses not as playing fields, but as landscapes. The purpose was to challenge and excite the participant physically and emotionally. Courses designed by an American and two Scots—A. W. Tillinghast (Baltusrol, Winged Foot), Alexander MacKenzie (Cypress Point, Augusta National), and Donald Ross (Seminole, Pinehurst)—have stood the test of time so well because of the remarkable imagination of the designers.

In the 1930s and '40s, no name was more synonymous with golf-course architecture than that of Robert Trent Jones. Immediately after graduating from Cornell in 1930, Jones became a partner with golf architect Stanley Thompson. Jones's design philosophy was that every hole should be a hard par, but an easy bogey. He followed that philosophy throughout his career—a career that would last until the 1990s and would include more than 450 courses.

For Jones and architects of his era, the demand for more golf courses seemed to be insatiable. (From 1945–1970, the number of golf courses in the U.S. more than doubled from five thousand to over eleven thousand.) The huge changes in technology meant that now golf courses could be built anywhere. And they were. Elaborate water systems, new construction techniques, and better machinery made them possible. From the desert to the arctic, there seemed no place safe from the advance of golf. The only impediment to the location of a golf course was money, something not in short supply in the postwar boom years.

## A Star Is Born

With the 1950s and 1960s came television. Television not only made new stars out of golf professionals like Arnold Palmer, it made stars out of the old courses and the men who designed them. Shell's *Wonderful World of Golf* began its broadcasts with architects describing the course and the different holes on it. The age of the architect as star was upon us.

New designers such as George Cobb, Joe Finger, Dick Wilson, Joe Lee, Tom Doak, and George Fazio emerged with a distinctly American style that made golf courses long and beautiful. Designer Peter Dye would go on to inspire a new generation of golf-course architects to revisit the old clubs in Scotland and in so doing understand the importance and role of the natural world. At Harbor Town, South Carolina (which Dye built in 1969), the course is a tight layout, with flat, simple, elegant little greens to match. The course was soon emulated around the country and around the world.

The great golfers like Nicklaus, Gary Player, Tony Jacklin, Tom Weiskoff, Palmer, Norman, and many others have made significant contributions to golf-course design around the world. They've added a great player's eye for detail and challenge. New architects have refocused their sights again on the principles of the natural world. It was partly a natural swing of the pendulum, but it also was being forced by an emerging environmental awareness that has forced the golf industry to look at land use and pollution problems that at one time were accepted practices at most golf courses.

## AT THE BEACH

DON'T PANIC WHEN you land in the sand. It happens to Tiger Woods and it'll happen to you. Play your ball off your left heel, with an open stance and your heels no more than six inches apart. The right foot is at a right angle to the target and your left foot should be turned out 45 degrees.

# Principles of Design

When the Inverness Club in Toledo, Ohio, began preparing to host the U.S. Open in 1920, organizers found it impossible to find impartial and authoritative information about how to properly tend to the turf. Their inquiries helped spur the USGA and the U.S. Department of Agriculture to collaborate in developing a wealth of scientific information for just those purposes. This ultimately led to the formation of the USGA Green Section later that year, which still exists today as the premier agency for providing information about golf-course development to the U.S. golfing industry.

It also led to the establishment of the National Association of Greenskeepers of America, in 1926, which first met in Toledo. Over the years it has sponsored numerous conferences and courses on matters of course design and maintenance, helping to further the science of course design.

Turf design today has become a science in itself, complete with its own specialists, and is a recognized area of study and research in many universities and laboratories. While all courses are unique, some main principles of golf course design do exist. The most important principle is that they should be designed to challenge, not to punish. Fairway bunkers and hazards should be situated to reward good play.

# In The Bunker

The USGA has a list of several recommendations for sand selection of bunkers. When selecting sand for a bunker, particle size, particle shape, penetrometer value, crusting potential, chemical reaction (pH), hardness, color, infiltration rate, and overall playing quality should be considered.

Course designers are encouraged to keep 4 to 6 inches of sand at the base of the bunker, and 2 to 4 inches across sloped bunker faces. Greenkeepers are also encouraged to keep the margins of the bunker clearly defined, so it's easy to determine whether a ball lies in the bunker or not. This alone is enough to constitute a day's work—and then some!

## On The Fairway

Perhaps one of the most tedious jobs is keeping the fairway grass mowed! And while different kinds of grass are always being developed for the golf course, the most common kind you'll find on the fairway is Kentucky bluegrass. The goal is to have a kind of grass that can stand being cut on a regular basis (about an inch) and is resilient to the abuse it receives from iron clubs.

## On The Green

The green, however, is perhaps the hardest area of all to keep in top shape. The challenge here is to have a type of grass that can stand being repeatedly cut short. Greens are usually kept at 1/8 to 1/10 of an inch high, so the grass here can't be of the kind that needs a lot of sun, since it has so little blade with which to catch the rays! To do that, some kind of creeping bentgrass is generally used here, which likes being kept short. Some courses even use it on the tee, where the grass is generally kept quite short, too.

An important development in green maintenance was the introduction of the Stimpmeter. This device, named after Edward S. Stimpson, measures the speed of putting greens. The Stimpmeter is a 36-inch aluminum bar with an extended V-shaped groove along its entire length. It also contains a ball-release notch that is designed to release a ball when the Stimpmeter is raised to an approximate 20-degree angle. The general range of Stimpmeter readings on U.S. golf courses is from 7 to 12 feet.

Under the right weather conditions, a healthy, vigorous, and well-prepared green can be maintained at a cutting height as low as 1/8 of an inch for short periods of times. Fast greens are very fragile, however, becoming susceptible to both diseases and pests.

---

## Bad Lies

WITH BAD LIES, forget distance and instead concentrate on good contact.

---

## Sidehill Lies

With sidehill lies, aim to the right of the target when the ball is above feet. Aim to the left of the target when the ball is below feet.

---

## Donald Ross

Born the son of a stonemason in Dornoch, Scotland, in 1872, Donald Ross worked during his early years as a carpenter. In the early 1890s the young carpenter, who would later become one of the most famous golf-course architects of his generation, had the good fortune to move to St. Andrews to work alongside the legendary Old Tom Morris.

Donald Ross was too ambitious to stay as an apprentice and left St. Andrews to become greenkeeper at Royal Dornoch. The land of opportunity was America, however, and legend has it that when Ross landed in Boston in 1899, he did so with two dollars in his pocket. There he quickly landed a job as greenkeeper at Oakley Country Club in Watertown, Massachusetts, greatly improving the course there and displaying the skills that would be in much demand the rest of his career.

Before Ross was a golf-course designer though, he was a golfer, and a very good one. His first taste of fame in America came as a player. He won the inaugural North and South Open as well as the Massachusetts Open, and competed in seven U.S. Opens from 1900–1911, his best performance being a fifth-place finish in 1903.

Impressed by his work in Watertown, Ross was invited by James Tufts to be the golf professional at the family-run resort in Pinehurst, North Carolina. When Tufts needed somebody to design and build his second course, Pinehurst Number 2, he turned to Ross. Although the course was completed in 1907, Ross would continue to work and improve it until his death in 1948.

The features of a Ross course include his use of the natural environment and a variety of green contours. His designs always rewarded both mental and physical skill. Ross also had an affinity for bunkers, one example being his design of Seminole, which opened in 1929 with 187 bunkers.

Two reasons why Ross was able to create as many courses as he did were his large personal workforce and his management style. He often used construction crews of as many as 3,000 men. During a site visit, Ross would often draft detailed plans and then have one of his foremen take over the project. Ross preferred to spend most of his time at his beloved Pinehurst or at his Rhode Island summer home.

Of the early golf-course architects, Donald Ross is the most well known. A modest and soft-spoken Scot, he designed or remodeled more than four hundred golf courses. One of the original members of the American Society of Golf Course Architects, Ross was consistently sought after for work between 1912 and 1948. While much of his work has been altered over the years, his significant contribution to the game of golf is undeniable.

---

### DOWNHILL LIES

PLAY THE BALL BACK in stance and lean a little left at address. Set your shoulders parallel to the slope and keep the clubhead low to the ground past impact.

---

## Course Work
## A New Club

The average cost of opening a golf course in America is $5 million.

### GOLF, ANYONE?

- There were 15,899 golf courses in the U.S. as of 2003, according to the National Golf Foundation.
- An additional 175 were added in 2004.
- There are 31,548 full-length golf facilities in the world, according to the Golf Research Group.

### Holy Ground

*"A golf course is to me a holy ground. I feel God in the trees, and the grass and the flowers, and in the rabbits and the birds and the squirrels; in the sky and the water. I feel that I am home."*
—Harvey Penick

## REAL ESTATE

There are 3,750 square miles of golf courses now occupying real estate in the United States—an area three times the size of Rhode Island—according to the Vail Nature Centre in Vail, Colorado.

## Seeded

The Sunningdale Golf Club, built outside London in 1901, was the first course with grass grown completely from seed.

## Old Hole

The Oakhurst Golf Club was founded in 1884 in White Sulphur Springs, Virginia. Its first hole is thought to be the oldest surviving golf hole in the U.S. It is now the number-one hole at the Homestead Resort.

## BACK DOOR

African American Joe Bartholomew grew up in New Orleans and entered the caddy ranks by the age of seven in 1887. He became an accomplished player and went on to attend college in New York to study golf-course design before moving back to New Orleans. He designed several courses in New Orleans, but because Bartholomew was black, many members of the courses refused to let him play on what he had designed.

## Slippery Slope

In 1985 the USGA introduced the "Slope System" to allow golfers to adjust their handicaps to allow for the relative difficulty of a golf course compared to players of their own ability.

## Still at the Beach

YOU'VE GOT YOUR STANCE, now you have to take your shot. The number-one rule in sand is to swing smoothly through the ball as you would with any other stroke. Have the blade open at impact, and hit the sand between 1 and 2 inches behind the ball.

### ISLAND GREEN

The Tournament Players Club at Sawgrass opened in 1981 with its controversial island green 17th hole, and immediately became the permanent host of the Tournament Players Championship. The TPC at Sawgrass is the prototype for many "stadium" courses around the United States.

### Favorite Movie

- 62 percent of golf course superintendents say their favorite golf movie is *Caddyshack*.
- 15 percent favor *Tin Cup*.
- 8 percent say *Happy Gilmore* is their favorite golf movie.

### Regis Who?

- 18 percent of golf-course superintendents say they would like to golf with Michael Jordan.
- 1 percent would choose Celine Dion.
- 0 percent say Regis Philbin.

### So There

In 1954, architect Robert Trent Jones received complaints that he had made the par-3 4th hole at Baltusrol too hard for the upcoming U.S. Open. He played the hole to see for himself and recorded a hole in one.

# Go Long

- 964 yards is the length of the longest golf hole in the world, located at Sano, Japan, according to the Guinness Book of World Records.
- The par on this hole is 7.

## Like Hell

THE WORLD'S BIGGEST TRAP is on Hell's Half Acre on the 585-yard 7th hole of the Pine Valley course, Clementon, New Jersey.

## WATER, WATER

In 1925, the first fairway irrigation system was developed in Dallas, Texas.

## Turfed

The USGA founded its famed Green Section to conduct research on turf grass in 1920.

## Pinehurst

- In 1916, the first miniature golf course opened in Pinehurst, North Carolina.
- In 1920, the first practice range opened in Pinehurst.

## WATER HAZARD

Four billion gallons of water are soaked up by golf courses in the U.S. annually, according to the Worldwatch Institute.

## Bunker Mentality

American and British Open winner Walter J. Travis was relentless in his harsh reviews of United States golf courses. He characterized cross-bunkers, a common design feature in early American courses, as a clear example of mindless course design. He produced illustrations of strategically placed bunkers along the fairway edges, a design philosophy and practice that is used today.

## In the Rough

Keep your thinking cap on, because club selection is crucial when your ball hits the rough. If the rough is extremely deep, you many need loft to get out of trouble, so go with a higher club. It is also a good idea to open the clubface up a bit, taking into account that the grass will push it back to square by contact.

## Long Putt

The world's largest green is the 695-yard 5th hole, a par 6 at the International Golf Club in Massachusetts, with an area in excess of 28,000 square feet.

## Size Is Everything

- 8,325 yards is the length of the world's longest course, the International Golf Club in Massachusetts, from the tiger tees.
- Par for the course is 77.

## If The Shoe Fits

In 1993, soft spikes were introduced to the golf world to protect greens from wear, signaling the demise of metal spikes.

## Heights

The world's highest golf course, the Tactu Golf Club in Morococha, Peru, sits 14,335 feet above sea level at its lowest point.

## Bent What?

Creeping bentgrass was developed for putting greens by the U.S. Department of Agriculture in 1977.

## 9 or 18?

62 percent of golf courses in the U.S. have 18 holes.

## All in a Year's Work

- In 1820, Alexander Monroe of the Aberdeen Golf Links (Scotland) became the first paid greenkeeper.
- Mr. Monroe was paid £4 annually.
- $63,000 is the average salary for a golf course superintendent in the U.S. today.

## Long Off the Tee

20 percent more space is required today to design golf courses due to the longer distances being achieved by players because of the advancement in the technology of clubs and balls, according to the American Society of Golf Course Architects.

## Which Course?

- 91 percent of avid golfers say golf courses are in better condition today compared to ten years ago, according to a survey by the Golf Course Superintendents Association of America.

- 93 percent believe superintendents are environmentally responsible.
- 90 percent say quality of course conditions is important in choosing a golf course.
- 33 percent say closeness to home is important.

## One and Two

Florida and California are the states with the most golf courses.

## GOING PUBLIC

- The Van Cortlandt Park Golf Course opened in New York in 1895, the first public golf course in America.
- It cost $624.80 to build the first nine holes of the course.

## It's Home

- 3.7 million U.S. golfers are permanent residents of a golf-course community, according to the National Golf Foundation.
- 48 percent of new golf course openings in 2003 were real estate related.

## Green Fees

- Americans spend $20 billion on green fees and dues annually.
- 81 percent of all golf spending is accounted for by green fees and dues.

## STATE BY STATE

- In the U.S., $37.30 is the average cost of weekend green fees in season with a cart, according to the National Golf Foundation.
- $85.70 is the average cost of this green fee in Hawaii, the most expensive in the nation.
- $23.80 is the average cost of this green fee in South Dakota, the lowest in the nation.

## Going to Walk, Walk, Walk

- 78 percent of golfers surveyed worldwide walk around the golf course, according to a survey by *Golf Digest*.
- 51 percent of American golfers walk the course.
- 1 percent of American golfers use a caddy.
- Singapore and the U.S. rank first and second as the countries where golfers are most likely to use a golf cart.
- India and Thailand rank first and second as the countries where golfers are most likely to walk using a caddy.

## First Cart

The first golf cart was invented in 1940, strictly for use by golfers with disabilities.

## TIMES ARE A CHANGIN'

- Computerized irrigation systems, the Internet, and satellite weather reports rank first, second, and third as the technological devices golf-course superintendents say they most rely upon, according to the Golf Course Superintendents Association of America.
- Alternative spikes, metal woods, golf carts, and golf-ball designs rank first, second, third, and fourth as the technological devices they say have had the most impact on the game.
- A decreased labor pool, increased operating costs, and the increased regulation of water rank first, second, and third as the most prevalent challenges in the coming years for maintaining a golf course.

## Plugged

Not all balls lay smoothly on the surface of the sand when your ball lands in the trap. Sometimes it plugs, and plugs call for a different measure. Here you close the clubface more and hit up to four inches behind the ball, giving you more of a chance to explode your ball out of the trap.

## ≡ *Old Tom Morris Award* ≡

Each year the Old Tom Morris Award is presented by the Golf Course Superintendents Association of America to an individual who "through a continuing lifetime commitment to the game of golf has helped to mold the welfare of the game in a manner and style exemplified by Old Tom Morris." Morris (1821–1908) was greenkeeper and golf professional at the St. Andrews Links Trust Golf Club of St. Andrews, Scotland; a four-time winner of the British Open (1861, 1862, 1864, and 1867); and ranked as one of the top links designers of the nineteenth century.

## Old Tom Morris Award Winners

| | | | |
|---|---|---|---|
| 1983 | Arnold Palmer | 1992 | Tom Watson |
| 1984 | Bob Hope | 1993 | Dinah Shore |
| 1985 | Gerald Ford | 1994 | Byron Nelson |
| 1986 | Patty Berg | 1995 | Dr. James R. Watson |
| 1987 | Robert Trent Jones Sr. | 1996 | Tom Fazio |
| 1988 | Gene Sarazen | 1997 | Ben Crenshaw |
| 1989 | Chi Chi Rodriguez | 1998 | Ken Venturi |
| 1990 | Sherwood Moore, CGCS | 1999 | Jaime Ortiz-Patiño |
| 1991 | William C. Campbell | 2000 | Nancy Lopez |
| 2001 | Tim Finchem | 2004 | Rees Jones |
| 2002 | Walter Woods | 2005 | Jack Nicklaus |
| 2003 | Pete Dye | | |

# ≥ *Did You Know?* ≥

- Did you know that cozy, quiet Pinehurst, North Carolina, the place many think of as the home of golf in America, has one area that is not so quiet—the driving range that the locals dubbed Maniac Hill?

- Did you know that members of the Pine Valley Golf Club deemed their course so difficult that they thought nobody would ever break 80? Enter a young golfer on the make named Arnold Palmer, reportedly taking all the bets members were willing to make. Palmer shot a 68 and walked away with a not inconsiderable payoff.

- Did you know Old Tom Morris regarded the design of the 18th green at St. Andrews as his major achievement? He had plenty of time to get it right. He looked at it from his shop window every day for forty years. Morris knew the land, he knew how it behaved, where it drained to, and where a golf ball would end up from any given shot.

- Did you know that legendary golf-course designer Alexander Mackenzie loved the golf course he built at Pasatiempo in California so much that he built his last home there in 1932 and his ashes were spread across it in 1934?

- Did you know that Augusta National is the only clay-based course designed by Alexander Mackenzie? Sand-based courses have higher percolation rates, so as a result Augusta National had drainage problems on Nos. 4, 10, and 11 that were corrected by future designers.

- Did you know that by the 1850s, newly created private clubs were hiring "greenkeepers" whose job it was not only to take care of their golf courses, but also to help design and build courses, teach golf lessons, make balls and clubs, and repair or improvise available equipment?

- Did you know that the development of the rail network was the most important contributing factor to the development of inland golf courses?
- Did you know that until 1870 a player teed off for the next hole from the green of the preceding hole?
- Did you know that James Tufts paid just a dollar an acre for the five thousand acres he purchased that includes Pinehurst No. 2?
- Did you know that during one five-year stretch in the 1960s the U.S. Open was played every year at a course that golf-course architect Robert Trent Jones either designed or had a hand in remodeling?

## THE DOWNSWING MOTION

To prove your downswing is a pulling motion, try this drill. Grip a three-foot-long piece of rope as if it were a golf club and swing it back. Let it flip over your right shoulder. Swing the rope down and through, letting the lower body lead the uncoiling action, pulling the rope taut and making the tip trail through the hitting area. The lower body must lead the upper body for the tip of the rope to whip through last.

## Robert Trent Jones

Jones was a superb scratch golfer before becoming the first dean of American golf-course architecture. He set a course record at the Rochester City Golf Championship and was low amateur at the 1927 Canadian Open. A stomach ulcer, however, put an end to any plans at a career playing golf.

When Jones decided on a line of study at Cornell University, he did something unusual for his era. He took courses—not necessarily leading toward a degree—that would allow him to become a golf-course architect. Those courses included agronomy, engineering, and landscape architecture; he also took courses in sketching from the Rochester Art School. Before he even finished school, he designed several greens at Sodus Bay Golf Club in New York.

Jones's work was good enough to get him noticed by Canadian golf architect Stanley Thompson and in short order they formed the company Thompson, Jones and Co., with offices in Toronto and New York. The partnership was fruitful enough that Jones and Thompson very quickly became the most influential architects of their generation.

Jones was influential in gaining acceptance for the concept of strategic design. Although it is difficult to characterize a typical Jones course because he designed so many, there certainly was a preference for length, often in excess of seven thousand yards. Jones's course were also characterized by huge, undulating greens and unusual looking bunkers.

Along with the baby boom after the war, there was also a golf boom, with the number of courses in the U.S. doubling over a twenty-five-year period. When Stanley Thompson passed on in 1953, Jones was alone at the top of the architectural heap and in huge demand. The Jones imprimatur on a golf course stamped it with respectability and sold memberships.

In total, Jones designed or remodeled more than 450 golf courses from the Caribbean to North Africa and Alaska to Switzerland and Japan. In America, his golf courses have included Winged Foot, Spyglass Hill, and The Dunes. No American architect has left a larger legacy.

Robert Trent Jones was the first recipient of the American Society of Golf Course Architecture Donald Ross Award for outstanding contributions to golf-course architecture. He has also been granted membership to the Royal and Ancient Golf Club of St. Andrews. In 1987, he was presented by the Golf Course Superintendents Association of America with the Old Tom Morris Award. Jones's two sons have continued the Jones tradition in the golf-course architecture profession, distinguishing themselves in their own right.

## Shanking

UNDERSTANDING HOW NOT to shank means you must understand why you shanked in the first place. Shanking can happen with woods, but seems more prevalent with irons. The worst thing about shanking is that it sends the ball in the opposite direction of your intended target. Make sure that you don't bring the club down in an outside-in trajectory. Watch yourself for faulty body action.

# 7

# The Country Club

It may have taken egalitarian America a little while to catch up with their clubbing cousins across the Atlantic, but when they did they took to clubbing with a vengeance. The Country Club in Brookline, Massachusetts, was only the beginning of a torrent of country clubs to spread across the U.S.

It is no surprise that in the conspicuous-consumption America of the turn of the century the country club came before the golf course. The country club, though, quickly became the "Golf and Country Club" and golf became the game of choice for the (mostly) men interested in moving up the social ladder.

What better way to differentiate yourself from the great unwashed masses than heading to the country for some good old-fashioned companionship and backslapping around the golf course? By the turn of the century, golf and country clubs numbered more than 1,000 but grew to more than 5,500 by the time of the Great Depression.

Although golf has become a more accessible sport for many people (public clubs exceeded private clubs for the first time in 1962), there are still clubs that rightly deserve the adjective "exclusive." Clubs like The Bridges in Rancho Santa Fe, California, Hamilton Farm Golf and Equestrian Club in Bedminster, New Jersey, The Vintage Club at Indian Wells, California, and Roaring Forks Golf Club in Basalt, Colorado, charge initiation fees that range from $300,000 to $1 million.

Memberships aren't exclusive enough, though, to prevent some businessowners from having more than one membership, so they have a place to go when they are on different coasts.

Membership does have its privileges, such as landing and storage space for your private plane or yacht, depending, of course, on how you are traveling. Because the market is understandably competitive for these types of members, there isn't anything a club won't do for its members, from laundry to gift shopping to fixing you up with a fishing pole and small boat to fish the lake where you may have lost your ball earlier in the day.

What private clubs are extremely good at is not divulging any information. When the newspaper daily, *USA Today*, attempted to survey exclusive clubs in 2003 on such mundane things as gender and race, only 5 percent agreed to answer. Like the old adage says, if you have to ask…

---

## Look Up…Way Up

WHEN YOUR TEE SHOTS look more like sand-wedge shots, you should make sure that you don't let your hands get too far ahead of the clubhead at impact. Also keep your head behind the ball throughout the swing. Keep your backswing shallow and maintain a shallow swing through impact. If you often find your tees smashed into the ground, it is a sign that your swing path is too steep.

# 8

# The Great Courses

## *Augusta National*

**E**very spring since 1934, the golf world has turned to a former nursery in Georgia to signal the official start to the golf season. No other golf course embodies perfection like Augusta National: blooming azaleas and dogwoods, fairways that look like carpeting, Paul-Newman-eyes blue water, rolling, speedy, and immaculately trimmed greens.

After successfully completing a 1930 grand slam—something not done in a single season before or since—Bobby Jones, at the tender age of 28, shocked the golf world and retired. Jones was not through with golf, however, but rather was casting about for a possible venue to establish a golf course of his own. Augusta National is that course and Jones's fingerprints are all over it.

Jones knew immediately that what was then a 365-acre indigo plantation was almost perfect for the golf course he wanted to build. That it was in Augusta was a bonus, because he had always had a soft spot for the area, his wife having come from there. An option of $70,000 was quickly taken out on the property and the deal to buy it struck shortly thereafter.

Jones hired well-known golf-course designer Dr. Alister MacKenzie to conceive the design. Jones had seen MacKenzie's work at Cypress Point and hoped that he could work the same magic at Augusta. No one, save MacKenzie and Jones themselves, knows whose stamp looms larger in the design of the course, but one thing for certain is that both men's imprints are there.

Jones hit literally thousands of golf balls to help MacKenzie determine how the course would play for the world's best golfers. There is also little dispute that Jones was actively involved with MacKenzie in the planning. Unfortunately for MacKenzie, he would die soon after construction and so never got a chance to see Augusta National in all of its splendor and glory.

The course opened in 1931 and Jones's invitational tournament (not yet called the Masters) was begun. The Masters has the unique distinction of being the only one of the majors played at the same venue every year. As a result, the Augusta National course is the most seen and probably best-known of any course in the world.

All great courses develop colorful histories of their own and Augusta is no exception. Sportswriter Herbert Warren Wind used the term "Amen Corner" to describe the second half of the 11th and 12th holes, and the first half of the 13th hole. The name was taken from a jazz record, "Shouting at Amen Corner."

Each hole at Augusta is adorned with a tree or shrub for which it is named. It is estimated that since the course was built, more than 80,000 plants of over 350 varieties have been added to the Augusta National landscape. Augusta National is most noted for the rhododendron, of which there are more than 30 varieties. The flowering season ranges from March to mid-April, perfect timing for the Masters.

There is also Ike's Pond, so-named after former President Dwight D. Eisenhower. During his second visit to Augusta National, he stated that he had found a perfect place for a dam to be built if the club ever decided to have a fish pond. Presidents apparently are listened to, as the pond was built, and the dam created.

Three bridges have been dedicated at Augusta: one commemorating Ben Hogan's record four-round score of 274 in 1953, one commemorating Byron Nelson's exceptional play on holes 12 and 13 at the 1937 Masters (as well as Ralph Guldahl's eagle-3 on 13 in 1939), and one commemorating Gene Sarazen's double eagle on 15 in 1935.

Augusta National has changed more than any other of the world's major courses. All that remains from Alister MacKenzie's features is his routing. Jones's and MacKenzie's love of the Old Course at St. Andrews is not as present anymore, but what Jones and MacKenzie both liked about the Old Course is that it emerged over time. So, too, has Augusta.

## READING THE GREEN

THE BEST VIEW of the contours of a green can be seen from between 50 and 100 yards out. Examine it, and see where you would like to hit your shot and how it might roll once you get it there.

## The Old Course at St. Andrews

There is absolutely no question that the most famous golf course in the world is the Old Course of the Royal and Ancient in St. Andrews, Scotland. Although golf historians have argued about the precise place of origin of the game, for most golfers around the world the point is moot. The Old Course represents the spirit of the game the way it was meant to be played.

Playing the Old Course at St. Andrews, golfers know they are walking with souls who traveled the same hallowed ground six hundred years earlier. They are traveling with fishermen and Willie Parks and Donald Ross and Old Tom Morris.

The course is not an easy course to get to know quickly. When Bobby Jones first came here, he thought it resembled a cow pasture more than a golf course. Toward the end of Jones's life he had revised that opinion. "If I had ever been sat down and told I was to play there and nowhere else for the rest of my life," said Jones, "I should have chosen the Old Course at St. Andrews."

The Old Course was not designed by any single architect but instead has evolved over time. There are, of course, people who played a major role in reshaping it—Daw Anderson, Old Tom Morris, and Alister MacKenzie—but the important architects were the nameless fishermen and shepherds who used it for hundreds of years.

Originally, the track through the Old Course was so narrow that golfers played to the same holes going out and coming in, using two different pin placements on each green. Originally there were twenty holes on the course, but as the game became increasingly popular, golfers would find themselves playing on the same hole but coming from different directions.

To relieve the mayhem, two holes were cut and those for the first nine were equipped with a white flag and those for the second nine with a red flag. When Old Tom Morris created a separate green for the first hole, it then became possible to play the course in a counterclockwise direction, rather than clockwise, which had previously been the norm. For many years, the course was played clockwise one week and counterclockwise the next.

The most striking feature of the course is its staggering number of bunkers (112), including the famous Hell on the long 14th, Strath on the short 11th, and the Road Bunker on the 17th. An unusual feature of St. Andrews is its double greens with the outward and inward holes cut from the same putting surface. These large greens can lead to putts of almost 100 yards.

The biggest trick St. Andrews has up its sleeve has nothing to do with the course at all—it is the weather. Winds can rise and rain can fall and just when you think you might finally gain advantage by having the wind at your back, it switches direction and plays against you.

## *Pebble Beach Golf Links*

The area around Pebble Beach began its life after the Civil War as a development by the Pacific Improvement Company, headed by the "Big Four" of railroad fame—Charles Crocker, Leland Stanford, Collis Huntington, and Mark Hopkins. It is here they opened Hotel Del Monte, near Monterey, hoping to become the Newport, Rhode Island, of the West. In 1897, the hotel built itself a 9-hole golf course.

In 1919, Sam Morse, a distant cousin of the inventor of the Morse Code, bought the operation from the Pacific Improvement Company. Morse quickly set out to buy even more land, acquiring the land for Pebble Beach Golf Links from Chinese fishermen who worked the area.

To develop the land as a golf course, Morse took a big chance and hired a California Amateur champion named Jack Neville to be his golf-course designer, even though Neville had very limited experience. The rest—as the expression goes—is history. The great American golf-course architect Robert Trent Jones paid Pebble Beach his highest compliment when he said it was unrivaled among oceanside courses.

The mistake many golfers and commentators make with Pebble Beach is to think of it as a links (low-lying seaside land) course; on the contrary, it is located on the craggy headlands that drop into Carmel Bay. Eight of the holes are set along those headlands, the ocean there to tease poorly hit golf balls into its midst, never to be seen again. On some days, with strong inland blowing winds, golfers are forced to aim at the ocean, hoping the wind beats the ball back to the fairway.

Many of its holes contain amazing ocean views. Small greens and narrow fairways, not to mention the ever-present wind, combine to make it a challenge and a feast for the eyes for any golfer. Pebble Beach has seen very few changes over the years, but perhaps the most significant change to the course occurred shortly after the course opened. In 1922, William Herbert Fowler changed the 379-yard par 4 to a staggering 548-yard par 5.

A tribute to its enduring difficulty and beauty is that as early as 1929, Pebble Beach played host to its first major, hosting the U.S. Amateur. It has gone on to host three more U.S. Amateur championships and no less than four U.S. Opens.

No golfer is as much associated with Pebble Beach as Jack Nicklaus. In 1961, he won the U.S. Amateur here and won the first U.S. Open ever held at the course in 1972. In 1982, he lost a tremendous battle with Tom Watson, after Watson chipped in for a birdie on the 17th hole.

In 1998, Nicklaus again became involved with Pebble Beach Golf Links, this time as a designer. The 5th hole originally was slated to play along the oceanfront, but Morse's original attempts to buy the property failed. Now with the land purchased, Nicklaus has placed the 5th where Morse originally had wanted—back along Pebble Beach's stunning oceanfront.

## On the Toe

SHOTS HIT HIGH on the toe are the result of a steep, outside-in swing. You can change this result by modifying your grip. Grip the handle with your fingers, making sure the V-shapes between your thumb and index finger are pointing at your right shoulder. What this does is make sure you have proper hand position at address.

# ⇶ *Pinehurst No. 2* ⇶

When legendary golf architect Donald Ross arrived in Pinehurst in the summer of 1900, he could not have known that it would be an association that would last a lifetime. Pinehurst No. 2, one of the masterpieces of golf-course architecture, had the rather unusual benefit of having an architect, Ross, thinking about it and perfecting it for almost fifty years.

Pinehurst the resort was established in 1895 by James Tufts, a New Englander who had the resources and the determination to spend as little time in the New England winters as possible. Tufts purchased 5,000 acres in the sandhills area of North Carolina and quickly turned it into a spa area for well-heeled northerners.

The game of choice for the well-heeled was, of course, golf, and Tufts had a 9-hole course built as early as 1898. He added another nine the next year, and to add an exclamation mark he had the biggest golf star in the world at that time, Harry Vardon, play the course.

Golf and the resort Tufts had built had became so popular that Tufts needed another course to satisfy demand. Ross was the local professional, so the task inevitably fell to him to begin the design of the new course. By the end of 1900, he had the first nine holes designed and constructed, completing the second nine in 1907.

One of the course's most striking aspects is the isolation of the holes. Each hole is separated by indigenous mature pine and dogwood, of which Ross took full advantage. Ross was proud enough to say that it was one of the fairest courses he had ever designed.

One of the most deceiving aspects of Pinehurst is the size of the greens. Although they appear comfortable in size, they are shaped to tail off, so only good to excellent shots count. The course itself can stretch to more than 7,000 yards, but was designed for shot-makers, not just long ball-hitters.

Champion golfers like Sam Snead and Tom Watson knew what it took to win at Pinehurst No. 2. "Pinehurst No. 2," said Snead, "has the ability to jump up and grab you, and if you don't pay attention for all 18 holes, you are a goner."

Ross's affection for Pinehurst is evident in every detail. In the 1930s, Ross replaced the old dirt greens with grass greens and extended it from under 6,000 yards to over 7,000. He designed and redesigned depending on new insights collected over the decades of his association with the course. The golf world has been the beneficiary.

## Royal Melbourne

The Royal Melbourne is Australia's—and one of the world's—finest and most beautiful golf courses. In a country that continues to produce some of the finest golf talent in the world, it is one of the best-kept secrets that it is also home to some of the world's most wonderful courses.

The history of the Royal Melbourne began in 1891 when a group of Melbournians established the Melbourne Golf Club on leased land near the Caulfield railway station. This was the club's first incarnation, but as increasing urban development continued, the club was moved to a racetrack and built among the heathland scrub of Sandringham to the city's south.

Again Melbourne's explosive population growth forced the club to sell the western corner of the course and reconfigure itself to the eastward, where an additional 68 acres of land was available. Although only six of the original holes were lost, the club decided that the entire course should be upgraded and redesigned.

The golf world had changed significantly since 1891. Golf had taken the world by storm and with this redesign, the committee struck to develop the course and took no chances. They hired Dr. Alister MacKenzie, who had just finished working with the Royal and Ancient on the Old Course at St. Andrews, to oversee the design.

MacKenzie cost the club a staggering £1000, but the club ended up recouping much of that by acting as MacKenzie's agent, finding work for him on other courses in Australia while he was there.

MacKenzie was as shrewd at business as he was designing courses. He quickly recognized the talents of Australian Open champion Alex Russell and head greenkeeper Mick Morcom. He explained his philosophies and ideas and the rest he left up to Russell and Morcom. The result is a masterpiece.

The course combines the skills of MacKenzie with some of the best golf-course land in Australia. The course is full of dramatic undulations and its fertile sandy soil and rugged appearance make each hole a feast for the eyes. When a later greenkeeper, Claude Crockford, came along, he added further value by making the large undulating greens some of the fastest and most interesting in the world.

Before MacKenzie started the project, he asked for a listing of all members' ages and handicaps with the intention of making the course enjoyable for golfers of any ability. The result is wide fairways that are playable for club players, but requires the best players to drive to the corners to get it close. It is a philosophy that still holds up today.

The word most often applied to Royal Melbourne is "character," and you see it not only in the greens, but in lumpy ridges and in MacKenzie's trademark bunkers. The par-4, 11th hole is considered the most difficult on the course. At 455 yards, the golfer has to drive far enough to get a shot at the green, but in typical

MacKenzie fashion, if you drive too far, you are in the trap. There are at least a half-dozen more holes that are equally exciting, and then, of course, there are those wonderful greens. Any golfing expedition to Australia simply wouldn't be complete without a visit to the Royal Melbourne.

## Against the Grain

FIGURING OUT THE LINE you want your putt to take is not your only responsibility once you are on the green. Examine how the green has been cut and remember that putts with the grain go faster and roll longer than those against it. So, yes, get a line on your putt, but take everything into account.

## Baltusrol

The fact that the Baltusrol Golf Course in New Jersey is still open today is perhaps one of the first indications of its esteemed place in American golf. While most courses and clubs were forced to close during the Great Depression, Baltusrol surged onward, not only remaining open, but also solvent. This bears witness to its great strength today.

On October 19, 1895, Louis Keller, publisher of the New York Social Register, and owner of 500 acres of land in Springfield Township, New Jersey, decided to build one of the finest golf courses in the world to that time. Fifty years earlier the land had been owned and farmed by a Scottish immigrant named Baltus Roll, from whom Keller got the name for his new golf course—the Baltusrol Golf Club. Even with only nine holes at the start, the course was quickly successful, so much so that the Club's membership jumped from thirty on opening day to nearly four hundred by early 1898.

Baltusrol soon became a place of many firsts. In 1901 it hosted one of the first U.S. Women's Amateurs, and in 1903 hosted one of the first U.S. Opens. In 1912, having built a impressive new clubhouse—the same one which stands today—after the previous one had been destroyed by fire, Baltusrol became the first golf club to host a U.S. president, William Howard Taft. On October 11, 1911, it also hosted a meeting of the USGA, which adopted a proposal to establish the first USGA Handicap System. And finally, in 1954, as golf expanded into the television world, Baltusrol led the way, hosting the U.S. Open that year and becoming one of the first golf clubs to be seen nationally on television.

Perhaps one of the most renowned assets for which Baltusrol is known is the "Creator of Baltusrol," A. W. Tillinghast. Long known as an avid golfer and frequent contributor to golf publications of the time, Tillinghast was hired in the 1920s to redesign the course. He did, constructing dual courses at the club, which were a roaring success. To this day, Tillinghast's successes at Baltusrol, and about sixty other courses he helped design or modify, have given him the reputation as one of golf's greatest course architects. While considered today by some as the dean of golf architecture, he is considered by many to have been one of the first to articulate the principles of golf-course design. As a patriarch of the game, Tillinghast was never a great golfer himself, but he knew every golfing great of the time, and his essays and writings contain some of the most in-depth personal accounts of those early days of golf.

The course itself is a sophisticated piece of work, and an impressive looking one at that. Having hosted the U.S. Open seven times, and a national championship in every decade of the twentieth century except one, it has seen numerous—and sometimes painful—revisions. First being expanded from nine to eighteen holes, the Old Course was again expanded into a dual course, becoming the two world-renowned courses that exist today. With rolling hills and beautiful fairways, the par-71, 6,975-yard Upper Course is a thing of beauty, capable of challenging the finest golfers.

When it comes to championships, Baltusrol can talk it up, and perhaps the 1967 U.S. Open is its greatest boast. That year it saw the emergence of golf's great Jack Nicklaus, who won the U.S. Open over the legendary Arnold Palmer—whom many had favored to win the tournament—shocking golfers all over the world.

## Carnoustie

For more than 400 years, the game of golf has been played in Carnoustie, Scotland. For more than 150 of those years, the Carnoustie Golf Course has hosted some of golf's greatest tournaments. It should, perhaps, come as little surprise that this course, being only 25 miles from the spiritual home of golf at the Royal and Ancient St. Andrews, has become a staple course in the golfing world.

In 1842, a large tract of land was purchased by some budding golfers from the Earl of Dalhousie, with the intent to build a golf course on the property. At first a 10-hole course was built, designed by legendary ball maker and professional Allan Robertson. The course would undergo some major changes over the years with none other than Tom Morris leading the charge to have Carnoustie's golf course brought up to 18 holes. In 1926, the course would take on its modern form, going through a complete redesign by another British Open champion, James Braid.

Carnoustie is a course known more for the demand it places on a golfer's skill than for its beauty. A rugged, flat course, it has a number of difficult holes, which can be mastered by only the finest of golfers. The 14th hole, for instance, is perhaps one of the most challenging holes in golf. It is nicknamed "Spectacles" after the twin sets of sand traps guarding the face of a ridge that runs across the fairway less than 100 yards from the green. The Championship Course, at 6,941 yards, commands a par of 75, while the 6,020 yard Burnside Course rests at a par of 68, and the Buddon Links a par of 66 at 5,420 yards.

Perhaps the most notable feature of Carnoustie is not its golf course, however, but the players it has produced who have contributed extensively to the world of golf. Around the turn of the century, 270 sons of Carnoustie left home and went around the world to teach, play, and expand the game of golf. At a time when the game of golf was expanding quickly, it was an excellent time to take on such an endeavor, and these sons of Carnoustie were so hugely successful that by 1926 their names were on national Open trophies of seven different countries, including the United States and Britain.

Perhaps the most famous of them is Mac Smith, whose brothers Willie and Alex both became U.S. Champions. Mac never managed a win at the U.S. Open, but he played hard, and his successes around the world earned him an outstanding reputation.

The golfing world owes a great debt to another son of Carnoustie, Stewart Maiden, whose brothers Allen and James both went on to win championships in Australia and America, respectively. While Stewart himself was never able to follow in his brothers' footsteps and become a golfing champion, he did have close contact with one of golf's greats: Bobby Jones. As one of

Jones's earliest teachers, Stewart was able to nurture the golfing legend early on and help lead Jones to become one of the greatest golfers the world has ever seen.

# Timeline: Turning the Century Clock

**1900** Harry Vardon tours U.S. and wins U.S. Open by two shots from J. H. Taylor.

**1902** Sandy Herd uses the Haskell ball to win the British Open from Harry Vardon and James Braid by a stroke.

**1904** Walter J. Travis is the first U.S. winner of the British Amateur and uses Schenectady center-shafted putter.

**1907** Frenchman Arnaud Massy is the first non-British player to win the British Open.

**1908**  Old Tom Morris, age 87, dies at St. Andrews.

**1910**  The R&A bans the center-shafted putter while the USGA keeps it legal, marking the beginning of a 42-year period with two official versions of *The Rules of Golf*.

**1911**  Johnny McDermott becomes the first American-born winner of the U.S. Open.

**1913**  Francis Ouimet, age 20, is the first Amateur to win the U.S. Open, beating Harry Vardon and Ted Ray in a play-off at Brookline.

**1914**  Walter Hagen wins his first U.S. Open. Harry Vardon wins his sixth British Open, a record to this day.

**1916**  PGA of America founded.

**1919**  Pebble Beach Golf Links opens.

**1921**  Jock Hutchison is the first American citizen to win the British Open. R&A and the USGA rule that the ball must he not more than 1.62 ounces in weight and 1.62 inches in diameter.

**1922**  Walter Hagen is the first American-born player to win the British Open.

**1922**  The Texas Open is inaugurated, the second-oldest surviving PGA Tour event.

**1922** Pine Valley Golf Club opens.

**1924** Joyce Wethered wins her fifth English Ladies' Amateur in a row.

**1924** The USGA legalizes steel-shafted golf clubs. The R&A does not follow suit until 1929, widening the breach in *The Rules of Golf.*

**1926** Bobby Jones wins the British Open.

**1926** Jess Sweetser is the first American to win the British Amateur title.

**1927** Walter Hagen wins his fourth consecutive USPGA title, his fifth in total.

**1927** U.S. beats Britain in the first Ryder Cup match at Worcester, MA.

**1929** Walter Hagen wins his fourth British Open.

**1929** R&A legalizes steel-shafted clubs, following a similar USGA ruling in 1926.

**1930** Bobby Jones wins the Grand Slam. He captures the U.S. and British Opens and the British and U.S. Amateurs titles.

**1931** Billy Burke is the first golfer to win a major championship using steel-shafted golf clubs.

*1932* Inaugural Curtis Cup match.

*1933* Hershey Chocolate Company sponsors the Hershey Open, becoming the first corporate title sponsor of a professional tournament.

*1934* The first Masters is played. Horton Smith is the first champion.

*1935* Glenna Collett Vare wins the U.S. Women's Amateur a record sixth time.

*1938* The 14-club rule is instituted by the USGA.

*1945* Byron Nelson wins 19 events in 31 starts, 11 of them are consecutive wins.

*1947* U.S. Open at St. Louis is first championship to be televised, albeit only locally.

*1947* Babe Zaharias is the first American to win the British Women's Amateur.

*1948* Ben Hogan wins his first U.S. Open at Los Angeles

*1949* Ben Hogan and his wife are almost killed in an automobile accident in Texas.

## Byron Nelson

In one of the great geographical flukes of all time, golf legends Ben Hogan and Byron Nelson happened to be caddies at the same golf club in Fort Worth, Texas. Most assuredly, members could never possibly have anticipated what they had in their midst.

Imagine, if you will, the annual Christmas caddy tournament where members would turn the tables and caddy for the caddies in a 9-hole tournament, a tournament in which Hogan and Nelson would compete against each other. They were both tied at three over after nine, so the members decided to delay the dinner to watch a 9-hole play-off in which Nelson won, draining a fifteen-footer on the last hole. The next time the two would meet again in a play-off would be the 1942 Masters.

Byron Nelson, or Lord Byron, as he later came to be known, had a run of sustained excellence that has never been achieved before or since in the history of golf. In 1944, Nelson won 13 of the 23 tournaments he entered and in 1945 he had 11 consecutive victories. To put an exclamation on this remarkable run, consider that Nelson had 113 consecutive top-20 finishes.

Nelson won two Masters, two PGA Championships, and the U.S. Open. He was also part of the Ryder Cup teams of 1937, 1939, 1947, and as a nonplaying captain in 1965. At over six feet, Nelson was one of the most powerful drivers of his generation. He was also the first tour player to make a successful transition from hickory to steel shafts.

Despite his wins on the golf course, there simply wasn't enough money to stop Nelson from retiring in 1946. By his own account, between 1936–42 where he'd won 19 times including four majors, his entire winnings were $25,495. His career winnings were $182,000. Typical winner's prize money for a single tournament today is close to a million dollars.

The knock against Nelson that he didn't face competition from Snead and Hogan during the war years is largely a myth. (Nelson was excused from going to war for medical reasons—it took his blood much longer to congeal than the average person's.) Snead, Hogan, and Sarazen were often in the field, and Nelson's scoring was such that it leaves little doubt about the greatness of this champion.

Nelson's career on the professional golfing tour may have been over, but his career in the larger world of golf was just beginning. When the television network ABC was scouting for recognizable expertise, they came to see Nelson. His affable manner and congenial southern drawl introduced him and the game of golf to a whole new audience.

Nelson was also a fine instructor and teacher. One of his students is the great Tom Watson, who continues to play excellent golf well past fifty years of age. Lord Byron is also known as one of the best storytellers on the circuit and is deservedly an icon in the great game of golf.

---

## Toe Shots

WHEN THE TOE of the clubhead contacts the ball, resulting in weak and erratic shots, swaying and resulting misalignment could be the cause. With the right tempo, let your lower body start the downswing, keep your elbow tucked against your side, and keep your left side firm through impact. Transfer your weight from the top of your swing diagonally toward the right of the target, while letting your right elbow come down.

---

**9**

# Presidential Golf

Golf as a game was built for politics, with its windows of opportunity for conversation and deal making. It should come as little surprise, then, that presidents from Taft to Bush have taken to it with such vigor. Fifteen U.S. presidents since the turn of the last century have hauled out the driver at one time or another.

The first mention of presidential golf came in 1909 when it was noted that President Taft was out playing a round of the game with steel magnate Henry Frick. That Taft golfed so often and with so many businessmen of the day led some to accuse him of letting business determine the agenda of the nation.

Whatever the effect on the affairs of state (and despite Teddy Roosevelt's caution that he should not be caught playing the sissy game), Taft's public fondness for the game spurred the growth of the sport in the U.S.

When Warren Harding became president, he merely continued the Taft tradition. Harding was a president who liked to have a good time. He played golf and poker twice a week and was known to sneak off to burlesque shows. Collectively, his advisors were known as the "Poker Cabinet" because they all played poker together.

The most famous of all the golfing presidents is Dwight D. Eisenhower. Eisenhower made enough trips to Augusta National during his presidency that he had a cabin built there, which became known as his vacation White House. Reports vary, but it is estimated he visited his cabin more than twenty times during his presidency.

The hard-charging former general did much to take the sissy label away from the game. Eisenhower's love affair for the game was such that he literally turned the backyard of the White House into a practice area, replete with putting green and an area to practice his short irons.

If Ike had legitimately removed the sissy label, he had firmly attached another—that of the country club. By the time John F. Kennedy came to the presidency, it was that elitist image he worried about projecting. In their book *Presidential Lies*, Shepherd Campbell and Peter Landau called Kennedy perhaps the best of all the presidential golfers, something he concealed lest the

American public think of him as belonging to the country-club set.

There was no glad-hander who loved the game more than President Clinton. When Hillary Rodham Clinton was thinking of a present for her husband's first Christmas as president, she decided on a set of golf clubs. And President Clinton took them out whenever he could—including one 2 a.m. match with a Southeast Asian leader, because the Secret Service was not sure they could guarantee safety later in the day.

The Bush presidents perhaps have the most legitimate claim to a golfing heritage of any U.S. presidents. President George W. Bush's great-grandfather, George Herbert Walker, was president of the U.S. Golf Association in 1920, and it is for him that the Walker Cup competition is named.

Both Bush presidents are famous not for the lengths of their drives but rather the speed with which they play a round of golf. Both Bush presidents like to get around 18 holes in no more than three hours. "My father's measure of success is not how low you score," said President George W. Bush, "but how fast you play."

## ≋ *Presidential Strokes* ≋

### MY FAVORITE

The U.S. Presidents that golf-course superintendents say they'd most like to play a round of golf with:

1. Kennedy
2. Eisenhower
3. Reagan

### Warren Harding

- In 1923, President Harding began serving as an honorary member of the United States Golf Association's executive committee.

- At hole No. 4 on the Chevy Chase golf course, Harding's butler was generally known to serve him a bootleg scotch and soda.

## Dwight Eisenhower

- Eisenhower made 22 trips to his beloved Augusta National in Georgia during his presidency.
- Eisenhower spent 222 days playing golf between 1953 and 1960.
- That equals 31 weeks of golf.
- President Eisenhower's handicap was 15.
- He first took up the game at age 37.
- He broke 80 three times in his life.

## THE KENNEDY YEARS

- President John F. Kennedy's preferred number of holes to play was nine.
- John F. Kennedy's $900 MacGregor woods sold for $772,500 at an auction in 1996.

## Bill Clinton: The Happy Golfer

- President Clinton had new work done on the White House putting green and had a chipping area added.
- Well known for making "billigans"—doing a shot over and over again until you get it right—the facts tell all about Clinton's golfing style.
- President Clinton generally makes 200 swings on the golf course in order to shoot an 82, according to First Off the Tee.

## Another Bush Legacy

- The opening round shot in the National Senior Tournament by Prescott Bush, father and grandfather of two U.S. presidents, was 66.

- He won the club title at Cape Arundel in Kennebunkport, Maine, eight times.
- He set a course record at Cape Arundel with a score of 66.

## ARE YOU DOIN' ANYTHING?

President George W. Bush's first date with future wife Laura was at a miniature golf course.

## Power Foursome

President Harding played regularly at the Chevy Chase Golf Club with what came to be known as the "senatorial foursomes" including, among others, President Woodrow Wilson's assistant secretary of the Navy, Franklin D. Roosevelt.

## Portrait of an Artist

The portrait of Bobby Jones that hangs on the walls of Augusta National was painted by President Eisenhower.

 ## TEMPER, TEMPER

President Taft's golf games were almost always covered by the national press. One trait the public learned about was that Taft often yelled at his ball for misbehaving and that the 300-plus-pound president was a very poor putter.

## Arnie for President

Arnold Palmer has played golf with six American presidents.

## Canadian Flu

After playing six holes of golf in Vancouver, Canada, President Harding became so weak that he jumped from the 6th to the 17th hole.

*"The beauty of golf is that you cannot play if you permit yourself to think of anything else."*—Howard Taft

*"The pat on the back, the arm around the shoulder, the praise for what was done right and the sympathetic nod for what wasn't are as much a part of golf as life itself."*
—Gerald R. Ford

*"One lesson you had better learn if you want to be in politics is that you never go out on a golf course and beat the president."*
—Lyndon B. Johnson

*"A lot more people beat me now."*—Dwight D. Eisenhower

*"That does look like very good exercise. But what is the little white ball for?"*—Ulysses S. Grant

*"It is true that my predecessor did not object as I do to pictures of one's golf skill in action. But neither, on the other hand, did he ever beat a Secret Service man."*
—John F. Kennedy

*"I deny allegations by Bob Hope that during my last game I hit an eagle, a birdie, an elk, and a moose."*
—Gerald R. Ford

*"I know I'm getting better at golf because I'm hitting fewer spectators."*—Gerald R. Ford

## Backswing

HOW FAR SHOULD YOU TAKE your club back on your backswing? Let your body be your guide. If you are falling off balance, you are going back too far. If you are not happy with how far you are going back, you can get incremental improvements with a stretching program. Remember, too, there is no substitute for a warmup before your match.

# Timeline: Five Decades of Change

**1950** Ben Hogan wins his second U.S. Open.

**1950** LPGA is founded, replacing the Women's Professional Golf Association.

**1951** USGA/R&A hold a rules conference to standardize rules for the game throughout the world. Stymie is abolished.

**1953** Ben Hogan becomes the first golfer to win the Masters, U.S. Open, and British Open in one year.

**1954** U.S. Open is televised nationally for the first time.

**1955** Last day of the British Open at St. Andrews is televised for the first time.

**1958** Arnold Palmer wins the Masters, his first major.

**1958** U.S. Tour prize-money reaches $1 million.

**1959** Bill Wright wins the U.S. Amateur Public Links, becoming the first African American to win a national championship.

**1961** Gary Player becomes the first foreign player to win the Masters.

**1961** Caucasians-only clause stricken from the PGA constitution, and at the Greater Greensboro Open Charlie Sifford becomes the first black golfer to play in a PGA co-sponsored tournament in the South.

**1962** Twenty-two-year-old Jack Nicklaus beats Arnold Palmer in U.S. Open play-off.

**1963** Arnold Palmer becomes the first professional to earn over $100,000 in official prize money in one calendar year.

**1965** Sam Snead wins the Greater Greensboro Open, his eighty-first Tour victory, a record.

**1967** Charlie Sifford wins the Greater Hartford Open, becoming the first African American to win a PGA Tour event.

**1969** Tony Jacklin becomes first Brit to win his national Open in 28 years.

**1970** Jacklin is U.S. Open Champion by seven strokes.

**1971** Lee Trevino wins U.S., Canadian, and British Opens—all within a period of three weeks.

**1972** Jack Nicklaus completes the first two legs of the modern Grand Slam winning the Masters and the U.S. Open (at Pebble Beach); but like Arnold Palmer, he loses the British Open, finishing second to Lee Trevino.

**1972** European Tour gets underway.

**1973** Jack Nicklaus wins the PGA Championship, breaking Bobby Jones's record for most major victories with fourteen.

**1974** Gary Player wins the British Open.

**1975** Lee Elder becomes the first African American golfer to play in the Masters.

**1979** Seve Ballesteros wins British Open.

**1980** Ballesteros becomes the first European to win the Masters.

*1981* Kathy Whitworth becomes the first woman to earn $1 million in career prize money.

*1986* Nicklaus wins his sixth Masters at age 46, becoming the oldest Masters winner on record in the process.

*1987* Nick Faldo wins his first of three British Opens with final round of 18 par.

*1988* Curtis Strange becomes first golfer to earn $1 million in a single season.

*1990* The R&A adopts the 1.68 inch diameter ball, and for the first time since 1910 the rules of golf are standardized throughout the world.

*1991* Phil Mickelson, an amateur, wins the PGA Tour's Northern Telecom Open.

*1993* An ownership group led by Joe Gibbs and Arnold Palmer announce plans for The Golf Channel.

*1994* U.S. and European PGAs block Greg Norman's World Tour plan.

*1995* Annika Sorenstam's first LPGA Tour win comes in the U.S. Women's Open.

*1996* Tiger Woods turns pro, wins two late-season PGA Tour events and is named Rookie of the Year. His first victory comes at the Las Vegas Invitational when he shoots 64 in the final round, then defeats Davis Love III on the first play-off hole.

**1998** At age 19, Se Ri Pak wins the U.S. Women's Open and the LPGA Championship. Pak's success begins a wave of Korean players joining the LPGA Tour.

**1999** Payne Stewart wins his second U.S. Open, but later in the year is killed in a plane crash.

**2000** Tiger Woods wins the U.S. Open at Pebble Beach by 15 strokes. He later adds the British Open and PGA Championship, becoming the first player since Ben Hogan in 1953 to win three majors in one year.

**2003** Annika Sorenstam plays in the PGA Tour Colonial, the first woman to play in a PGA Tour event since Babe Didrikson Zaharias in 1945. Sorenstam misses the cut.

**2004** Tiger Woods surpasses $40 million in career earnings.

## Ben Hogan

Ben Hogan was a small man—diminutive in stature, not in courage or determination—who grew up poor in Fort Worth, Texas. Poverty and the suicide of his father clearly shaped his tenacious character. Despite a career that included towering victories, he never became a media darling in the traditional sense. It was always Hogan's clubs that did his talking. He became the best golfer of his generation and one of the best golfers of all time.

Hogan was a loner and never one of the boys. While beers were being shared in the clubhouse, Hogan was famously on the driving range. Nobody else may have known, but Hogan knew he was meant for golf and he practiced it with a determination like no other player in the game at that time.

Poverty would continue to visit Hogan over and over again well into his thirties. Twice he had to quit the golf tour to return home to Texas to make money. It didn't help that up until 1940 the only event Hogan managed to win was a four-ball tournament.

That all changed in 1940 when he won the North and South event and in the process became the leading money winner on tour. Hogan's career was in flight. He would again be the leading money winner in 1941 and 1942. Just when Hogan seemed poised for greatness, along came the war years, largely keeping Hogan away from the game until after the war.

In 1946, he picked up where he had left off. He became the leading money winner again and captured his first major in the PGA Championship. In the combined 1946–47 season, he had a total of 21 wins, a number that would grow to 62 by the end of his career.

The Hogan ascendancy to the top of the golf pecking order seemed assured when in 1948 he captured his first U.S. Open title and his second PGA Championship. Then once again fate seemed to intervene against Hogan. Exhausted and wanting to spend time in a new house, Hogan and his wife Valerie were involved in a collision with a ten-ton Greyhound bus.

Hogan threw himself over his wife in the passenger seat to protect her, and in so doing he avoided being impaled. The injuries to Hogan were life threatening and when he finally pulled through he had been away from golf for eleven months. When the golfing public saw photos of Hogan in their local papers, they were shocked by his gauntness.

In 1950, a hobbled Hogan decided to enter the Los Angles Open as an experiment to see if he was capable of playing golf again. The experiment worked. He tied Sam Snead for the lead. He would capture the U.S. Open later that year, and captured it two more times before the end of his career. In total, his other majors included two Masters, two PGA Championships, and one British Open. In 1953, he won the Masters and the U.S. and British Opens, but couldn't compete in the PGA Championships because of a conflict of dates.

The most enduring legacy of Hogan was his belief in himself. Despite poverty, size, and injury, he would not be denied. This quiet Texan is one of the greats of the game.

## Target Practice

ALL GOOD GOLFERS pick out a target and know before they swing where they'd like to hit the ball. A trick many professionals use is to pick out a target ten to fifty yards out from their ball, keeping in mind that it is easier to aim at a target closer to you than it is to aim at one 250 yards down the fairway.

# Golf Crazy

## A LOVE/HATE RELATIONSHIP

*"They call it golf because all of the other four-letter names were taken."—Ray Floyd*

## Over The Moon

Astronaut Alan Shepard used a 6-iron at "Fra Mauro Country Club" on the moon in 1971.

## Art

*"What other people may find in poetry or art museums, I find in the flight of a good drive—the white ball sailing up into the blue sky, growing smaller and smaller, then suddenly reaching its apex, curving, falling, and finally dropping to the turf to roll some more, just the way I planned it."*
*—Arnold Palmer*

## WHERE'S OLLIE

• 542 rounds (9,756 holes) is the number of rounds completed by Ollie Bowers of Gaffney, South Carolina, in one calendar year.

## Good for Something

*"Golf and sex are about the only things you can enjoy without being good at either."* *—Jimmy Demaret*

# Tips in Prose

*"I have a tip that can take five strokes off anyone's golf game.*
*It is called an eraser." —Arnold Palmer*

*"Putting is like genetics. I'm in the horse business, so I've studied*
*genetics for twenty-five years; and I've played golf for a lot longer.*
*And the conclusions I've reached about putting and genetics are:*
*number one, success is what works;*
*and number two, I know a lot about nothing."*
*—Gary Player*

*"To play well you must feel tranquil and at peace.*
*I have never been troubled by nerves in golf because I felt*
*I had nothing to lose and everything to gain."*
*—Harry Vardon*

*"More matches are lost through carelessness at the beginning*
*than any other cause." —Harry Vardon*

*"The older I get the better I used to be."—Lee Trevino*

## FORE-TY

- Freddie Tait bet his friends at the Royal Cinque Ports Golf Club that he could bang a ball in 40 shots or less from the clubhouse at Royal St. George's to the Royal Cinque Ports Golf Club, a three-mile distance.
- On stroke 32, he put the ball through the clubhouse window at the Cinque Ports club.

## Winston's Take

*"Golf is a game whose aim it is to hit a very small ball
into an even smaller hole with weapons
singularly ill-designed for the purpose."*
—Sir Winston Churchill, former British prime minister

## Final Round

Bing Crosby died in 1977 after completing a round of golf in
Spain. His Bing Crosby National Pro-Am continued for several
years, but after relations soured between the PGA Tour and the
Crosby family, AT&T took over sponsorship of the event.

## Where Am I?

- In 1992, Simon Clough and Boris Janic completed 18-hole
  rounds of golf in five countries (France, Luxembourg, Belgium,
  Holland, and Germany) in one day, walking each course.
- It took them 16 hours, 35 minutes to complete their journey.

## Shhhhhh

*"The first thing a television viewer realizes when watching a golf
tournament is how the sport tends to make one inclined to
whisper and avoid sudden movements, such as walking to the
refrigerator [during] a possible birdie putt."*
—Peter Alfano, sports commentator

## Even in Japan

- At the end of World War II, there were 300 golf courses in Japan.
- Today there are 2,400.
- The typical cost to join one of many exclusive golf clubs in Japan
  was $2.8 million (U.S.) when the golf market peaked in the early
  1990s, according to Suguru Matsuzaki of the brokerage house
  Juchi.

## Love Thy Enemy

*"Golf is good for the soul. You get so mad at yourself you forget to hate your enemies."—Will Rogers*

## Left to Right

- It took Floyd Satterlee Rood 114,737 strokes when he played from the Pacific Ocean to the Atlantic, using the United States as his golf course, from September 14, 1963, to October 3, 1964.
- He lost 3,511 balls along the way.
- He traveled 3,397.7 miles.

## Night Work

Ian Colston, aged 35, played 401 holes at the Bendigo Golf Club in Victoria from November 27 to 28, 1971, making him the golfer to have played the greatest number of rounds in 24 hours.

## Speed Golf

- It took 77 players 10 minutes and 30 seconds to complete the Kern City Course in California on August 24, 1984.
- They played 18 holes.
- The course was 6,502 yards long.
- They used one ball.
- They scored 80.

## Forty

*"Golf is a fascinating game. It has taken me nearly forty years to discover that I can't play it."—Ted Ray*

## Playing Catch

The lowest recorded score ever for throwing a golf ball around 18 holes (more than 6,000 yards) was 82. It was accomplished by Joe Flynn at the 6,228-yard Port Royal Course in Bermuda on March 27, 1975.

## ALL WORK

*"If you watch a game, it's fun. If you play it, it's recreation. If you work at it, it's golf." —Bob Hope*

### Six, Please

- Thad Daber scored 73 on the 6,037-yard Lochmore Golf Course in Cary, North Carolina, on November 10, 1985, when he won the World One-Club Championship.
- He used a 6-iron throughout the game.

### Play Thru

- It took Steven Ward 222 strokes to play the 6,212-yard Pecos Course in Reeves County, Texas, on June 18, 1976.
- The young Mr. Ward's age at the time was 3 years, 286 days.

### LONG HITTERS

- Australian meteorologist Nils Lied drove a ball 2,640 yards across ice at Mawson Base, Antarctica, in 1962.
- Liam Higgins at Baldonnel Military Airport in Dublin drove a Spalding Top-Flite ball 634.1 yards on the airport runway on September 25, 1984.

### Perfect Stroke

- Jack Nicklaus holed a putt from 110 feet at the 1964 Tournament of Champions, and Nick Price did the same in the 1992 PGA, making them the longest-holed putts in a major tournament.

- Robert Tyre "Bobby" Jones Jr. is reputed to have holed a putt from 100 feet at the 5th green in the first round of the 1927 British Open at St. Andrews.
- 140 feet and 2 inches was the length of a putt sunk on the 18th at St. Andrews by Bob Cook in the International Four-Ball Pro Am Tournament on October 1, 1976.

## Unusual Tournaments

In the 1890s, Rudyard Kipling invented snow golf when he was living in Vermont. He painted his golf balls red so that they could be located in the snow.

## TEE TIME

One of the drills suggested by some instructors is when you get to the practice range, set up a series of tees a half-foot apart. After a couple of practice swings, close your eyes and swing so that now you are hitting the tees in order (not stopping), showing to yourself that you have a swing that is repeatable and that you don't get psyched out by having to hit the ball.

## Keep Your Eye on The Ball

The Maine Supreme Court forced the Fort Kent Golf Course to pay a patron $40,000 after a golf ball bounced off an abandoned railroad track on the course, striking the woman and breaking her nose.

## Like This, Honey

The highest ever single-hole golf score was 166, recorded during a qualifying round for the Shawnee Invitational for Ladies in Pennsylvania in 1912, after a young lady and her stroke-counting husband set out in a boat to chip her floating ball, which had landed in the Binniekill River, back to shore.

### I'll Mow

- 27 percent of U.S. men say that the White House lawn would be their top lawn-mowing assignment, according to the Murray Mowing Survey.
- 16 percent chose the Pebble Beach Golf Course as their top mowing assignment, the second most popular choice.

### Craziest

- Japan, South Korea, and the U.K. rank 1, 2, and 3 as the countries with the highest number of sports fans who watch golf, according to a survey by Ipsos-Reid.
- Japan, the U.S., the U.K., and South Korea rank 1, 2, 3, and 4 as the countries with the highest number of sports fanatics who play golf.

---

### Shooting Your Age

The oldest golfer ever to play a round is believed to be Arthur Thompson of British Columbia, Canada, at age 103. He is believed to have shot his age.

---

### The Babe

Babe Ruth was first introduced to golf at age 21 as a pitcher with the Boston Red Sox, but it wasn't until he became a member of the Yankees, who held their spring training trips in St. Petersburg, Florida, that the Babe really became a golfing fanatic.

## Play the Clarinet

When Davis Love II first began to teach golf as an instructor, he turned to legendary instructor Harvey Penick for advice. "Learn to play the clarinet or saxophone—something new," Penick said. Love attributes that advice to making him one of the best instructors in the game.

## Survival of the...

Did you know that one of the greatest golf writers of all time, Bernard Darwin, is the grandson of naturalist Charles Darwin?

### EXPENSIVE HOOKER

*Life Magazine* paid golfer Ben Hogan $20,000 in 1955 for a feature story in which Hogan revealed his "secret" technique that he learned years earlier for straightening out a terrible hook.

## Brown Bomber

Many people around former heavyweight boxing champion Joe Louis believe that Louis lost to Max Schmeling in 1936 because he had lost his focus. He had taken up golf in 1935 and became a fanatic.

## Mini Golf

In the early 1900s, miniature golf was actually the short game of regulation golf. The name quite frequently used in the early years was "Garden Golf" and it was played with a putter on real grass. In the 1920s and '30s, "rails" or "bumpers" started to appear, confining the ball within a boundary. The playing surface was changed to hard-pressed cottonseed hulls, which created a smoother putting surface. The game of mini golf was extremely popular among movie stars and celebrities, which helped spawn new links all across the nation. During the 1930s, there were approximately 30,000 links throughout the country with over 150 rooftop courses in New York City.

## Ice Golf

Ice golf was known as early as the seventeenth century. A painting by the Dutch painter Aert van der Neer (1603–1677) shows players with clubs in their hands attempting to get a ball into a hole in the ice covering a frozen canal in Holland. At that time the game was called "kolven."

Today, the World Ice Golf Championship is played 360 miles north of the Arctic Circle in Uummannaq, Greenland. Freezing glaciers and huge icebergs frame the course and continue to move slowly all year round—even in March the "green" is cut literally days before the event. Temperatures can fall to minus 50 degrees Celsius with the wind-chill factor.

The course is laid out in March on the fjord ice, close to the town, a week prior to the actual championship. Its shape is determined by the positions of icebergs in the fjord. The foundation is variable and can be very different from hole to hole. On one side of an iceberg there can be a lot more snow than on the other.

### RULES OF THE WORLD ICE GOLF CHAMPIONSHIP

The competition is played in accordance with *The Rules of Golf* as approved by the Royal and Ancient Golf Club of St. Andrews 2000, and additional local rules and conditions of competition as approved by the tournament committee.

## Not Your Usual Game

- The course is nine holes…par 35 or 36, with two sets of nine holes played, one in the morning and one in the afternoon.
- Greens are white and the ball is orange. Possible risks include losing a ball to a polar bear.

---

## Nancy Lopez

A little more than a year after getting her first set of golf clubs, 9-year-old Nancy Lopez won her first tournament. Less than a year later she won the state championship for her age group. As a 12-year-old, she won the New Mexico Women's Amateur, followed by two U.S. Junior Girls Championships. In high school, Lopez played on the boys' team, helping them to two state championships.

In 1975, Lopez entered the U.S. Women's Open as an amateur and finished in a tie for second. Lopez went on to Tulsa University and was named to the All-American team and named Tulsa University's Female Athlete of the Year. The lure of professional golf beckoned, and Lopez turned professional after her sophomore year at Tulsa.

She was an immediate sensation. In 1977, she was named Rookie of the Year. The following year Lopez won nine tournaments, including a record-setting five in a row, and was named LPGA Player of the Year. In 1979, she captured eight more tournaments and again was named Player of the Year. By the end of her career she would win the LPGA Championship three times and be named Player of the Year four times. She was also a four-time leading money winner.

Lopez was one of the first women golfers to capture the imagination of both the male and female golfing public. She had it all—a powerful swing, wonderful concentration—and was a maestro on the greens.

Lopez was also a feisty competitor who never gave up on a shot or a tournament and was one of the best closers in the game. She had spunk, style, and barrels of charisma, and the public and players warmed to her like no other female player in the television age. After her first season on the professional circuit, attendance tripled. She was the shot-in-the-arm women's golf needed and soon sponsors and television networks were lining up to get a piece of the action.

By the time she was 30, Nancy Lopez had won enough tournaments (35) to qualify for the LPGA Hall of Fame, making her the youngest qualifier. She has now won a total of 48 tournaments of her career and served as a role model for a generation of women golfers.

## Home on the Green

CONSIDERING THAT a typical golfer makes 38 to 42 putts per round, not nearly enough attention is paid to the putting stroke. Want to shave strokes off your game? Spend as much time on the practice green as you do on the practice range.

# The Majors

very sport has its crowns against which its great players are measured. Football has the Vince Lombardi trophy; hockey, the Stanley Cup; and baseball has the World Championship Trophy. In golf, the measure of greatness is the majors: the Masters, the British Open, the U.S. Open, and the PGA Championship.

The great Jack Nicklaus says the majors are the only reliable indicator; the only tournaments where you know you will be competing against the best players in the world. Winning one major can be the crowning achievement in a career. Winning more than one is a sign of greatness. Winning them all becomes the stuff of legend.

The fans know it. The media know it. More important, the players know it. The majors let us watch the world's best golfers compete against each other in a four-day battle that can be one of the most exciting spectacles in sport.

## ≣ Major Winners ≣

### Most Wins

| | | | |
|---|---|---|---|
| Jack Nicklaus | (18) | Gary Player | (9) |
| Walter Hagen | (11) | Tom Watson | (8) |
| Ben Hogan | (9) | Tiger Woods | (8) |

## ONLY ONES

- Bobby Jones is the only player who has won all four majors in one season.
- Bobby Jones and Tiger Woods are the only players who have held all four majors at one time.

## Sure Bet

- Bobby Jones received no money when he completed the original Grand Slam, winning the U.S. and British Amateurs and the U.S. and British Opens in the same year in 1930.
- Professional Bobby Cruickshank, who bet on Jones to complete the Slam at 120–1 odds, won $60,000.

## Broadway Bound

In 1953, New York City threw a ticker tape parade for Ben Hogan after he won the British Open. Hogan had already won the U.S. Open and Masters earlier in the year.

---

### FOR THE RECORD

Five golfers have won both the U.S. Open and the Masters in the same year (Tiger Woods, Ben Hogan, Arnold Palmer, Jack Nicklaus, and Craig Wood).

---

## Lefty

- In 1963, Bob Charles was the first left-hander to win a major—the British Open.
- In 2004, lefty Phil Mickelson won the Masters and in so doing became only the third left-handed winner of a major in the history of golf.

## The Big Three

To BECOME A GOOD PUTTER of the ball, you need three qualities. You need the ability to read greens, the ability to judge distance and breaks, and lastly you need a good stroke. Put all three of those together and you'll be the envy of your golf friends.

## Major Trivia

### WORLD'S NUMBER ONE

In 1996, the European Tour, Japan Golf Tour, PGA Tour, PGA Tour of Australia, and Southern Africa Tour formed the International Federation of PGA Tours. The alignment would lead to the World Golf Championships and the first widely accepted worldwide golf ranking system, thereby determining who plays in the majors.

### Final Day Leader

- In 1986, Greg Norman held the lead on Sunday morning in each of the four major championships.
- He was able to win only the British Open.
- Bobby Jones is the only other golfer who had previously held the Sunday morning lead in each Grand Slam event.

### Favorite Major

- 73 percent of avid golfers (25 rounds per year or more) say that the Masters is their favorite tournament to watch, according to a survey by *Golf Magazine*.
- 15 percent say it's the U.S. Open.
- 7 percent prefer the British Open.
- 5 percent favor the PGA Championship.

## Major Leaguers

*"Achievement is largely the product of steadily raising one's levels of aspiration and expectation."*
—Jack Nicklaus

*"The more I practice, the luckier I get."*—Gary Player

*"What does it take to be a champion? Desire, dedication, determination, concentration, and the will to win."*
—Gene Sarazen

## Between the Ears

*"Competitive golf is played mainly on the 5 1/2-inch course— the space between your ears."*—Bobby Jones

*"The person I fear most in the last two rounds is myself."*
—Tom Watson

*"What a shame to waste those great shots on the practice tee."*
—Walter Hagen

*"I play with friends, but we do not play friendly games."*
—Ben Hogan

*"Don't play too much golf. Two rounds a day are plenty."*
—Harry Vardon

## Bobby Jones

One of the greatest legends in golf is that of Atlanta lawyer Bobby Jones. At the height of his game and at the tender age of 28, Jones retired after winning four majors in a single season, a feat not accomplished before or since.

On a cold December day in 1971, golfers on the Old Course at St. Andrews stopped play and the flag on the clubhouse was lowered to half-mast. It was for Bobby Jones the legend, but it was also for somebody they had come to know beyond the game of golf.

For anybody who has ever seen footage or photographs of Bobby Jones, it is hard to imagine him as the sickly kid he was. Maybe it was the country air or the change of scenery, but when the Jones family moved digs to the Georgia countryside when Bobby was six, he began to flourish. Gone was the sickliness, and he began to play sports. One of those sports, as we all know, was golf.

If imitation is the sincerest form of flattery, then the golf-course professional at East Lake golf club from whom a young Jones began to learn the game should be flattered indeed. Jones began by mimicking the swing of Stewart Maiden, a swing that became the envy of the golfing world.

By the time Jones was nine he had won the Atlanta Athletic Club junior title, defeating a 16-year-old opponent. When he was 13, he won an invitational tournament in Birmingham, Alabama. As a 14-year-old, Jones won the Georgia Amateur and in 1916 he made U.S. Amateur history, becoming the youngest player ever to qualify for and play in a U.S. Amateur Championship. Jones didn't win, but he beat a former U.S. Amateur champion before eventually losing in the third round to defending champion Bob Gardner.

Like Jack Nicklaus and Tiger Woods after him, Jones's showing at the U.S. Amateur made him a legitimate star. The young 14-year-old was a "can't miss." He was the next big thing.

Problem was that the expectation was too much and too soon. When Jones picked up his ball in frustration after hitting into a bunker at the British Open in 1921, it was as if all of the promise had just disappeared. The British press was merciless in its condemnation of Jones, but what nobody knew was that inside, Jones would channel that humiliation and energy into a champion's heart. Far from being the end, it was just the beginning.

The lean years would continue until 1923 when the floodgates finally opened and Jones began to fulfill and exceed all that was expected of him. In that fateful year, he fought through a terrible finish and grueling 18-hole play-off to win the U.S. Open.

Between 1923 and 1930, Jones dominated the game of golf, winning at least one national championship every year and 13 of 21 major championships he entered. He was so completely dominant during that period that his two primary rivals—Walter Hagen and Gene Sarazen—never won any U.S. or British Open in which Jones played.

In 1926, Jones became the only amateur to win both the U.S. and British Open championships in the same year, a feat grand enough to earn him a ticker-tape parade down Broadway in New York City. In 1927, he returned to St. Andrews to defend his Open title and in the process erased the bitter disappointment he had suffered six years earlier. Declaring that the trophy would remain in St. Andrews if he should win, Jones endeared himself to the people of St. Andrews, forming a bond with the birthplace of golf that would flourish for all time.

## CAN YOU SAY GRAND SLAM?

In 1930, Jones accomplished the unthinkable by winning the U.S. and British Open and Amateur Championships all in the same year. This tremendous feat, later dubbed the Grand Slam, has never been accomplished before or since. Having already dominated both professionals and amateurs, there seemed to be no limit to the number of tournaments Jones could win. Just over a month after winning the Grand Slam, Bobby Jones shocked the world and retired.

Perhaps Bobby Jones's greatest legacy to the game of golf was his design of Augusta National. Still considered one of the finest golf courses in the world, Augusta opened in 1933 and is home to the Masters, one of the four major tournaments played today. Though he played the game almost three quarters of a century ago, Bobby Jones is forever woven into the very fabric of golf. He was simply one of the greatest the game of golf has ever seen.

---

### CHIPPING AWAY

IF AT ALL POSSIBLE you should always walk off the distance on short pitches and chips. That way you get a lay of the land and an idea where you want to put the ball.

---

# British Open

The oldest and arguably the most prestigious of the four majors is the British Open. Oddly enough, the first British Open wasn't really an open at all. In 1860, the Earl of Eglinton and Colonel James Fairlie of the Prestwick Golf Club cooked up the idea to host the "Open" and had letters sent to all the leading clubs in the area inviting them to send their top three players. The problem was that the letters didn't go out until October and only eight people showed up to play in the first championship.

The result: Willie Park beat Old Tom Morris by two strokes in the three round championship on the 12-hole course. For his effort Park received a handsome belt of red leather affixed with a silver buckle and decorations.

The following year the Open was declared open to the whole world. The announcement wasn't enough to bring a flood of new challengers (it jumped to twelve), but what it did begin was a legacy of sorts. This time Tom Morris was victorious, and by 1872 Tom Morris and his son, Young Tom Morris, had won four championships apiece. When Young Tom Morris won three in a row from 1868–1870, the bylaws clearly stated that the belt was his to keep.

Awarding Young Tom Morris the belt in perpetuity did pose one problem: What now for the new champion? In order to find the "green" for a new trophy, the Royal and Ancient Golf Club and the Honourable Company of Edinburgh Golfers were invited to contribute £10 each in turn for the right to stage the Open. The three clubs agreed to pony up with £10 for a new claret jug that today every golf fan knows is one of the most prestigious and sought after trophies in the world of sports.

One of the consequences of being a world power like the British Empire was that the game of golf spread rapidly outside its own borders. Soon real challengers from all parts of the globe began to arrive and compete in what was now a true open. Despite the challengers, Great Britain still maintained its sway as a Scot, an Englishman, and a Channel Islander managed to have one of the greatest runs in sport history.

## The Big Three

During a period of twenty years (from 1894–1914), J. H. Taylor, James Braid, and Harry Vardon won the Open sixteen times, and together they became known as the great triumvirate. Braid and Taylor had five victories each and Vardon remains the only person to this day to capture the Open six times.

The center could not hold forever, though, and in 1921 American Jock Hutchison became the first American to win the

Open, opening the floodgates to a series of American winners that would last from 1924–1933. The stylish American Walter Hagen would capture the British Open four times between 1922–29, a feat only surpassed by one other American by the name of Tom Watson.

Walter Hagen and Gene Sarazen (Sarazen captured the title in 1932) were at the height of their powers during this period, but the man who most intrigued golf enthusiasts on either side of the pond was a young Atlanta lawyer named Bobby Jones.

## Jones Arrives

Jones was derided by the British public and press in his first British Open showing for having a violent temper, but it was an image of Jones that would not last. When he won the last of his three British Open championships, it was as if he had conquered Britain itself. In the magical season of 1930 he captured all four major titles and retired immediately from competitive golf at the tender age of 28. He had become a legend.

Play was suspended during the war years, but immediately after the war the British Open began to be dominated by South African Bobby Locke and Australian Peter Thomson, capturing the title four times each in a ten-year stretch from 1949–58. That stretch was brought to an end by another South African, Gary Player.

American interest in the British Open would be rekindled with the arrival of Arnold Palmer, who would capture the title twice. In Palmer's wake would follow new British Open champions like Tom Watson, Jack Nicklaus, and Lee Trevino, beginning another American run at the championship.

Like all runs, though, it came to an end. It was time for Europeans to assert themselves and none did that better than Spain's Severiano Ballesteros, who won the British Open three times. Sandy Lyle would follow him, becoming the first Scot since James Braid in 1910 to add his name to the silver claret jug. England's Nick Faldo would also have a grand run, winning the British Open three times. Faldo may have won a fourth time were it not for Greg Norman, who finished with a spectacular 64 to win the first of two championships.

The 1990s and early 2000s have seen another run of American players hoisting the silver claret. Names like Tiger Woods, Ernie Els, John Daly, David Duval, and Mark O'Meara. No doubt new turns and new wrinkles await this most extraordinary of championships.

## Low Ball

MANY GOLFERS FEEL most comfortable (and safer) teeing the ball higher. True, you are more likely to catch a ball teed higher, but many pros find teeing the ball lower gives them increased accuracy.

# *British Open Record Book*

## Show Me the Money

### YEAR AND FIRST PRIZE (IN POUNDS STERLING)

| Year | Prize | Year | Prize |
|------|-------|------|---------|
| 1894 | £30 | 1938 | £100 |
| 1899 | £30 | 1981 | £25,000 |
| 1904 | £30 | 1949 | £300 |
| 1911 | £50 | 1985 | £65,000 |
| 1922 | £75 | 1993 | £100,000 |
| 1928 | £100 | 2003 | £700,000 |
| 1934 | £100 | | |

# Winner's Circle

| | | | |
|---|---|---|---|
| 2004 | Todd Hamilton | 1971 | Lee Trevino |
| 2003 | Ben Curtis | 1970 | Jack Nicklaus |
| 2002 | Ernie Els | 1969 | Tony Jacklin |
| 2001 | David Duval | 1968 | Gary Player |
| 2000 | Tiger Woods | 1967 | Roberto de Vicenzo |
| 1999 | Paul Lawrie | 1966 | Jack Nicklaus |
| 1998 | Mark O'Meara | 1965 | Peter Thomson |
| 1997 | Justin Leonard | 1964 | Tony Lema |
| 1996 | Tom Lehman | 1963 | Bob Charles |
| 1995 | John Daly | 1962 | Arnold Palmer |
| 1994 | Nick Price | 1961 | Arnold Palmer |
| 1993 | Greg Norman | 1960 | Kel Nagle |
| 1992 | Nick Faldo | 1959 | Gary Player |
| 1991 | Ian Baker-Finch | 1958 | Peter Thomson |
| 1990 | Nick Faldo | 1957 | Bobby Locke |
| 1989 | Mark Calcavecchia | 1956 | Peter Thomson |
| 1988 | Seve Ballesteros | 1955 | Peter Thomson |
| 1987 | Nick Faldo | 1954 | Peter Thomson |
| 1986 | Greg Norman | 1953 | Ben Hogan |
| 1985 | Sandy Lyle | 1952 | Bobby Locke |
| 1984 | Seve Ballesteros | 1951 | Max Faulkner |
| 1983 | Tom Watson | 1950 | Bobby Locke |
| 1982 | Tom Watson | 1949 | Bobby Locke |
| 1981 | Bill Rogers | 1948 | Henry Cotton |
| 1980 | Tom Watson | 1947 | Fred Daly |
| 1979 | Seve Ballesteros | 1946 | Sam Snead |
| 1978 | Jack Nicklaus | *1940–45 Not played* | |
| 1977 | Tom Watson | 1939 | Richard Burton |
| 1976 | Johnny Miller | 1938 | R. A. Whitcombe |
| 1975 | Tom Watson | 1937 | Henry Cotton |
| 1974 | Gary Player | 1936 | Alfred Padgham |
| 1973 | Tom Weiskopf | 1935 | Alfred Perry |
| 1972 | Lee Trevino | 1934 | Henry Cotton |

| | | | |
|---|---|---|---|
| 1933 | Denny Shute | 1894 | J. H. Taylor |
| 1932 | Gene Sarazen | 1893 | William Auchterlonie |
| 1931 | Tommy Armour | 1892 | Harold Hilton |
| 1930 | Robert Jones Jr. | 1891 | Hugh Kirkaldy |
| 1929 | Walter Hagen | 1890 | John Ball |
| 1928 | Walter Hagen | 1889 | Willie Park Jr. |
| 1927 | Robert Jones Jr. | 1888 | Jack Burns |
| 1926 | Robert Jones Jr. | 1887 | Willie Park Jr. |
| 1925 | James Barnes | 1886 | David Brown |
| 1924 | Walter Hagen | 1885 | Bob Martin |
| 1923 | Arthur Havers | 1884 | Jack Simpson |
| 1922 | Walter Hagen | 1883 | Willie Fernie |
| 1921 | Jock Hutchison | 1882 | Robert Ferguson |
| 1920 | George Duncan | 1881 | Robert Ferguson |
| *1915–19 Not played* | | 1880 | Robert Ferguson |
| 1914 | Harry Vardon | 1879 | Jamie Anderson |
| 1913 | J. H. Taylor | 1878 | Jamie Anderson |
| 1912 | Edward Ray | 1877 | Jamie Anderson |
| 1911 | Harry Vardon | 1876 | Robert Martin |
| 1910 | James Braid | 1875 | Willie Park |
| 1909 | J. H. Taylor | 1874 | Mungo Park |
| 1908 | James Braid | 1873 | Tom Kidd |
| 1907 | Arnaud Massy | 1872 | Tom Morris Jr. |
| 1906 | James Braid | *1871* | *Not played* |
| 1905 | James Braid | 1870 | Tom Morris Jr. |
| 1904 | Jack White | 1869 | Tom Morris Jr. |
| 1903 | Harry Vardon | 1868 | Tom Morris Jr. |
| 1902 | Alexander Herd | 1867 | Tom Morris Sr. |
| 1901 | James Braid | 1866 | Willie Park |
| 1900 | J. H. Taylor | 1865 | Andrew Strath |
| 1899 | Harry Vardon | 1864 | Tom Morris Sr. |
| 1898 | Harry Vardon | 1863 | Willie Park |
| 1897 | Harold Hilton | 1862 | Tom Morris Sr. |
| 1896 | Harry Vardon | 1861 | Tom Morris Sr. |
| 1895 | J. H. Taylor | 1860 | Willie Park |

> ## Distribution
>
> IN YOUR STANCE make sure weight is distributed evenly. Stand with your toes pointed slightly outward. You've just positioned yourself to take a competent stroke at your ball.

## MOST VICTORIES

6: Harry Vardon (1896, 1898, 1899, 1903, 1911, 1914)

5: James Braid (1901, 1905, 1906, 1908, 1910); J. H. Taylor (1894, 1895, 1900, 1909, 1913); Peter Thomson (1954, 1955, 1956, 1958, 1965); and Tom Watson (1975, 1977, 1980, 1982, 1983)

## MOST TIMES RUNNER-UP OR JOINT RUNNER-UP

7: Jack Nicklaus (1964, 1967, 1968, 1972, 1976, 1977, 1979)

6: J. H. Taylor (1896, 1904, 1905, 1906, 1907, 1914)

## Most Top-Five Finishes

16: J. H. Taylor; Jack Nicklaus

15: Harry Vardon; James Braid

## OLDEST WINNERS

Old Tom Morris (1867), 46 years, 99 days old

Harry Vardon (1914), 44 years, 41 days old

Roberto de Vicenzo (1967), 44 years, 93 days old

## Youngest Winners

Young Tom Morris (1868), 17 years, 5 months, 8 days old
Willie Auchterlonie (1893), 21 years, 24 days old
Severiano Ballesteros (1979), 22 years, 3 months, 12 days old

## Lowest Winning Scores

267: Greg Norman (66, 68, 69, 64), Royal St. George's, 1993
268: Tom Watson (68, 70, 65, 65), Turnberry, 1977; Nick Price
    (69, 66, 67, 66), Turnberry, 1994
269: Tiger Woods (67, 66, 67, 69), St. Andrews, 2000

## Biggest Margin of Victory

13 strokes: Old Tom Morris (1862)
12 strokes: Young Tom Morris (1870)
8 strokes: J. H. Taylor (1900 and 1913); James Braid (1908);
    Tiger Woods (2000)
6 strokes: Bobby Jones (1927); Walter Hagen (1929); Arnold
    Palmer (1962); and Johnny Miller (1976)

## Lowest Aggregate by an Amateur

281: Iain Pyman (68, 72, 70, 71), Royal St. George's, 1993; Tiger
    Woods (75, 66, 70, 70), Royal Lytham and St. Anne's, 1996
282: Justin Rose (72, 66, 75, 69), Royal Birkdale, 1998
283: Guy Wolstenhome (74, 70, 71, 68), St. Andrews, 1960

## Most Wins by Amateurs

3: Bobby Jones (1926, 1927, 1930)
2: Harold Hilton (1892, 1897)
1: John Ball (1890)
Roger Wethered lost a play-off in 1921

# LONGEST COURSE

7,361 yards, Carnoustie (1999)

## Courses Most Often Used

St. Andrews, 26
Prestwick, 24
Muirfield, 15
Sandwich, 13
Hoylake, 10
Royal Lytham, 10
Royal Birkdale, 8

Royal Troon, 7
Musselburgh, 6
Carnoustie, 6
Turnberry, 3
Deal, 2
Royal Portrush and Prince's, 1

## Successive Victories

4: Young Tom Morris (1868–72) (no championship in 1871)
3: Jamie Anderson (1877–79); Bob Ferguson (1880–82); Peter
  Thomson (1954–56)
2: Old Tom Morris (1861–62); J. H. Taylor (1894–95); Harry
  Vardon (1998–99); James Braid (1905–06); Bobby Jones
  (1926–27); Walter Hagen (1928–29); Bobby Locke
  (1949–50); Arnold Palmer (1961–62); Lee Trevino (1971–72);
  Tom Watson (1982–83)

## Highest Number of Rounds Under 70

33: Jack Nicklaus; Nick Faldo
27: Tom Watson
23: Greg Norman
21: Lee Trevino
20: Severiano Ballesteros; Nick Price

# First Players to Break 70 in the Open

1904 Royal St. George's:
68: J. H. Taylor
69: James Braid (3), Jack White (4)

## Champions in Three Decades

| | |
|---|---|
| Harry Vardon | (1896, 1903, 1911) |
| J. H. Taylor | (1894, 1900, 1913) |
| Gary Player | (1959, 1968, 1974) |

## Youngest and Oldest Competitor

Young Tom Morris (1865), 14 years, 4 months, 4 days old
Gene Sarazen (1976), 74 years, 5 months, 8 days old

## Lowest Individual Round

63: Mark Hayes, 2nd round Turnberry (1977); Isao Aoki, 3rd round Muirfield (1980); Greg Norman, 2nd round Turnberry (1986); Paul Broadhurst, 3rd round St. Andrews (1990); Jodie Mudd, 4th round Royal Birkdale (1991); Nick Faldo, 2nd round, and Payne Stewart, 4th round, Royal St. George's (1993)

## Lowest Individual Round by an Amateur

66: Frank Stranahan, 4th round Troon (1950); Tiger Woods, 2nd round, Royal Lytham and St. Anne's (1996); Justin Rose, 2nd round Birkdale (1998)

*Source: The British Open*

## No Ordinary Jug

The famous claret jug was made by Mackay Cunningham and Company of Edinburgh and was presented to the winner of the British Open in 1873 and every subsequent year for almost half a century. Cost of the original was £30. That all changed when Atlanta lawyer Bobby Jones won the Championship at St. Andrews in 1927. The Championship Committee of the R&A decided that "in future the original Open Championship Cup would be retained in possession of the Royal and Ancient Golf Club and that a duplicate be obtained for presentation to the winners."

### Why a Jug?

Because many social foursomes played for or wagered bottles (and on many occasions cases) of claret. Claret and port were the most popular drinks in the clubhouse, and many strange wagers were conceived in the bar after overindulging. One young, spry gentleman wagered he could drive a feathery from the Old Course to Cupar—over nine miles—in less than 1,000 shots. He did and won two cases of claret.

# ⇒ *British Open Trivia* ⇐

## It Never Rains But It Pours

- 179 was the winning score of the 1873 Open Championship, after torrential rains had soaked the course the night before. According to the rules of the time, a one-stroke penalty was recorded if a player moved his ball from casual water on the course. It was the highest score ever recorded for the 36-hole Open.

## SENIORS

British Open winners can play in the tournament without qualifying until age 65.

## JUST ONCE

*"I wish that every man who plays golf could play St. Andrews once."*—Gene Sarazen

## Aussie Rules

In 1954, Peter Thomson became the first Australian to win a major tournament with a victory in the British Open.

## What Odds

Odds of 500 to 1 were given by British bookmakers on 2003 British Open winner Ben Curtis winning the British Open.

##  NO MONEY BELT

- Old Tom Morris received £3 in prize money when he came in second to Willie Park in the first British Open.
- Willie Park received no prize money when he won the first British Open, making due with the title "The Champion Golfer" for that year.

## For All Time

Young Tom Morris, who had won the British Open four successive times (so often, in fact, that they gave him the championship belt to keep), was 24 years old when he died on Christmas day.

## Room and Board

• $14,000 is the weekly cost of staying at Harburn House near Edinburgh—advertised as being less than a two-hour commute to St. Andrew's—during the week of the British Open.

---

### COW PATTIE

*Q: "What abandoned course is that?"*
*A: "That, sir, is no abandoned course. That is where we play the Open Championship."*
—Sam Snead's conversation with a fellow passenger
upon arriving by train at St. Andrews in 1946

---

## Harry Vardon

Golf historians have been able to make a very good case that Harry Vardon may have been the greatest of them all. He is the only one of a great triumvirate (the other two being J. H. Taylor and James Braid) to capture six British Opens, a record that remains to this day. He was runner-up four more times, and across the pond he captured the U.S. Open once and was runner-up twice, the second of those as a fifty-year-old.

Vardon was born a Channel Islander in 1870, far away from the hotbed of golf in Scotland. As a result, he was unhindered and unencumbered by the prevailing swings and common practices on the courses there. When he played golf at all, Vardon played on a 50-yard course with handmade clubs made from oak and a marble ball.

Vardon's older brother, Tom, was a good enough golfer that he landed a job as a professional at an English club. Young Harry was interested in seeing whether he might be able to follow in his brother's footsteps and entered tournaments in England and Scotland. He did well enough in them to land him a series of positions as professional like his brother.

In 1896, Vardon began his assault on the British Open, beating J. H. Taylor and becoming the first Englishman to win the event. The Vardon win was more than just a victory, though. There was something peculiar about this young man that many golfers and golf watchers had never seen before: the Vardon grip and swing.

The swing was rhythmic, closer in to the body than was the prevailing practice in most of Scotland at the time. Vardon also had a wider stance and an interlocking grip (to this day called the Vardon grip) that must have made him a very peculiar sight indeed.

### JUST LIKE HARRY

Vardon was also said to have used lighter clubs than those used by golfers in Scotland, and when one of them broke, he often borrowed or replaced it with a lady's club. As the victories began to pile up, all of these Vardon peculiarities began to be emulated and, within a decade, everybody was golfing like Harry Vardon.

Vardon was the first celebrity golfer to be as much in demand in North America as he was at home. He traveled across the U.S., putting on well-attended exhibitions that served to further popularize the game here.

Three of Vardon's victories were with the guttie and three after the introduction of the rubber ball, a testimony to his skill and adaptability. The last of his major victories came with his win at the 1914 British Open (he also captured the French Open that same year) although he would be a competitive force into his fifties.

The quiet, charming Channel Islander spent thirty-four years as the professional at South Hertfordshire Golf Club near London. During the course of his lifetime, he did what no golfer had done before him—he changed the way the game was played.

## Bad Form

NOT EVERYBODY WHO PLAYS the game is blessed with perfect golfing posture. The best way to correct poor posture is to keep your back straight and bend your knees.

**1 3**

# U.S. Open

The first U.S. Open took place quietly in 1895 at Rhode Island's Newport Golf and Country Club. The tournament had such little standing in the public consciousness at the time that it was considered a sideshow to the U.S. Amateur Open, which was also taking place at the 9-hole Newport course that weekend.

A young Englishman, 21-year-old Horace Rawlins, emerged from the 11-man field to win it. He completed the 36-hole, single-day tournament with a score of 173, taking home the first-place prize money of $150, plus a $50 gold medal. In 1898, the tournament was extended to 72 holes over a three-day period, closing with 36 holes on the final day. That remained the format until 1965, when the U.S. Open went to four 18-hole daily rounds.

Young Horace Rawlins was the first of sixteen consecutive British champions who would win the U.S. Open in its early years. Indeed, Scotland's Willie Anderson won it three years in a row, from 1903 to 1905.

## Arrival of Ouimet

In 1911, however, something unprecedented happened. A young American, the youngest champion ever even to this day, John J. McDermott, went on to become the first American to claim the U.S. Open title. When 20-year-old American Francis Ouimet did the same thing in 1913, coming from out of nowhere to beat two British golf legends—Harry Vardon and Ted Ray—the golf world stopped to catch its breath.

The victory represented more than just a victory, it represented the beginning of a subtle shift in the number of Americans consistently beating their British rivals in major championships. It also had the effect of causing a tremendous upsurge in American interest in the game.

In 1922, another kid, a 20-year-old who had quit school in sixth grade, had copped the U.S. Open title. It was a fairy-tale story that captivated the American public again and made the name Sarazen one of the most famous in golf for almost half a century.

By 1930, the year the brilliant U.S. Amateur Bobby Jones captured all four majors in a season, the shift from British to American dominance was complete. Since 1930, only five foreign players have won the U.S. Open title—England's Tony Jacklin, Australia's David Graham, and the South African trio of Gary Player, Ernie Els, and Retief Goosen. If you take a quick glance at the list of names who have won what is effectively the U.S.'s national golf championship, you see names like Sarazen, Hagen, Jones, Hogan, Palmer, Nicklaus, Payne Stewart, and Tiger Woods.

The history of the U.S. Open has been intertwined with the development and history of golf in the U.S. Great champions like Sarazen, Jones, Nicklaus, and Palmer made their mark here, but none have made their mark more so than the great Ben Hogan.

In 1950, after a full year away from the game of golf because of a crippling car crash, Hogan came to the U.S. Open at Merrion to win the second of four U.S. Open championship titles and make him one of the greatest U.S. Open champions in the history of the event.

Bridesmaids have a way of staying bridesmaids and that certainly appeared the case for Ken Venturi. In 1958, at the U.S. Open, the likable Venturi lost by two strokes. In 1960, it would happen again when Arnold Palmer birdied the last two holes to steal victory by a single stroke from Venturi.

By 1963, Venturi didn't even qualify for the U.S. Open and it looked like opportunity had passed him by. In 1964 however, the golf gods smiled down on Venturi. He came from behind to beat Palmer and Tommy Jacobs in one of the biggest and most cheered victories in U.S. Open history.

Another champion whose greatness was on display at the U.S. Open was Tiger Woods. In 2000, he put together what many observers consider to be the most awesome display of golf ever seen. He destroyed the field at Pebble Beach, and in the process smashed U.S. Open records, including most strokes under par at any point (12), lowest 36-hole total (134) and biggest winning margin (15).

The U.S. Open is played at a different course each year, though a number of courses have hosted the tournament more than once. The host course is prepared to United States Golf Association (USGA) specifications and the course is designed to make it play considerably more difficult than it would normally. Fairways are generally narrower, rough is deeper, and par-5 holes are often shortened slightly to become long par-4s.

Golfers often complain about the difficulty of the Open course, but listen to this response from USGA executive Frank Tatum: "We had no intention of confounding the best players in the world. We simply wanted to identify who they were."

## Opened and Closed

OPENED AND CLOSED STANCES are used for different shots. For drives, for example, you should have a square or slightly closed stance, meaning you should line up square to the line of the shot. An opened stance, used for chips, places your foot across the line of the shot, giving you greater control over your club rather than balance.

# ⚕ *U.S. Open Record Book* ⚕
## Show Me the Money

| Year | Amount | Year | Amount |
|------|--------|------|--------|
| 1895 | $150 | 1960 | $14,400 |
| 1905 | $200 | 1970 | $30,000 |
| 1915 | $300 | 1980 | $55,000 |
| 1930 | $1000 | 1990 | $220,000 |
| 1940 | $1,000 | 2000 | $800,000 |
| 1950 | $4,000 | 2003 | $1,080,000 |

## WINNER'S CIRCLE

| Year | Winner | Year | Winner |
|------|--------|------|--------|
| 2004 | Retief Goosen | 1983 | Larry Nelson |
| 2003 | Jim Furyk | 1982 | Tom Watson |
| 2002 | Tiger Woods | 1981 | David Graham |
| 2001 | Retief Goosen | 1980 | Jack Nicklaus |
| 2000 | Tiger Woods | 1979 | Hale Irwin |
| 1999 | Payne Stewart | 1978 | Andy North |
| 1998 | Lee Janzen | 1977 | Hubert Green |
| 1997 | Ernie Els | 1976 | Jerry Pate |
| 1996 | Steve Jones | 1975 | Lou Graham |
| 1995 | Corey Pavin | 1974 | Hale Irwin |
| 1994 | Ernie Els | 1973 | Johnny Miller |
| 1993 | Lee Janzen | 1972 | Jack Nicklaus |
| 1992 | Tom Kite | 1971 | Lee Trevino |
| 1991 | Payne Stewart | 1970 | Tony Jacklin |
| 1990 | Hale Irwin | 1969 | Orville Moody |
| 1989 | Curtis Strange | 1968 | Lee Trevino |
| 1988 | Curtis Strange | 1967 | Jack Nicklaus |
| 1987 | Scott Simpson | 1966 | Billy Casper |
| 1986 | Ray Floyd | 1965 | Gary Player |
| 1985 | Andy North | 1964 | Ken Venturi |
| 1984 | Fuzzy Zoeller | 1963 | Julius Boros |

| 1962 | Jack Nicklaus | 1927 | Tommy Armour |
|------|---------------|------|--------------|
| 1961 | Gene Littler | 1926 | Bobby Jones |
| 1960 | Arnold Palmer | 1925 | W. MacFarlane |
| 1959 | Billy Casper | 1924 | Cyril Walker |
| 1958 | Tommy Bolt | 1923 | Bobby Jones |
| 1957 | Dick Mayer | 1922 | Gene Sarazen |
| 1956 | Cary Middlecoff | 1921 | James M. Barnes |
| 1955 | Jack Fleck | 1920 | Edward Ray |
| 1954 | Ed Furgol | 1919 | Walter Hagen |
| 1953 | Ben Hogan | *1917–18 Not played* | |
| 1952 | Julius Boros | | *due to World War I* |
| 1951 | Ben Hogan | 1916 | Charles Evans Jr. |
| 1950 | Ben Hogan | 1915 | Jerome Travers |
| 1949 | Cary Middlecoff | 1914 | Walter Hagen |
| 1948 | Ben Hogan | 1913 | Francis Ouimet |
| 1947 | Lew Worsham | 1912 | John McDermott |
| 1946 | Lloyd Mangrum | 1911 | John McDermott |
| *1942–45 Not played* | | 1910 | Alex Smith |
| | *due to World War II* | 1909 | George Sargent |
| 1941 | Craig Wood | 1908 | Fred McLeod |
| 1940 | Lawson Little | 1907 | Alex Ross |
| 1939 | Byron Nelson | 1906 | Alex Smith |
| 1938 | Ralph Guldahl | 1905 | Willie Anderson |
| 1937 | Ralph Guldahl | 1904 | Willie Anderson |
| 1936 | Tony Manero | 1903 | Willie Anderson |
| 1935 | Sam Parks Jr. | 1902 | Laurie Auchterlonie |
| 1934 | Olin Dutra | 1901 | Willie Anderson |
| 1933 | Johnny Goodman | 1900 | Harry Vardon |
| 1932 | Gene Sarazen | 1899 | Willie Smith |
| 1931 | Billy Burke | 1898 | Fred Herd |
| 1930 | Bobby Jones | 1897 | Joe Lloyd |
| 1929 | Bobby Jones | 1896 | James Foulis |
| 1928 | Johnny Farrell | 1895 | Horace Rawlins |

> ## Down Under
>
> NEW AND EVEN EXPERIENCED PLAYERS often complain about not getting under the ball with their irons. Players see pros taking a divot with their irons, so the object becomes taking the divot and not the ball. Wrong. The divot is taken after you make contact with the ball.

## Most Victories

4: Willie Anderson (1901, 1903, 1904, 1905); Robert T. Jones Jr. (1923, 1926, 1929, 1930); Ben Hogan (1948, 1950, 1951, 1953); and Jack Nicklaus (1962, 1967, 1972, 1980)

## MOST TIMES RUNNER-UP OR JOINT RUNNER-UP

4: Robert T. (Bobby) Jones Jr. (1922, 1924, 1925, 1928); Sam Snead (1937, 1947, 1949, 1953); Arnold Palmer (1962, 1963, 1966, 1967); and Jack Nicklaus (1960, 1968, 1971, 1982)

## Most Top-Five Finishes

11: Willie Anderson; Jack Nicklaus
10: Alex Smith; Walter Hagen; Ben Hogan; Arnold Palmer

## Most Top-Ten Finishes

18: Jack Nicklaus     14: Gene Sarazen
16: Walter Hagen      13: Arnold Palmer
15: Ben Hogan         12: Sam Snead

## Oldest Winners

Hale Irwin (1990), 45 years, 15 days old
Raymond Floyd (1986), 43 years, 9 months, 11 days old
Ted Ray (1920), 43 years, 4 months, 16 days old

## YOUNGEST WINNER

John J. McDermott (1911), 19 years, 10 months, 14 days old

## Lowest Winning Scores

272: Jack Nicklaus (63, 71, 70, 68), Baltusrol G.C. (Lower
     Course), 1980; Lee Janzen (67, 67, 69, 69), Baltusrol G.C.
     (Lower Course), 1993; and Tiger Woods (65, 69, 71, 67),
     (12 under par), Pebble Beach G.L., 2000
273: David Graham (68, 68, 70, 67), Merion G.C. (East Course),
     1981

## Best Comeback by Winner, Final Round

7 strokes: Arnold Palmer (72, 71, 72, 65), Cherry Hills C.C., 1960
6 strokes: Johnny Miller (71, 69, 76, 63), Oakmont C.C., 1973
5 strokes: Johnny Farrell (77, 74, 71, 72), Olympia Fields C.C.,
           1928; Byron Nelson (72, 73, 71, 68), Philadelphia
           C.C., 1939; and Lee Janzen (73, 66, 73, 68), The
           Olympic Club, San Francisco, 1998

 ## BIGGEST MARGIN OF VICTORY

15 strokes: Tiger Woods (272), Pebble Beach G.L., 2000
11 strokes: Willie Smith (315), Baltimore C.C., 1899

## Amateurs to Win the Championship

Francis Ouimet, The Country Club, Brookline, MS, 1913
Jerome D. Travers, Baltusrol G.C., Springfield, NJ, 1915
Charles Evans Jr., Minikahda Club, Minneapolis, MN, 1916
Robert T. Jones Jr., Inwood (NY) C.C., 1923; Scioto C.C.,
     Columbus, OH, 1926; Winged Foot G.C., Mamaroneck, NY,
     1929; Interlachen C.C., Edina, MN, 1930
John Goodman, North Shore C.C., Glenview, IL, 1933

## Oldest Players to Make the Cut

61: Sam Snead, 1973 (tied for 29th)

58: Jack Nicklaus, 1998 (tied for 43rd)

57: Sam Snead, 1969 (tied for 38th); Dutch Harrison, 1967 (tied for 16th); Jack Nicklaus, 1997 (tied for 52nd)

## Lowest Score 18 Holes

63 (8 under): Johnny Miller, final round, Oakmont C.C., 1973

63 (7 under): Jack Nicklaus, first round, Baltusrol G.C., 1980; Tom Weiskopf, first round, Baltusrol G.C., 1980

## Lowest Score by Non-Winner, 72 Holes

274 (6 under): Isao Aoki (68-68-68-70), Baltusrol G.C., 1980; Payne Stewart (70-66-68-70), Baltusrol G.C., 1993

## Largest 54-Hole Lead

10: Tiger Woods (205), Pebble Beach G.L., 2000

 7: James Barnes (217), Columbia C.C., Chevy Chase, MD, 1921

 6: Fred Herd (244), Myopia Hunt Club, S. Hamilton, Mass., 1898; Willie Anderson (225), Baltusrol G.C., Springfield, NJ, 1903; Johnny Goodman (211), North Shore G.C., Glenview, IL, 1933

## Largest Lead after 54 Holes (Non-Winner)

5: Mike Brady, Brae Burn C.C., West Newton, MS, 1919

## Highest Score by Winner, First Round

91: Horace Rawlins, Newport (RI) G.C., 1895

SINCE WORLD WAR I

78 (6 over): Tommy Armour, Oakmont (PA) C.C., 1927

78 (7 over): Walter Hagen, Brae Burn C.C., West Newton, MS, 1919

76 (6 over): Ben Hogan, Oakland Hills C.C., Birmingham, MI, 1951; Jack Fleck, Olympic Club, San Francisco, CA, 1955

## Lowest Score by Winner, Fourth Round

63 (8 under): Johnny Miller, Oakmont (PA) C.C., 1973

65 (6 under): Arnold Palmer, Cherry Hills C.C., Englewood, CO, 1960

65 (5 under): Jack Nicklaus, Baltusrol G.C., Springfield, NJ, 1967

## HIGHEST WINNING SCORE

331: Willie Anderson, Myopia Hunt Club, South Hamilton, MS, 1901 (won in play-off)

293: Julius Boros, The Country Club, Brookline, MS, 1963 (won in play-off)

290: Jack Nicklaus, Pebble Beach (CA) G.L., 1972

## Highest Score, One Hole

19: Ray Ainsley, 16th Hole (par-4), Cherry Hills C.C., Englewood, CO, 1938

## Most Sub-Par Rounds, Career

37: Jack Nicklaus

## ROUNDS IN THE 60S

29: Jack Nicklaus

## Sub-Par 72-Hole Totals

7: Jack Nicklaus

## Most Times Led after 54 Holes

6: Robert T. Jones Jr.
4: Tom Watson

## MOST TIMES LED AFTER 18, 36, OR 54 HOLES

11: Payne Stewart
10: Alex Smith
9: Robert T. Jones Jr.; Sam Snead; Arnold Palmer

## Most Times Low Amateur

9: Robert T. (Bobby) Jones Jr.

## Low 72-Hole Score by an Amateur

282: Jack Nicklaus, Cherry Hills C.C., Englewood, CO, 1960

## WINNERS OF BOTH U.S. OPEN AND U.S. AMATEUR

Francis Ouimet (1913 Open; 1914, 1931 Amateurs)
Jerome D. Travers (1915 Open; 1907, 1908, 1912, 1913 Amateurs)
Charles Evans Jr. (1916 Open; 1916, 1920 Amateurs)*
Robert T. Jones Jr. (1923, 1926, 1929, 1930 Opens; 1924, 1925, 1927, 1928, 1930 Amateurs)*
John Goodman (1933 Open; 1937 Amateur)
Lawson Little (1940 Open; 1934, 1935 Amateurs)
Arnold Palmer (1960 Open; 1954 Amateur)
Gene Littler (1961 Open; 1953 Amateur)
Jack Nicklaus (1962, 1967, 1972, 1980 Opens; 1959, 1961 Amateurs)
Jerry Pate (1976 Open, 1974 Amateur)
Tiger Woods (2000, 2002 Opens; 1994, 1995, 1996 Amateurs)
*Won both the same year

# Evolution of U.S. Open Scoring Records

| 1895 | 173 | Horace Rawlins | (91, 82) |
|------|-----|----------------|----------|
| 1896 | 152 | James Foulis | (78, 74) |
| 1898 | 328 | Fred Herd | (84, 85, 75, 84) |
| 1899 | 315 | Willie Smith | (77, 82, 79, 77) |
| 1900 | 313 | Harry Vardon | (79, 78, 76, 80) |
| 1902 | 307 | Laurie Auchterlonie | (78, 78, 74, 77) |
| 1904 | 303 | Willie Anderson | (75, 78, 78, 72) |
| 1906 | 295 | Alex Smith | (73, 74, 73, 75) |
| 1909 | 290 | George Sargent | (75, 72, 72, 71) |
| 1916 | 286 | Charles Evans Jr. | (70, 69, 74, 73) |
| 1936 | 282 | Tony Manero | (73, 69, 73, 67) |
| 1937 | 281 | Ralph Guldahl | (71, 69, 72, 69) |
| 1948 | 276 | Ben Hogan | (67, 72, 68, 69) |
| 1967 | 275 | Jack Nicklaus | (71, 67, 72, 65) |
| 1980 | 272 | Jack Nicklaus | (63, 71, 70, 68) |
| 1993 | 272 | Lee Janzen | (67, 67, 69, 69) |
| 2000 | 272 | Tiger Woods | (65, 69, 71, 67) |

## Consecutive Wins

3: Willie Anderson (1903, 1904, 1905)

2: John J. McDermott (1911, 1912); Robert T. Jones Jr. (1929, 1930); Ralph Guldahl (1937, 1938); Ben Hogan (1950, 1951); and Curtis Strange (1988, 1989)

*Source: United States Golf Association*

## WARM UP

What clubs to begin with? Most pros begin with soft or half-swings, warming up their muscles and preparing for the full swings to follow. They also start with their shorter clubs, working up to hitting driver. Another tip is always to make your last practice shots with the club you'll be using off the first tee.

# ≋ *U.S. Open Trivia* ≋

## Lucky 7

Chick Evans had seven clubs in his bag when he won the 1916 U.S. Open

## Runner-Ups

- Bobby Jones was the runner-up at the U.S. Open eight times in a nine-year period.
- Arnold Palmer lost the U.S. Open in a play-off three times.

## You're the One

- Andy North won two events during his professional career.
- Both of them were U.S. Opens.

## Trade You

- Sixth grade dropout Gene Sarazen earned $500 for winning the 1922 U.S. Open.
- $1.08 million in prize money was awarded in 2004.

## Amateurs

- The U.S. Open has been won by an amateur eight times.
- Four of those were by Robert (Bobby) Jones.

## Decade

- 10 is the number of years for which a champion receives a full exemption into the field.
- 15 is the number of the top finishers that are exempt from qualifying for next year's U.S. Open.

## You Want In?

- 1.4 is the U.S. Golf Association Handicap Index at which any amateur or professional golfer can apply to play in the U.S. Open.
- 8,500 people apply annually to play in the U.S. Open.

## YOU WANT TO BE ON TV?

- 55 million people typically watch the U.S. Open on television in the U.S.

## The Longest Yard

- 289 yards was the longest drive at the 1928 U.S. Open.

---

## Gene Sarazen

When Gene Sarazen captured his first U.S. Open in 1922, he was proof-positive of the American dream. He had to quit school by sixth grade to help support his family. Luckily for the golfing world, when he began to apprentice with his carpenter father at sixteen he developed pleurisy and was instructed to find a more suitable employment outdoors.

Sarazen quickly landed that outdoor job, becoming an assistant pro at a local golf club. Although he had played on the public courses as a kid and practiced during his recuperation, his job as assistant pro allowed him to practice until he felt he had it perfect.

In 1922, as a brash 20-year-old, the golfing world saw that perfection. He came from behind to capture the first of two U.S. Open titles. For immigrant America and for the working class, Sarazen's victory represented more than just a win at a major, it meant they too could take up the game of golf and they too could win a major.

Sarazen was no flash in the pan. By the time his career ended, he had won seven major titles and is one of only five players to have won a career Grand Slam (capturing the Masters, U.S. and British Opens, and PGA Championship), the others being Ben Hogan, Gary Player, Jack Nicklaus, and Tiger Woods.

Perhaps because of his humble beginnings, Sarazen was ever alert to opportunity to earn a dollar. He played exhibition matches all over the globe. He also developed and marketed the sand wedge. Reporters, players, and the public admired his pluck. Sarazen's appeal was such that tournaments still wanted him in their field even though his best playing days were behind him. In the PGA Championship, he was both its youngest winner and, at seventy, its oldest participant.

Whatever business success Sarazen had off the course, he knew it all related to his performance on the course. During his long career, he won thirty-two PGA Tournaments, captured seven major titles, and was a member of the American Ryder Cup team on six occasions.

Sarazen was introduced to a whole new generation of golf fans as a television commentator with *Shell's Wonderful World of Golf*. He claimed that more people knew of him as a commentator than as a winner of tournaments.

Not true of the golfing world. By any measure, his was an extraordinary career. Gene Sarazen was inducted into the World Golf Hall of Fame in 1974.

## On Your Knees

TEE UP YOUR BALL, then kneel and get ready to stroke it with your driver. What this allows you to see is how your backswing coils your back, shoulders, and hips together. The trick now is to use this knowledge off the tee.

14

# The Masters

When Atlanta lawyer Bobby Jones captured all four majors and promptly retired in 1930, he was by no means finished with golf. He had always considered building his ideal golf course, so when a couple of investment bankers who wintered in the area approached Jones with some potential land that they thought he might like, he said he would take a look.

Although Jones was approached many times before, the minute Jones laid his eyes on what was then the Fruitland Nursery, he knew this was it. Today, of course, it is known as Augusta National Golf Club and the tournament Jones began in 1934 called the Augusta National Invitational Tournament (he thought Masters sounded too snooty) was begun. He was going to bring in his old combatants—all of the world's best golfers—and see what happened.

The first Augusta National Invitational was such a huge hit, plans were quickly drawn up for the following year. In the second year, Gene Sarazen won the tournament, thanks to what has become one of the most famous shots in golf.

## Shot Heard 'Round the World

With four holes to play, Sarazen was three strokes behind Craig Wood, who was already finished for the day. Two hundred and thirty-five yards from the hole on the par-5 15th, Sarazen let rip with a 4-wood. The ball bounced and bounced, dribbling into the hole for a double eagle. Sarazen had tied Wood with a single stroke and won the next day in a play-off. The press dubbed it "the shot heard 'round the world."

The Augusta National Invitational and, later, the Masters (Jones finally gave in to the name change in 1939) has been front-page news ever since. The first of the four majors, it is compulsory viewing for any golf fan. The green jacket and the Masters seem today as much a part of spring as daffodils and tulips. For many in the northern hemisphere, the golf season doesn't really begin until after the Masters.

The Masters is arguably the best known of the four majors. It is the only major played at the same course year after year, and television has seen to it that even those who have never been to Augusta seem to have great affection for it.

After the great triumph by Sarazen, other great stars made their mark at Augusta. Jimmy Demaret became the first person to win the Masters three times. The boyhood rivals Ben Hogan and Byron Nelson continued their rivalry at Augusta. In the second of his two Masters victories, Nelson beat Hogan in an 18-hole play-off by a single stroke.

Hogan was not to be denied, though. He captured his first Masters title in 1951, after the golfing world thought his career was over as a result of a debilitating car crash. For good measure, Hogan would repeat the feat in 1953.

## Modern Triumvirate

After Hogan came the modern triumvirate of Arnold Palmer, Gary Player, and Jack Nicklaus. All handsome, all ripe for a new age: the television age. In the nine-year period between 1958–1966, they won a total of eight Masters titles—Palmer four times, Nicklaus three, and Player once. Although Palmer's victories would stop at four, Nicklaus would go on to win six times and Player three times.

Although the Masters had been dominated by Americans, after the modern triumvirate it was now time for the Europeans to stand up and have their run. Seve Ballesteros of Spain won two Masters championships. He was joined by Bernhard Langer, Nick Faldo, Ian Woosnan, and the Scot Sandy Lyle. Ballesteros would later be joined by fellow countryman Jose Maria Olazabal.

Americans, of course, were not done. Tiger Woods burst onto the scene in 1997, capturing the first of three Masters championships. He was joined by Mark O'Meara and Phil Mickelson. No matter who the champion or where they're from, the Masters will always be one of the most important golf tournaments in the world.

Part of the charm of the Masters is its tradition. The green jacket can only be worn by members and the Masters champion, and only by the Masters champion as long as he or she remains champion. The course is also cordoned off so that the players have more room than in any other golf event in the world. Then, of course, there is the prize money, which now exceeds the million-dollar mark. As with the other majors, along with a win at the Masters come the endorsement deals and all of the benefits of modern professional golf. More than anything, what a victory at the Masters means for the champion is that over the course of four days, he played and beat the best players in the world.

---

### CHIN UP

KEEPING YOUR CHIN UP as you swing through the ball helps keep your back straight.

---

## Masters Record Book

### Show Me the Money

#### FIRST PRIZE MONEY BY YEAR

| | | | |
|---|---|---|---|
| 1934 | $1,500 | 1976 | $40,000 |
| 1946 | $2,500 | 1986 | $144,000 |
| 1956 | $6000 | 1996 | $450,000 |
| 1966 | $20,000 | 2004 | $1,080,000 |

### Winner's Circle

| | | | |
|---|---|---|---|
| 2004 | Phil Mickelson | 2000 | Vijay Singh |
| 2003 | Mike Weir | 1999 | Jose Maria Olazabal |
| 2002 | Tiger Woods | 1998 | Mark O'Meara |
| 2001 | Tiger Woods | 1997 | Tiger Woods |

| 1996 | Nick Faldo | 1966 | Jack Nicklaus |
|------|------------|------|---------------|
| 1995 | Ben Crenshaw | 1965 | Jack Nicklaus |
| 1994 | Jose Maria Olazabal | 1964 | Arnold Palmer |
| 1993 | Bernhard Langer | 1963 | Jack Nicklaus |
| 1992 | Fred Couples | 1962 | Arnold Palmer |
| 1991 | Ian Woosnam | 1961 | Gary Player |
| 1990 | Nick Faldo | 1960 | Arnold Palmer |
| 1989 | Nick Faldo | 1959 | Art Wall |
| 1988 | Sandy Lyle | 1958 | Arnold Palmer |
| 1987 | Larry Mize | 1957 | Doug Ford |
| 1986 | Jack Nicklaus | 1956 | Jack Burke Jr. |
| 1985 | Bernhard Langer | 1955 | Cary Middlecoff |
| 1984 | Ben Crenshaw | 1954 | Sam Snead |
| 1983 | Seve Ballesteros | 1953 | Ben Hogan |
| 1982 | Craig Stadler | 1952 | Sam Snead |
| 1981 | Tom Watson | 1951 | Ben Hogan |
| 1980 | Seve Ballesteros | 1950 | Jimmy Demaret |
| 1979 | Fuzzy Zoeller | 1949 | Sam Snead |
| 1978 | Gary Player | 1948 | Claude Harmon |
| 1977 | Tom Watson | 1947 | Jimmy Demaret |
| 1976 | Raymond Floyd | 1946 | Herman Keiser |
| 1975 | Jack Nicklaus | 1942 | Byron Nelson |
| 1974 | Gary Player | 1941 | Craig Wood |
| 1973 | Tommy Aaron | 1940 | Jimmy Demaret |
| 1972 | Jack Nicklaus | 1939 | Ralph Guldahl |
| 1971 | Charles Cody | 1938 | Henry Picard |
| 1970 | Billy Casper | 1937 | Byron Nelson |
| 1969 | George Archer | 1936 | Horton Smith |
| 1968 | Bob Goalby | 1935 | Gene Sarazen |
| 1967 | Gay Brewer | 1934 | Horton Smith |

## Most Victories

6: Jack Nicklaus (1963, 1965, 1966, 1972, 1975, 1986)

4: Arnold Palmer (1958, 1960, 1962, 1964)

3: Jimmy Demaret (1940, 1947, 1950); Sam Snead (1949, 1952, 1954); Gary Player (1961, 1974, 1978); Nick Faldo (1989, 1990, 1996); and Tiger Woods (1997, 2001, 2002)

2: Horton Smith (1934, 1936); Byron Nelson (1937, 1942); Ben Hogan (1951, 1953); Tom Watson (1977, 1981); Seve Ballesteros (1980, 1983); Bernhard Langer (1985, 1993); Ben Crenshaw (1984, 1995); and Jose Maria Olazabal (1994, 1999)

## Most Times Runner-Up

4: Ben Hogan (1942, 1946, 1954, 1955); Jack Nicklaus (1964, 1971, 1977, 1981); Tom Weiskopf (1969, 1972, 1974, 1975)

3: Johnny Miller (1971, 1975, 1981); Greg Norman (1986, 1987, 1996); Tom Watson (1978, 1979, 1984); Raymond Floyd (1985, 1990, 1992); and Tom Kite (1983, 1986, 1997)

## WIRE-TO-WIRE CHAMPIONS

| Craig Wood | (1941) | Jack Nicklaus | (1972) |
| Arnold Palmer | (1960) | Raymond Floyd | (1976) |

# Most Top Fives

15: Jack Nicklaus
9: Ben Hogan; Tom Kite; Arnold Palmer; Sam Snead; Tom Watson

## Most Top Tens

22: Jack Nicklaus
17: Ben Hogan
15: Gary Player; Sam Snead; Tom Watson
14: Byron Nelson

## Widest Margin of Victory

12 strokes, Tiger Woods (1997)

## Best Comebacks

After 18 Holes: 7 strokes, Nick Faldo (1990)
After 36 Holes: 8 strokes, Jack Burke (1956)
After 54 Holes: 8 strokes, Jack Burke (1956)

### OTHERS

8 strokes: Gary Player (1978, final round)
6 strokes: Nick Faldo (1996, final round)
5 strokes: Art Wall (1959, with 7 holes to play)
3 strokes: Fuzzy Zoeller (1979, with 3 holes to play); Nick Faldo
   (1989, with 3 holes to play)

## Oldest Winner

Jack Nicklaus (1986), 46 years, 2 months, 23 days old

## Youngest Winner

Tiger Woods (1997), 21 years, 3 months, 14 days old

### OLDEST FIRST-TIME WINNER

Mark O'Meara (1998), 41 years, 3 months, 29 days old

### Youngest First-Time Winner

Tiger Woods (1997), 21 years, 3 months, 14 days old

### Oldest Second-Time Winner

Ben Crenshaw (1995), 43 years, 2 months, 29 days old

### YOUNGEST SECOND-TIME WINNER

Jack Nicklaus (1965), 25 years, 2 months, 21 days old

### Oldest Third-Time Winner

Gary Player (1978), 42 years, 5 months, 8 days old

### Youngest Third-Time Winner

Jack Nicklaus (1966), 25 years, 2 months, 20 days old

### OLDEST FOURTH-TIME WINNER

Arnold Palmer (1964), 34 years, 7 months, 2 days old

### Youngest Fourth-Time Winner

Jack Nicklaus (1972), 32 years, 2 months, 19 days old

### Youngest/Oldest Fifth-Time Winner

Jack Nicklaus (1975), 35 years, 2 months, 23 days old

### AVERAGE WINNER'S AGE

32.65 years

## Average First-Time Winner's Age

31.58 years (41 winners, 16 under age 30)

## Number of Attempts before First Victory

1: Horton Smith (1934); Gene Sarazen (1935); Fuzzy Zoeller (1979)

2: Jimmy Demaret (1940); Herman Keiser (1946)

3: Byron Nelson (1937); Ralph Guldahl (1939); Claude Harmon (1948); George Archer (1969); Bernhard Langer (1985); Tiger Woods (1997)

4: Arnold Palmer (1958); Art Wall (1959); Tom Watson (1977); Seve Ballesteros (1980); Larry Mize (1987); Mike Weir (2003); Ian Woosnam (1991)

5: Henry Picard (1938); Doug Ford (1957); Gary Player (1961); Jack Nicklaus (1963)

6: Gay Brewer (1967); Charles Coody (1971); Craig Stadler (1982); Nick Faldo (1989)

7: Jack Burke (1956); Sandy Lyle (1988); Vijay Singh (2000)

8: Craig Wood (1941); Jose Maria Olazabal (1994)

9: Bob Goalby (1968); Fred Couples (1992)

10: Sam Snead (1949); Ben Hogan (1951); Cary Middlecoff (1955)

11: Tommy Aaron (1973)

12: Raymond Floyd (1976)

13: Ben Crenshaw (1984)

14: Billy Casper (1970)

15: Mark O'Meara (1998)

## AVERAGE NUMBER OF ATTEMPTS BEFORE FIRST VICTORY

6 (41 Players)

# Number of Attempts before Second Victory

3: Horton Smith
6: Jimmy Demaret; Arnold Palmer
7: Jack Nicklaus; Seve Ballesteros; Nick Faldo; Tiger Woods
8: Byron Nelson; Tom Watson
11: Bernhard Langer
12: Ben Hogan
13: Jose Maria Olazabal; Sam Snead
17: Gary Player
24: Ben Crenshaw

## Average Number of Attempts before Second Victory

9 (15 players)

## LOWEST SCORE

276: Tiger Woods (winner), 2002
278: Tom Watson (T2), 1978; Nick Faldo (winner), 1990

## Low 72 Holes

270: Tiger Woods (1997)
271: Jack Nicklaus (1965); Raymond Floyd (1976)
272: Tiger Woods (2001)

## Low Amateur

281: Charles R. Coe (72, 71, 69, 69), 1961
Source: Augusta National Inc.

## Masters Trivia
### The King

Arnold Palmer has played in fifty Masters.

### Foreigners

- In 1961, Gary Player became the first international winner of the Masters.
- In 2004, the Masters welcomed its first Chinese player.

### CHAMPION'S DINNER

In 1952, the "Champion's Dinner" (also known as the Masters Club) began when defending champion Ben Hogan gave a dinner for all previous winners. Each year since, the defending champion selects the menu and acts as host for the Tuesday night dinner.

### It's How You Play the Game

Bobby Jones finished 13th at the first Masters in 1934. Even though he had retired from golf by that time, he played in the first Masters because the club was not yet on a firm financial footing and it was expected Jones would be a huge draw.

# A Little Green

- In 1937, Augusta National members were urged to buy and wear a green jacket during the Masters Tournament so that patrons would be able to identify a reliable source of information.
- In 1949, the tradition of awarding the Green Jacket began at the Masters, given to winner Sam Snead.
- Three times it was not necessary for the preceding champion to give the winner the Green Jacket, because they were the preceding winner (Jack Nicklaus, Nick Faldo, and Tiger Woods).

## PLAYING FAVORITES

- 53 percent of golf-course superintendents say the Masters is their favorite tournament, according to the Golf Course Superintendents' Association of America.

## Not Plural

Only one hole is not protected by bunkers at Augusta.

## Short Game

1991 Masters champion Ian Woosnam is 5 feet 4.5 inches tall.

## OUT TO PASTURE

From 1943–45, the Masters was not played because cattle and turkeys were being raised on the grounds to help with the war effort.

## Magnolia Lane

The sixty-one large magnolia trees that line both sides of Magnolia Lane date back to the late 1850s and were planted as seeds by the Berckmans, who owned Fruitland Nurseries. Magnolia Lane, which is approximately 330 yards long and stretches from the entrance gate to the clubhouse, was paved in 1947.

## Mirror, Mirror

HOW PERFECT OR TERRIBLE is that swing of yours? In most instances golfers don't know. One of the cheapest ways of finding out how your form looks is practicing alongside a mirror. You don't have to pay a pro, and you don't have to get a family member to bring the digital recorder. Better still, you can make changes and improvements on the fly.

## Jack Nicklaus

Born in Columbus, Ohio, in 1940, Jack Nicklaus is considered to be the greatest golfer of the modern era and arguably the greatest in the game's history. Strangely enough, young Jack's introduction to the game of golf came from a father who only took up the sport to help with an ankle injury he had sustained. Young Jack tagged along as his caddy.

To say young Jack was a quick study would be an understatement. By age thirteen, he had already shot a 69, and he was very quickly becoming a legitimate phenomenon in golfing circles. Nicklaus wouldn't disappoint those who were predicting great things of him. In 1959, at the age of nineteen, he won his first of two U.S. Amateur titles. As an amateur, he was also runner-up at the U.S. Open in 1960, and in 1961 he led Ohio State to an NCAA title.

The role model for Jack, as it was for many young golfers of his era, was Bobby Jones, the Atlanta lawyer who retired at 28 and never turned professional. Despite giving some thought to remaining an amateur and following in the footsteps of his chemist father, the lure of making a living from the sport he loved was just too compelling.

And what better way to introduce himself to the world of professional golf than to win the 1962 U.S. Open. In 1963, in just his second full year as a professional, he would add two more majors in the Masters and PGA Championship. Arnold Palmer may have been the "King of Golf," but now he had to make room for the "Golden Bear." The legend was just beginning and soon the Nicklaus Sunday afternoon charge became compulsory television viewing for anybody even remotely interested in golf.

In a quick scan of any golf record book, you see the name of Jack Nicklaus under almost every category. Almost every golf and sporting magazine has called Nicklaus the greatest golfer of the century. Who could argue? Eighteen major professional championships (seven more than his closest competitor, and ten more than Tiger Woods); an incredible nineteen runner-ups in the majors, and nine third-place finishes.

## GOLDEN BEAR

The "Golden Bear" is the only player in history to have won each of the game's majors at least twice (six Masters, five PGA Championships, four U.S. Opens, three British Opens), and is the only player to have completed the career "Grand Slam" on both the regular and senior tours. He has played on six Ryder Cup teams, captained two other Ryder Cup teams, and served as U.S. Captain for the 1998 and 2003 President's Cup.

In a career that spanned five decades, he had 73 official tour victories (113 around the world) and 58 second-place finishes. He was the leading money winner eight times and PGA Player of the Year five times. The unusual combination of raw power and touch made Nicklaus like poetry on the golf course. He was one of the greatest putters of all time, as well as one of the longest hitters on the tour. He popularized the "power fade" which became a Nicklaus trademark.

---

### TARGETING

ON THE DRIVING RANGE, place a couple of pylons on route to your intended target. Now, instead of shooting for a faraway target, aim for the pylons closest to you and make adjustments accordingly.

---

## PGA Championship

The PGA Championship began as an outgrowth of the formation of the Professional Golf Association (PGA) of America. When thirty-four fellow golf professionals joined with Walter Hagen in 1916 to form the PGA of America, it seemed like a logical next step to have a tournament they could call their own.

At that initial meeting was department-store mogul Rodman Wanamaker. He was convinced that interest in golf was on the cusp of exploding and he wanted to be part of it. Wanamaker agreed to provide a trophy and the initial purse of $2,580 for the event in exchange for the right to sell golf gear more cheaply than pros could sell it in their pro shops. The winners share was set at $500, a diamond medal, and the Wanamaker Trophy. The PGA Championship was born and is now considered one of the four majors and one of the most prestigious titles in golf.

Today, of course, the winner's share exceeds a million dollars. Perhaps more importantly, every winner of the PGA Championship receives five-year exemptions from qualifying for the PGA Tour, the Masters, and the U.S. and British Opens. With the lucrative purses available on today's tour, this represents an extraordinary financial opportunity for a professional golfer.

Sharp-shooting Englishman Jim Barnes won the inaugural championship, then won it again in 1919 when the tournament was resumed after the war years. The championship quickly grabbed the attention of golfers on both sides of the Atlantic and the PGA Championship became a fixture on the world golf landscape.

## Want That Win

Flashy Walter Hagen would see to it that an American would soon have his name inscribed on the championship trophy. Before the 1920s were out, Hagen would win the championship five times. Tiny Gene Sarazen would chip in with three of his own victories in the 1920s and early 1930s.

In the late 1930s to mid-1940s, no name was more synonymous with the PGA Championship than that of Byron Nelson. In the 1939 Championship, he was defeated by Henry Picard in the finals, but that only made him hungrier. In 1940, he won the event and was runner-up every year until 1945, when he won again.

After the war years and the retirement of Nelson, the winners of the PGA Championship and Wanamaker Trophy included golfing legends like Ben Hogan and Sam Snead, who would capture the title two and three times, respectively. In 1958, to accommodate requests made by television, the PGA Championship changed its format from match play to stroke play.

In 1962, South African Gary Player became the first non-American to win the event since 1947. Player would repeat the feat a decade later. This, however, was the era of Jack Nicklaus, and the Golden Bear would dominate the PGA Championship as he did others.

## Second Time Around

When Nicklaus won his first of five championships going away in 1971, he was the first player to complete the modern era Grand Slam for the second time. He would also place runner-up two more times and finish in the top five fourteen times.

Two of golf's greatest, Arnold Palmer and Tom Watson, could not make a break through at the PGA Championship. The most heartbreaking loss for Watson came in 1978. Going into the final round, John Mahaffey was a full seven strokes (in fact, he was tied for 47th place after the first round) behind Tom Watson. Watson finished with a 73, good only for a tie with Mahaffey and Jerry Pate. Mahaffey was on a roll, though, and won the event with a 12-foot birdie putt on the second play-off hole.

In 1984, the charming Lee Trevino won his second PGA Championship and, in 1986, Bob Tway chipped in for birdie on the 18th against luckless Greg Norman. In 1991, the PGA Championship allowed the ninth reserve to play for the Championship because Nick Price decided to take the event off due to the birth of his son. The player had never played the Crooked Stick, Indiana, course before, but went on to win and carry with him the press labeled moniker of "Wild Thing." He was, of course, John Daly.

Nick Price would not miss the following year's tournament, capturing the first of two titles and establishing himself as one of the best golfers in the world. In 1999, a new era was entered and it became the battle of young guns…the next generation. Twenty-three-year-old Tiger Woods squared off against 19-year-old Spaniard Sergio Garcia. Woods came out on top by one stroke, becoming the fifth youngest winner in PGA Championship history.

In 2000, Woods was looking to win the trifecta (he had already won the British and U.S. Opens) and looking to become the first back-to-back winner of the PGA Championship since 1937. In a thrilling three-hole play-off, Woods won by a single stroke.

What began with a small gathering in New York has grown into one of the most prestigious events of the golf year. From Hagen to Woods, the history of the PGA Championship is the history of professional golf writ large.

## Half Shot

PRACTICE HALF and three-quarter shots by adjusting your backswing, not your downswing. Experiment with gripping down on your clubs to develop a feel for a change in distance.

## PGA Championship Record Book
### Show Me the Money

#### WINNER'S SHARE BY YEAR

| Year | Share | Year | Share |
|------|-------|------|-------|
| 1916 | $500 | 1973 | $45,000 |
| 1933 | $1,000 | 1983 | $100,000 |
| 1944 | $3,500 | 1993 | $300,000 |
| 1954 | $5,000 | 2003 | $1,080,000 |
| 1963 | $13,000 | | |

# WINNER'S CIRCLE

| | | | | |
|---|---|---|---|---|
| 2003 | Shaun Micheel | | 1971 | Jack Nicklaus |
| 2002 | Rich Beem | | 1970 | Dave Stockton |
| 2000 | Tiger Woods | | 1969 | Ray Floyd |
| 1999 | Tiger Woods | | 1968 | Julius Boros |
| 1998 | Vijay Singh | | 1967 | Don January |
| 1997 | Davis Love III | | 1966 | Al Geiberger |
| 1996 | Mark Brooks | | 1965 | Dave Marr |
| 1995 | Steve Elkington | | 1964 | Bobby Nichols |
| 1994 | Nick Price | | 1963 | Jack Nicklaus |
| 1993 | Paul Azinger | | 1962 | Gary Player |
| 1992 | Nick Price | | 1961 | Jerry Barber |
| 1991 | John Daly | | 1960 | Jay Hebert |
| 1990 | Wayne Grady | | 1959 | Bob Rosburg |
| 1989 | Payne Stewart | | 1958 | Dow Finsterwald |
| 1988 | Jeff Sluman | | 1957 | Lionel Hebert |
| 1987 | Larry Nelson | | 1956 | Jack Burke |
| 1986 | Bob Tway | | 1955 | Doug Ford |
| 1985 | Hubert Green | | 1954 | Chick Harbert |
| 1984 | Lee Trevino | | 1953 | Walter Burkemo |
| 1983 | Hal Sutton | | 1952 | Jim Turnesa |
| 1982 | Raymond Floy | | 1951 | Sam Snead |
| 1981 | Larry Nelson | | 1950 | Chandler Harper |
| 1980 | Jack Nicklaus | | 1949 | Sam Snead |
| 1979 | David Graham | | 1948 | Ben Hogan |
| 1978 | John Mahaffey | | 1947 | Jim Ferrier |
| 1977 | Lanny Wadkins | | 1946 | Ben Hogan |
| 1976 | Dave Stockton | | 1945 | Byron Nelson |
| 1975 | Jack Nicklaus | | 1944 | Bob Hamilton |
| 1974 | Lee Trevino | | 1943 | Not played |
| 1973 | Jack Nicklaus | | 1942 | Sam Snead |
| 1972 | Gary Player | | 1941 | Vic Ghezzi |

| 1940 | Byron Nelson | 1928 | Leo Diegel |
|------|--------------|------|------------|
| 1939 | Henry Picard | 1927 | Walter Hagen |
| 1938 | Paul Runyan | 1926 | Walter Hagen |
| 1937 | Denny Shute | 1925 | Walter Hagen |
| 1936 | Denny Shute | 1924 | Walter Hagen |
| 1935 | Johnny Revolta | 1923 | Gene Sarazen |
| 1934 | Paul Runyan | 1922 | Gene Sarazen |
| 1933 | Gene Sarazen | 1921 | Walter Hagen |
| 1932 | Olin Dutra | 1920 | Jock Hutchison |
| 1931 | Tom Creavy | 1919 | James M. Barnes |
| 1930 | Tommy Armour | *1917–18 Not played* | |
| 1929 | Leo Diegel | 1916 | James M. Barnes |

## Rhyme and Reason

WHEN YOU ARE PRACTICING your putting and you are looking to determine how your feel and accuracy are working, remember to practice short putts to see how your accuracy stands up and to practice long putts for weight and feel. Together they'll give you a good idea about the state of your putting.

## Most Money Won

$2,2583,062 by Tiger Woods, spanning 7 championships
$1,080.000 by Shaun Micheel, in 1 championship
$1,040,448 by Nick Price, spanning 19 championships
$1,004,362 by Phil Mickelson, spanning 11 championships
$995,550 by Rich Beem, spanning 3 championships
$996,150 by David Toms, spanning 7 championships
$967,378 by Vijay Singh, spanning 12 championships
$842,098 by Steve Elkington, spanning 13 championships

$795,917 by Justin Leonard, spanning 9 championships
$763,058 by Davis Love III, spanning 17 championships
$650,000 by Chad Campbell, spanning 2 championships
$627,644 by Jim Furyk, spanning 9 championships
$618,220 by Jay Haas, spanning 24 championships
$605,325 by Fred Funk, spanning 14 championships
$600,767 by Paul Azinger, spanning 18 championships
$594,523 by Kenny Perry, spanning 13 championships
$565,510 by Greg Norman, spanning 22 championships
$549,600 by Bob May, spanning 2 championships
$542,869 by Steve Lowery, spanning 9 championships
$541,031 by Mark Brooks, spanning 16 championships
$533,465 by Ernie Els, spanning 12 championships
$519,660 by Mark Calcavecchia, spanning 16 championships
$516,714 by Sergio Garcia, spanning 5 championships
$491,736 by Scott Hoch, spanning 23 championships
$475,071 by Nick Faldo, spanning 21 championships
$451,958 by Tom Watson, spanning 31 championships
$436,755 by Jack Nicklaus, spanning 37 championships

## MOST VICTORIES

5: Walter Hagen (1921, 1924, 1925, 1926, 1927); Jack Nicklaus
    (1963, 1971, 1973, 1975, 1980)

## Most Times Runner-Up

4: Jack Nicklaus
3: Byron Nelson; Arnold Palmer; Billy Casper

## Most Top-Three Finishes

12: Jack Nicklaus
5: Lanny Wadkins; Gary Player
4: Billy Casper

## MOST TOP-FIVE FINISHES

14: Jack Nicklaus
6: Billy Casper; Gary Player
5: Nick Price; Greg Norman; Lanny Wadkins

## Most Top-Ten Finishes

15: Jack Nicklaus
10: Tom Watson
14: Ray Floyd
13: Billy Casper
12: Sam Snead
8: Gary Player

## Oldest Winner

Julius Boros (1968), 48 years, 4 months, 18 days old

## YOUNGEST WINNER

Gene Sarazen (1922), 20 years, 5 months, 22 days old

## Lowest Winning Scores

270: Tiger Woods (66, 67, 70, 67), Valhalla GC, 2000; Bob May (72, 66, 66, 66), Valhalla GC, 2000
267: Steve Elkington (68, 67, 68, 64), Riviera CC, 1995; Colin Montgomerie (68, 67, 67, 65), Riviera CC, 1995

## Best Comeback by Winner

7 shots: John Mahaffey (1978)
6 shots: Bob Rosburg (1959); Lanny Wadkins (1977); Payne Stewart (1989); Steve Elkington (1995)

## HIGHEST FIRST-ROUND SCORE
## BY WINNER

75  (4 over): John Mahaffey      (1978)
74  (2 over): Payne Stewart      (1989)

## Lowest First-Round Score by Winner

63 (7 under): Raymond Floyd (1982)
64 (6 under): Bobby Nichols (1964)

## Lowest Scoring Average

| 69.00 | (4 rounds) | Shaun Micheel |
|---|---|---|
| 69.00 | (1 round) | Jimmy Demaret |
| 70.07 | (28 rounds) | Tiger Woods |
| 70.13 | (8 rounds) | Bob May |
| 70.25 | (4 rounds) | Andy Oldcorn |
| 70.50 | (10 rounds) | Greg Chalmers |
| 70.50 | (6 rounds) | Franklin Langham |
| 70.50 | (4 rounds) | Robin Freeman |

## LOWEST SCORING AVERAGE
## MINIMUM 25 ROUNDS

| 70.07 | (28 rounds) | Tiger Woods |
|---|---|---|
| 70.73 | (30 rounds) | Justin Leonard |
| 70.81 | (42 rounds) | Phil Mickelson |
| 70.91 | (34 rounds) | Jim Furyk |
| 71.02 | (47 rounds) | Steve Elkington |
| 71.18 | (38 rounds) | Jerry Pate |
| 71.33 | (33 rounds) | Calvin Peete |
| 71.37 | (128 rounds) | Jack Nicklaus |

## Most Appearances

37: Jack Nicklaus; Arnold Palmer
31: Tom Watson; Raymond Floyd
28: Lanny Wadkins; Tom Kite
26: Ben Crenshaw
25: Hale Irwin; Larry Nelson

## Most Subpar Rounds

53: Jack Nicklaus
41: Tom Watson
33: Jay Haas; Nick Faldo
31: Greg Norman
30: Raymond Floyd
28: Nick Price; Lanny Wadkins; Hale Irwin
27: Fred Couples

### Four Rounds in the 60s Same PGA Championship

1964: Arnold Palmer (68-68-69-69)
1979: Ben Crenshaw (69-67-69-67)
1984: Lee Trevino (69-68-67-69)
1993: Paul Azinger (69-66-69-68); Greg Norman (68-68-67-69); Nick Faldo (69-66-69-68)
1995: Steve Elkington (68-67-68-64); Colin Montgomerie (68-67-67-65); Jeff Maggert (66-69-65-69); Bob Estes (69-68-68-68); Steve Lowery (69-68-68-69)
1998: Steve Elkington (69-69-69-67)
2001: David Toms (66-65-65-69); Phil Mickelson (66-66-66-68); Steve Lowery (67-67-66-68)

## Wire-To-Wire Winners

Bobby Nichols    (1964)
Raymond Floyd    (1969)
Raymond Floyd    (1982)
Hal Sutton    (1983)
Tiger Woods    (2000)

## Champion Breakdown by Native Country

72: United States
4: South Africa; Australia
2: Scotland; England
1: Fiji

## Age Breakdown of Winners

7 between 20–24 years old
18 between 25–29 years old
38 between 30–34 years old
18 between 35–39 years old
2 between 40–44 years old
2 between 45–50 years old

*Source: PGA of America*

## Commitment

SOME PEOPLE JUST CAN'T commit, but Vijay Singh has said commitment was one of the chief reasons for his success in 2004. Commitment in the golf sense means that once you've decided on your shot, commit to it, believe it, because if you don't believe, nobody else will.

# *PGA Championship Trivia*
## Gone Missing

When PGA Championship officials went to present the Wanamaker trophy to 1928 winner Leo Diegel, the trophy was nowhere to be found. Former winner and five-time champion Walter Hagen, who was supposed to return it, thought he left it somewhere in a taxicab. The trophy showed up two years later in a Detroit warehouse owned by none other than the Walter Hagen Golf Company.

## REDUCE, REUSE, RECYCLE

In 1974, Lee Trevino won the PGA Championship using an old putter he found in the attic of the house he was renting at the time.

## In the Army

- In 1942, Sam Snead asked for and received permission from his recruiting officer to enlist a few days late so he could participate in the PGA Championship.
- He subsequently won three PGA Championships, including 1942.

## Going Abroad

- 1930 was the last year in which a European-born player, Tommy Armour, won the PGA Championship.

## NOT AN ALL-AMERICAN GAME

It took five years after the PGA Championship was started in 1916 before it would be won for the first time by an American-born PGA professional, Walter Hagen.

## He Just Keeps Going...And Going...

Walter Hagen won the PGA Championship in four consecutive years (1924–27), making him the only person in the twentieth century to win the same major this many times consecutively.

## A SPECTATOR SPORT

- 100,000 people line the fairway to watch the PGA Championship each year.
- 900 members of the media are credentialed.

## Time for a Change

In 1958, the PGA switched from match play to stroke play.

---

## Walter Hagen

Colorful, flamboyant characters like Walter Hagen, or the "Haig" as he was called, come along once a generation. Golf was his ticket to fame, fortune, and the ladies. (He made two brief and unsuccessful attempts at marriage.) So cocksure was this black-smith's son that he appeared to be to the manor born.

When you came to watch Hagen, you not only got extraordinary golf, you got Hagen the master showman. And he was impossible to miss. It was Hagen who introduced colorful clothing to the golf course. He was always fastidiously dressed, showing up to play in multicolored plus fours, two-tone shoes, and tank top. He was the very embodiment of the brash American.

When he showed up to play at the British Open in 1920, he was prevented from entering the clubhouse through the front door because he was a professional. To counter the snobbery, Hagen not-so-quietly hired out a Rolls Royce (which he used as a changing room) with a footman, and set himself up outside the clubhouse entrance. At another event, he refused to go into the clubhouse to accept his prize because he was forbidden to use it earlier on the basis of his professional status.

Hagen summed up his philosophy on life and golf to one reporter this way: "I never wanted to be a millionaire, just to live like one," he said. He, of course, did earn a million dollars during the course of his career and he lived like it. He always traveled by limousine and when in London partied with the elite at the Savoy.

Despite the fact that it appeared that Hagen was often just rolling out of bed from an all-night party, he was always immaculately dressed and ready for the challenge on the golf course. His record speaks for itself. He won a total of eleven majors, including four British Opens and five PGA Championships.

In 1916, Walter Hagen gathered together with thirty-four fellow golf professionals to form the PGA of America. He was almost single-handedly responsible for bringing respectability to "professional golf" and Gene Sarazen has gone on record as saying that every professional golfer who has ever earned a dollar should give a tip of their hat to Walter Hagen.

As a player, Hagen was deadly from within a hundred yards and with his putter. He was also a psychologist, able to talk to the crowds as he strolled up to his ball that may have been in impossible rough. It made his competitors crazy or scared...or both.

The professional circuit, such as it was, wasn't quite big enough for the larger-than-life world of Walter Hagen. He traveled the world putting on exhibitions from Japan and Australia to South America and even Africa. On many occasions trick golfer Joey Kirkwood would go along for the ride and the dough, of which for Hagen there was never enough. Even when it was clear he had made a million from the game, he said, "I'm the only golfer to have earned a million and spent two."

---

### Overtime

YOU'VE JUST HAD a terrible round, or maybe you just couldn't hit your wedges. Instead of going home right after your round, take the time to go to the practice tee, practicing only with the clubs that didn't work for you out on the course.

---

## To Be a Caddy

Caddy comes from the French *cadet*, a title the French used to describe young boys in the army who did the physical work of portering or moving of equipment. In Scotland, and later exported around the world, the word "caddy" took on the meaning of a person responsible for carrying the golf clubs of a golfer.

With a single ball costing as much as a week's wages, golf in the eighteenth and nineteenth centuries was a game largely reserved for the wealthy and nobility. Many golfers had two caddies: a forecaddy, who would be used as a forward caddy or lookout and whose responsibility it was to keep his eyes focused on those precious early balls; the other caddy was there to select the right club, and was expected to tee up the ball and attend to the flag stick.

Over time, the gentry weren't satisfied with merely having their bag touted. They wanted advice, and often they wanted to win the not-inconsiderable wagers that were being placed on matches.

## Club Caddy

This ushered in the era of the club caddy—a caddy who knew the course like the back of his hand and who just might be able to offer some timely advice that would make the difference in a tight match. It was a hardscrabble living, if it was a living at all. One caddy who had a remedy for the penurious conditions was Trap Door Willie Johnson.

Johnson falsely claimed to have one leg shorter than another, so he could stuff a special boot he had made with the golf balls of his patrons. He was known to be generous enough to sell them back to his patrons—at a later date, of course—at a much-reduced rate.

At the turn of the twentieth century, the upper crust of American society embraced golf, and caddies with it, as yet another opportunity to emulate their prosperous British cousins. The problem was that on both sides of the Atlantic, public courses were entering the fray; furthermore, as the propertied class often had to leave the golf course to attend to business affairs, caddies were left alone to work on their swing.

## Caddy to Pro

When former caddies like Walter Hagen and Gene Sarazen turned professional, the upper class still contented themselves with the notion that it was crass and déclassé to play for money. Those early professionals, however, turned into fine golfers, who then turned into legends.

The two most famous caddies are Ben Hogan and Byron Nelson, who caddied at the same Fort Worth, Texas, golf club. Before they played-off at the Masters, they had a play-off in the Christmas caddy's tournament at the Fort Worth club where they worked (Nelson won by a stroke). Eventually it seemed as though everybody who was winning on the professional circuit had spent some time in the caddyshack.

The biggest enemy of the caddy has been the arrival of the golf cart. In a little over thirty-five years, it has made the caddy almost obsolete in North America. Current estimates are that less than 10 percent of clubs in North America have caddies at all.

With the tremendous money available in professional golf today, caddies are former golf professionals themselves. Caddies like former Tiger Woods caddy Mike Cowan even manage to become minor B-list celebrities in their own right. What has been lost with the demise of the caddy has been the long apprenticeship that at one time made great champions.

# The Caddy File

## A PRO

- At age 16, a 1909 USGA ruling calls all caddies, caddy masters, and greenkeepers professional golfers.
- Although the rule was later modified, it was completely reversed in 1963.

## The First

- 1682 is the year of the first recorded instance of a caddy, Andrew Dickson, carrying clubs for the Duke of York.

## Arm-Y

- Early caddies carried their player's clubs in their arms. Later crude bags were fashioned, making the caddy's job a lot easier.

## LABOR COSTS

- $15 is the price to rent a cart for members of the Pinehurst Resort in North Carolina.
- $40 plus tip is the price for a caddy.

## The Commish

One of the caddies at Sunset Ridge Country Club in Illinois was a young man named Peter Ueberroth. He would go on to become the Major League Baseball commissioner from 1984–89.

## A Caddy and a Scholar

Caddy Eddie Lowery was only ten years old when he caddied for Francis Ouimet when he went on to win the U.S. Open in 1913. It was the biggest turning point in American golf. Lowery went on to establish the Francis Ouimet Caddy Scholarship Fund in 1949. In its first year the fund awarded $4,600 to thirteen students. In 2003–04 it awarded $975,000, making it the largest "caddy" fund in the U.S.

## FLUFF

Mike "Fluff" Cowan, Tiger Woods's first caddy on the professional circuit, got his start in the business after being fired from a job as assistant pro at a Maine golf club. Cowan and a friend decided to catch up with the PGA tour in Hartford, Connecticut, to see if they could land some work. That was in 1976 and he, of course, has been a caddy ever since.

## Really Big Shew

Ed Sullivan and Gene Sarazen were both caddies at the Apawamis Golf Club when American Francis Ouimet beat British golf legend Harry Vardon in 1913.

## American Made

In 1933, the Professional Golf Association of America (PGA) named George Jacobus, a former caddy, its first American-born president of the PGA.

## ARN

Arnold Palmer began caddying at age eleven at the Pennsylvania golf club where his father was the pro.

## Gardening Champ

Six-time British Open champion Harry Vardon's first job was as a gardener to a gentleman who enjoyed golf. Vardon would sometimes caddy for him and be given the opportunity to use proper equipment to play a few strokes.

## Teed Up

G. Leslie Smith wrote this in 1892 about a caddy that apparently had a few too many "wee nips." "He could not tee the ball properly," Smith wrote, "and fell down."

## You Can Be Replaced

*"My caddy had the best answer for why I carry two putters:*
*'Just to let the other one know it can be replaced.'"*
—Larry Nelson

### Fore!

The word "fore" comes from a time when golfers (usually noblemen) had two caddies. One carried the bag and one was a forecaddy, whose job it was to go ahead and keep an eye on his lordship's balls. Golfers would issue a warning yell to alert forecaddies that a ball was on route.

## The Tipping Point

GOLF IS A GAME that is rarely played alone, and often played with different people. To get used to either zoning out people (think front of the clubhouse) or better still relishing competition, put a sawbuck on it. It lets you get used to pressure.

## Did You Know?

- Did you know that caddies in Japan take a break for lunch after the first nine?
- Did you know that rules prevent a caddy from shielding a player from the elements while taking a stroke?

---

### Bruce Edwards

Every once in a great, long while, people pause to pay homage not to greatness but rather to gentleness and human decency.

They did that when ALS (Lou Gehrig's disease) claimed the life of Tom Watson's long-time caddy Bruce Edwards in 2004.

Just three weeks before the 48-year-old Edwards was supposed to get married, Watson was worried about some unusual symptoms his friend was exhibiting and insisted that he see his doctor at the Mayo Clinic. What Edwards found out was that he had ALS and probably one to three years to live.

As it turns out, it was one year, but what an extraordinary year it was. Together Watson and Edwards shot a 65 at the U.S. Open to hold a share of the lead and capture the imagination of the American public. Watson became the first pro to play in all nine majors on the PGA Tour and Champions Tour, and he won two and placed second in two others.

Edwards and Watson had been in lock step since 1973, when Edwards first went on Watson's bag. They argued, but mostly they laughed and reveled in each other's company. When Byron Nelson was asked why Watson seemed to be playing so well in 2003, he quietly said it was because he had something to play for.

When Edwards died in 2004, it was the day after his father picked up the Ben Hogan Award on his son's behalf. The Hogan Award is given to someone who continues to be active in golf despite a disability or disease. There was never a more fitting candidate than Bruce Edwards.

## Bump and Run

SOMETIMES IF THERE'S no trouble in front of the green, use a mid-iron instead of a sand wedge to hit a low and running shot to the green. Sometimes the better and safer play is to bump and run the ball along the ground instead of lofting it up into the air.

# 17

# Business Links

**F**irst came the monarchs, James IV, James VI, and Mary, Queen of Scots. After the monarchs inevitably came the noblemen. And so they did, twenty-two of them, to form the St. Andrews Golf Club in Scotland in 1754.

In America of 1894, a similar band of American aristocrats, including master architect Stanford White, financier Charles Schwab, and steel mogul Andrew Carnegie—captains of industry all—founded the first incorporated golf club in America, Shinnecock Hills. (Henry Taft was also among them; in fifteen years, he would be president of the United States.) Golf and business have been inextricably linked ever since.

In Britain, nobles may have wanted to talk of the world and culture; in America, the talk was business. One of the most dedicated of early America golfers also happened to be one of the world's first billionaires.

Having been retired for only four years as head of the Standard Oil Company, John D. Rockefeller only picked up a club by accident while on vacation in 1899 (he was 60 years old at the time). He was hooked, and for the next thirty-three years of his life he played every day at 10:15 a.m.

In the communist world, one of the first acts of the new governments was to eliminate the trappings of capitalism. One of those trappings was golf. In communist China, for example, Shanghai closed the better of its two courses, changing it into a public park. By 1949, China had closed down all of its courses. In Russia, a country known for its love of sport, only a single solitary course existed as late as 1989. It was designed by American Robert Trent Jones Jr.

When former Communist Party president Leonid Brezhnev approached U.S. oil magnate Armand Hammer on what to do to attract U.S. business investment, Hammer told him they would need to offer three things: limousines, a business center, and golf.

The communist political and military elite everywhere continued to know the power of the game of golf as a networking tool. As professor Ken Jowitt remarks, "How else can we explain that Saudi princes, Japanese businessmen, Argentine colonels, and Russian politicians all play golf?" Today, golf is experiencing an explosion in China as budding young capitalists discover the importance of golf in making a deal.

Golf has become essential to success in business. The PGA, for example, teams up budding college business students with PGA professionals, with their "Golf: For Business and Life" program. The Executive Women's Golf Association does the same thing for women. Starting with just 28 members in 1991, it now has more than 17,000 members across North America.

It's partly because of the nature of the game—long walks on the course give plenty of time to observe somebody who wants your money. Part of it too is the simple camaraderie that develops from spending a few hours together on the links. Whatever the reason, there's no denying the importance golf plays in the corporate world.

## *Executives on the Golf Course*
### LET'S MEET

- 9 percent of business executives say that their most successful business meetings happened on the golf course, according to a survey by Robert Half International.

# Let's Make a Deal

- 97 percent of business executives feel that golfing with a business associate is a good way to establish a close relationship, according to a survey by Starwood Hotels and Resorts.
- 92 percent of executives say it's a good way to make new business contacts.
- 43 percent say that some of their biggest deals have been done on the golf course.
- 45 percent believe that playing golf makes clients more likely to give you business.
- 20 percent would let a client beat them if they thought it would get them more business.
- 81 percent of deals are closed a few days after a round of golf.

## Best Time To Talk Business

1. The "19th Hole"
2. The Back Nine

### THE 19TH HOLE

- 81 percent of business executives say the 19th hole is very or somewhat important when doing business on the golf course.

### The Fortune Handicap

- The average handicap of a Fortune 500 CEO who golfs is 15, according to *Golf Digest's* annual survey of Fortune 500 CEO golfers.
- The average number of rounds of golf they play a year is 29.
- $8,283,141 is the total average compensation received each year by a Fortune 500 CEO who regularly golfs (including stock options, bonuses, etc.).

# Favorite Courses of Fortune 500 CEOs

1. Augusta National
2. Pebble Beach
3. Pine Valley

## FAVORITE OVERSEAS COURSE OF FORTUNE 500 CEOs

1. Royal Dornoch, Scotland

## Most Admired Golfers of Fortune 500 CEOs

1. Arnold Palmer
2. Tiger Woods
3. Jack Nicklaus

# Freebies

- 73 percent of corporations use golf and golf-related products for company events, such as golf balls, shirts, hats, and caps, according to a survey by Potentials.
- $4.3 million is the average promotional budget for those companies who participated in the survey.

## CHARITY

- $150,000 was contributed to the World War I war effort in 1918 after a fundraising tour by a group of young kids called the Dixie Kids—featuring Atlanta teenagers Perry Adair, Watts Gunn, Bobby Jones, and Alexa Stirling.
- 140,000 charitable events are held on U.S. golf courses annually, generating $3.2 billion.

## Bunkered

BUNKERS CAN BE ANYWHERE, as we can all attest. Different bunkers call for different shots. The fairway bunker is different because you not only want to make sure you get out, but often you also want some distance. Select slightly more club for the yardage you are looking at, because you should be choking down on your club to account for your feet being in the sand.

# *Play Nice*
## Playing Hooky

- 10 percent of CEOs and executives have called in sick to play golf, according to a Starwood Hotels and Resorts survey.
- 47 percent often find themselves daydreaming about golf while at work.
- 11 percent say golf is more important to them than sex.
- 92 percent of executives say that golf is a good way to relieve business stress.

## PLACE YOUR BETS

- 87 percent of CEOs say they place wagers on their golf games, according to Starwood Hotels and Resorts survey.
- The average wager is $589.

## Above Board...Really

- 82 percent of business executives admit to cheating on the golf course, according to a Starwood Hotels and Resorts survey.
- 55 percent admitted the same in 1993.
- 86 percent admitted to cheating in business.

- 87 percent have played with someone who cheated on their golf score.
- 82 percent say they hate people who cheat when they play golf.
- 57 percent of Americans say that if they saw their boss improve a lie in the rough, they would call him or her on it, according to a *Golf Digest* study.
- 96 percent of Argentineans would rat out their boss.

## Top Golfing Sins of Executives on the Golf Course

1. Improving your lie a little.
2. Allowing partners to cheat on their score.
3. Not counting a missed tap-in.
4. Taking a mulligan without asking.

## ON AND OFF THE LINKS

- 59 percent of business executives say the way a person plays golf is very similar to the way he or she conducts their business affairs, according to a Starwood Hotels and Resorts survey.
- 75 percent feel it demonstrates one's level of competitiveness and motivation.
- 73 percent say playing golf together gives you time to get to know another person's true character.
- 67 percent say a person who cheats at golf would probably cheat in business.
- 57 percent say a hothead on the golf course is typically someone who is also bad tempered in the office.

## Must You?

- 85 percent of executives have been embarrassed by someone's bad behavior on the golf course.

# Mood Swing

- 12 percent of American golfers say a bad round of golf puts them in a bad mood for the rest of the day, according to a survey by *Golf Digest*.

## WORST BEHAVIORS EXECUTIVES HAVE WITNESSED

1. Vulgar and abusive language.
2. Throwing or breaking clubs.
3. Throwing clubs into a lake or pond.
4. Excessive drinking.

## Love The Kids, But...

- 11 percent of executives would rather get a hole in one than see their child get a game-winning home run.

## *It's Only Money* Rockefeller

- John D. Rockefeller spent $27,537.80 on golf in 1906, according to his account book for that year.
- That would be roughly equivalent to $450,000 today.
- It took Rockefeller 64 strokes to play the first 9 holes of his life, in 1899.
- Rockefeller usually went 5 strokes over par at the age of 80 when playing 9 holes.
- It usually took him 25 strokes to play 6 holes at the age of 91.

## THAT'S A DOOZY

A four-passenger, fully loaded Duesenburg Estate Golf Car features a 36-volt electric motor, rack and pinion steering, AM/FM compact disc player, roll-up side curtains, chrome side pipes, and a gold-plated Doozy hood ornament. Price tag: $28,000.

## Give Me Green

- 71 percent of Americans would rather be rich than a good golfer, according to a survey by *Golf Digest*.

## *Everybody's Doing It*
## More than the Ol' Boys' Club

- 43 percent of male executives say that if more women played golf, they'd succeed more in business, according to a survey by Starwood Hotels and Resorts.
- 69 percent of female executives say the same.
- 23 percent of female executives say they have closed a major deal on the golf course.
- 43 percent of male executives say the same.

## HOW YOU PLAY THE GAME

- 75 percent of women executives say that how a person plays golf says a lot about how they conduct business.
- 58 percent of men say the same.
- 70 percent of female business executives say golf outings are useful in predicting business behavior, according to a survey by Oppenheimer Funds.
- 73 percent say they are useful in developing new relationships.
- 23 percent have closed a deal on the golf course.

## Even the Chinese Are Doing It

- There are approximately 100,000 golfers in China, according to T. K. Pen, a Taiwanese-American investor who owns courses in Beijing and Xiamen.
- In 1994, there were 3 golf courses in Beijing.
- Today there are over 30.
- In all of China today there are 180 courses.

## Up and Down

IT MAY BE OBVIOUS, but if you are hitting uphill, you need to hit more club; when you are hitting downhill, you need to hit less club. Usually you would club one club up or down, excluding unusual weather conditions.

## Tom Watson

Born in Kansas City, Missouri, the knock against Watson in his early years was that he had all the stuff of greatness but couldn't win. He soon proved that wrong and must be considered one of the greatest golfers of the modern era.

In 1975, he won his first of five British Opens and established himself as the biggest challenger to Jack Nicklaus for the title of the world's best golfer. To watch these two titans clash as they did in the British Open at Turnberry in 1977 and the U.S. Open in 1982 was to see golf played at its highest level.

At Turnberry in Scotland, Nicklaus and Watson were tied after two rounds and as a result were in the final pairing for round three. Here again they matched each other shot for shot, both shooting a 66 and set for a Sunday showdown. Nicklaus matched his Saturday score, again shooting a 66. On any other day it would have been good enough to ensure victory, but Watson shot a 65 to win.

Watson's only U.S. Open win came at Pebble Beach in 1982.

Nicklaus and Watson were again matching each other stroke for stroke and were tied with two holes to play. On the par-3, 17th hole, Watson hit his tee shot into the rough off the green. He faced an extremely difficult shot downhill on a very fast green. It was a chip that hit the flagstick and dropped for a birdie. Watson would birdie 18 for good measure and a two-stroke victory.

In addition to his five British Open victories, Watson also won a Masters and the already mentioned U.S. Open. He was five times a leading money winner and was named the USPGA Player of the Year six times. He was awarded the Vardon trophy for the lowest stroke average three times, and in 1986 was awarded the Bobby Jones Award for sportsmanship and contributions to the game.

Watson's Midwestern charm and determination was never more in evidence than when he helped put a very public face on Lou Gehrig's disease, after his caddy Bruce Edwards contracted the disease. His stalwart support was typically underplayed by a modest Watson, proving once again what lies beneath is a champion's heart.

## RULES OF THUMB

THERE ARE RULES, then there are rules of thumb. One you must follow, the other you may choose not to, but you do so at your peril. Around the green, remember these simple rules of thumb. Putt whenever you can, that is providing you can roll the ball cleanly. Chip and run when you can't putt, and pitch only when you have no other option.

# 18

# All Aces, Baby...

The bases-loaded grand slam in baseball, the Hail Mary in football, or the slam dunk in basketball don't compare to the hole in one in golf. It is simply the most exciting shot in golf. This is our story of the odds, the prizes, and the people who've scored them.

## Parting Shot

*"Man blames fate for other accidents but feels personally responsible for a hole in one."*
—Martha Beckman

## Go Baby

- 31 percent of golfers surveyed say a hole in one is the most exciting shot to watch, according to a survey by *Golf Magazine*.
- 30 percent say a hole-out from the fairway is the most exciting.
- 24 percent find watching an escape from the trees the most exciting.
- 13 percent find watching an 80-foot putt drop the most exciting.
- 2 percent like to watch a tee shot go into the drink.

## FIRST ACES

- In 1868, Young Tom Morris scored the first recorded hole in one.
- In 1959, Patty Berg hit the first hole in one for a woman in a LPGA tournament.

# What Are the Odds?

- The odds of an amateur golfer hitting a hole in one are 12,600 to 1.
- The odds of a male professional or top amateur hitting a hole in one are 3,708 to 1.
- The odds of a female professional or top amateur hitting a hole in one are 4,648 to 1.
- The chances of making two holes in one in a round of golf are 1 in 67 million.

## Be Insured

The Japanese spend $210 million a year on hole-in-one insurance because it is traditional in Japan to share one's good luck by sending gifts to all your friends when you get an ace.

## SEE ONE-HANDED

One-handed golfer Bill Hilsheimer, a retired photo engraver, achieved three holes in one in a six-month period in 2003–2004.

## What a Payday

The National Hole in One Association offers insurance to hole in one tournaments. They've included some unusual pay-outs, including the rather blasé $1 million in cash, but also airplanes, an oil well, and even a casket at a funeral director's tournament.

## Four Aces

- Four golfers—Doug Weaver, Mark Wiebe, Jerry Pate, and Nick Price—hit aces on the par-3 6th hole on the same day at the 1989 U.S. Open at Oak Hill.
- The odds against four professionals achieving four holes in one in a field of 156 are 332,000 to 1.

## LONG BALL

- Marie Roke of Wollaston, Massachusetts, aced a 393-yard hole—the longest ace ever recorded by a woman.
- The longest hole in one ever recorded was by Robert Mitera at the 10th at Miracle Hills Golf Club at Omaha, Nebraska, on October 7, 1965, at 447 yards. A 50mph gust carried his shot over a 290-yard drop-off.

## Unique Accomplishment

- Two holes in one on two successive par-4s at Del Valle CC, California, were scored by Norman Manley, an amateur from Long Beach. It is the first and only time this feat has been accomplished.

## Three Aces

- Dr. Joseph Boydstone recorded 11 aces in one calendar year at Bakersfield Country Club in California.
- He recorded three in one round.

## ALL ACES

- The most holes-in-one in a year was 28, by Scott Palmer in 1983 at Balboa Park in San Diego, California.
- The most holes-in-one in a career was 68, by Harry Lee Bonner from 1967 to 1985, most of them at his 9-hole home course of Las Gallinas, San Rafael, California.

## Oldest

The oldest person ever to hit a hole in one was Otto Bucher from Switzerland in 1985 at La Manga's 130-yard 12th hole. He was 99 years old.

## British Open Aces

In the 1973 British Open Championship at Troon, two holes-in-one were recorded, one by the youngest and one by the oldest player in the tournament: Gene Sarazen and amateur David Russell.

## SUPREME

Sandra Day O'Connor is the only U.S. Supreme Court justice to hit a hole in one.

## Happy New Year

Jenny Ritchie set a hole in one on the last day of 1999 and another on the same hole on the first day of 2000 at New Zealand's Wanganui Golf Club, her 5th and 6th holes in one during 34 years of playing golf.

## Long Days

In 1951 in New York, 1,409 players held a competition to see who could get a hole in one. This competition was held over several days at short holes on three New York golf courses. Each player was allowed a total of five shots, for a total of 7,045 shots. The closest ball finished 3 1/2 inches from the hole.

## LONG NIGHTS

In 1940, American professional Harry Gonder hit a total of 1,817 balls over 16 hours and 25 minutes trying to achieve a hole in one on the 160-yard hole. He had two official witnesses and caddies to tee and retrieve balls and count strokes. His best effort was an inch from the hole.

# Ace Profile by Hole-In-One.com

- Average age of a hole-in-one golfer: 43.9501 years
- Average handicap of a hole-in-one golfer: 12.5622
- Average number of years playing golf: 15.3907 years
- Percent of hole-in-one golfers: male 80 percent/female 20 percent
- Percent of golfers registering first ace: 76.97 percent
- Day of week most holes in one occur: Friday
- Day of week least holes in one occur: Sunday
- Date when most aces occurred: June 29, 2003
- Golf hole most frequently aced: Hole 8.88
- Average par for the aced hole: Par 3.01
- Average yardage of aced hole: 149.99 yards
- Club most used in making an ace: 7-iron

## Ace States

1. California with 1,063 aces
2. Florida with 971 aces
3. Michigan with 523 aces
4. Illinois with 491 aces
5. Ohio with 443 aces

## ACE COUNTRIES

1. USA with 10,377 aces
2. Canada with 543 aces
3. United Kingdom with 256 aces
4. Australia with 51 aces
5. Ireland with 40 aces

*Source: Hole-in-one.com, reprinted with permission.*

## Mark McCormack

With the arrival of television came the arrival of the modern business manager. Players made money in endorsements and exhibitions in the era before television, but a young Yale law graduate named Mark McCormack was the first to recognize just how much potential there was.

McCormack had a genuine love for golf. He had competed in both the U.S. and British Amateurs. In 1960, the 29-year-old McCormack approached a 31-year-old Arnold Palmer and a partnership was born that would launch both men into financial stratospheres they could not have imagined.

Palmer became one of the most bankable stars of his generation and soon became known as much for his business acumen as for the game he played on the course. The big fish was Palmer, but soon two other emerging superstars came knocking at McCormack's door—Jack Nicklaus and Gary Player. Together they represented the modern triumvirate and they were all in the McCormack stable.

As his clients became incredibly wealthy, so did McCormack. Soon the company he founded, IMG Group, was signing people across all sports. He added, for instance, French skier Jean-Claude Killy and made major inroads in tennis in 1968 when he signed Rod Laver. At one point he also had Bjorn Borg, John McEnroe, Ivan Lendl, Chris Evert, and Martina Navratilova.

Other tennis and golf stars that are with or have been with IMG include Andre Agassi, Pete Sampras, Tim Henman, the Williams sisters, and golf stars Colin Montgomerie and Sergio Garcia.

Both tennis and golf magazines were calling him the most powerful man in those sports. In 1990, *Sports Illustrated* cut to the chase and simply called him "The Most Powerful Man in Sports."

When a new talent named Tiger Woods came on the scene, it seemed almost inevitable that he would end up with McCormack's company—and he did. First thing on the agenda was a huge $100-million-plus contract for Woods with Nike.

McCormack passed away in 2003 at the age of 72. In a career that spanned forty years, he changed the face of sports and there are many athletes with huge bank accounts who will forever be in his debt.

## OVERSWINGING

MEN AND WOMEN who have played the game have always wanted to hit the ball farther and farther. One of the consequences of wanting to hit the ball farther is overswinging. Under the guise of obtaining more power, some golfers attempt to extend the arc of their club by over-rotating on their backswing. What this does unfortunately is take you out of your natural arc, so remember to stay with the natural contours of your body.

# Roar of a Tiger

Born Eldrick Woods on December 30, 1975, he grew up in Cypress, California, the son of an African American and former army lieutenant colonel father, Earl Woods, and a Thai mother, Kultida. Earl quickly pinned the nickname "Tiger" to his son, after a Vietnamese soldier and friend, Vuong Dang Phong, with whom he had served in Vietnam.

Tiger was practically born with a golf club in his hand, swinging his first golf club at the age of nine months. By the age of two, Tiger appeared on the *Mike Douglas Show* engaging in a putting contest with legendary entertainer and golf aficionado, Bob Hope. Later, he would be featured on CBS, NBC, ABC, and ESPN.

At the age of eight, Tiger won the Optimist International Junior Championship, an event he would win four more times. From 1991–1993, Woods won three consecutive U.S. Junior Amateur Championships, becoming both the youngest winner and the only person to have won the event more than once.

Tiger would go on to repeat that feat as an amateur, becoming the only person to win three consecutive U.S. Amateur Championships. It was an achievement good enough to earn Tiger his first PGA Tour invitation to the Nissan Los Angeles Open at the tender age of sixteen.

## STANFORD

The next stop for Tiger was Stanford University, where he would lead the team to the Pac-10 and NCAA Championships in 1996, in the process being named both the Fred Haskins and Jack Nicklaus College Player of the Year. He was also a first team All-

American in both 1995 and 1996, Pac-10 Player of the Year, and Stanford's Male Freshman of the Year for all sports in 1995.

Turning professional in August 1996, he won two out of his first six events and earned an incredible $800,000 in just eight weeks. His Masters victory in 1997 made him the youngest to ever win the title and in June of the same year, Tiger became the youngest player to ever become number one on the official world golf rankings (21 years, 24 weeks). From 1999–2000, Tiger Woods compiled six consecutive PGA Tour wins, the second most in a row of all time, next only to Byron Nelson's 11 in 1945.

The year 2000 saw Tiger Woods put together one of the greatest years in the history of golf. He set or tied twenty-seven PGA Tour records and won three majors, becoming the youngest player ever to complete a career Grand Slam and only the fifth golfer ever to accomplish this feat.

In addition to the majors, he also had eleven PGA tournament victories. At the U.S. Open at Pebble Beach, Woods literally crushed the competition, winning by a record 15 strokes. At St. Andrews, he set a new mark for lowest score in relation to par and incredibly he did not hit into any of the course's 112 bunkers. He earned a record $9,188,321 on the PGA Tour in 2000, becoming the Tour's all-time career money leader.

In 2001, Tiger captured the Masters again, becoming the only player to hold all four professional major titles at the same time. In 2002, Tiger Woods won both the Masters and the U.S. Open, becoming the first player since Jack Nicklaus in 1972 to accomplish this feat. That same year, he won his thirtieth career PGA Tour victory, setting the record for most wins before the age of 30. In 2002, he also became the youngest player to win seven majors, at the age of 26.

In 2003, Tiger beat Byron Nelson's record of 113 consecutive cuts made. He has had an incredible run of consecutive weeks as the number-one-ranked player in the world. In 1996, he established the Tiger Woods Foundation to promote the health, education, and welfare of children through community-based programs. It is a legacy he says he hopes will be bigger than his exploits on the golf course.

## A Beautiful Thing

*"There isn't a flaw in his golf or his makeup. He will win more majors than Arnold Palmer and me combined...he has the finest fundamentally sound golf swing I've ever seen."—Jack Nicklaus*

### Distance and Control

THERE ARE SEVERAL ROLES the wrists play in your golf swing, but two of those are to control the club throughout the golf swing and to provide power through impact. If your wrists are weak it will be very hard to accomplish these actions. Do exercises to strengthen your wrists specific to their role in the golf swing. One good exercise is to stand with your arm hanging at your side. Grab a golf club in one hand towards the end of the grip. Raise the club as high as you can only by cocking your wrist and keeping your arm at your side. Lower and repeat until you have accomplished a set of 15 repetitions.

# Tiger File

### BEATS DAD
At age 11, Tiger beat his father at golf for the first time.

### BOYS WILL BE BOYS

- Tiger won his first pitch, putt, and drive contest at age 2.
- Tiger shot 48 for nine holes at age 3.
- Tiger began working with former PGA Player Randy Duran at age 4.
- Tiger scored his first hole in one at age 12.

### MEDIA SAVVY
- Tiger first underwent media training at age 3 and first appeared on the television show *That's Incredible* at age 5.

### PUTTS
- At age 7, he sank 80 four-foot putts in a row.

### PSYCHOLOGY
- He had a sports psychologist at age 13.

### SHOWDOWN
- 65 percent of Americans think Tiger Woods is one of the best golfers ever, according to a poll by Harris Interactive.
- 10 percent feel he actually is the best golfer ever.
- 46 percent of golfers feel Tiger Woods would beat Jack Nicklaus if the two faced off in a game of golf.
- 14 percent say the game would be a tie.

### CELEBRITY POWER

- 26 percent of Americans surveyed say they would be more likely to purchase a product endorsed by Michael Jordan, the highest-ranked sports celebrity on the list, than if it were endorsed by Tiger Woods or Lance Armstrong.
- 19 percent say they'd be more likely to choose a product endorsed by Tiger Woods, the second-highest sports celebrity on the list.

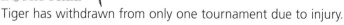

### ALL IN A NAME

- The retail value of an autographed Tiger Woods photograph is $1,000.
- In a single autograph session, Tiger Woods can generate product sales of $2 million.

### WEAR MY HAT

- Nike paid Woods $8 million to wear its brand name when he first broke into the professional ranks.
- Titleist paid him $4 million to use its clubs.
- $77 million is the estimated annual revenue generated by Tiger Woods's endorsements today.
- Mark McCormack's first deal for golfer Arnold Palmer to endorse equipment for Wilson Sporting Goods in 1960 was for $5,000.

### TIGER IS HERE

Tiger Woods's involvement in a golf event generates $250,000–$400,000, according to officials of the PGA, Nike, and Senior golf circuits.

### INJURY-FREE

Tiger has withdrawn from only one tournament due to injury.

- There have been two winners of the U.S. Open and U.S. Junior Amateur: Johnny Miller (1973 Open; 1964 Junior) and Tiger Woods (2000, 2002 Opens; 1992 and 1993 Junior).
- There has been only one winner of the U.S. Junior Amateur, U.S. Amateur, and U.S. Open: Tiger Woods (1991–1993 Juniors; 1994–1996 Amateurs; 2000, 2002 U.S. Open).
- In 1996, Tiger tied the British Open record for an amateur.
- No amateurs other than Tiger have ever made the cut at the Masters (Tiger made it in 1996).

## HOW FAST?

The average speed at which the head of Tiger's driver moves is 122 mph.

## LASER VISION

In 1999, Tiger Woods underwent successful laser eye surgery.

## MOM'S BOY

Tiger Woods's mother handmade his clubhead cover. The words "Love from Mom" in Thai are stitched on it.

## SEEING RED

Tiger Woods always wears the color red on the final day of the tournament, because his mother feels that it's lucky and a "power color" for him.

## UNIVERSITY DAYS

- "Urkel" was Tiger's nickname during his two years at Stanford University.
- Economics was Tiger's major at Stanford.

- Steve Williams, Tiger's caddy, has also caddied for Ray Floyd and Greg Norman.
- Mike (Fluff) Cowan was Tiger Woods's first caddy.

## ON THE MENU

After his record-setting 12-stroke victory at the 1997 Masters, Tiger Woods got to select the menu for the 1998 Masters Champions dinner: cheeseburgers, grilled chicken sandwiches, french fries, and strawberry or vanilla shakes!

## GOOD SPORT

In 1996 and 2000, *Sports Illustrated* named Tiger Sportsman of the Year.

## GOOD PRESS

- Tiger's name first appears in *Golf Digest* magazine when he was 5 years old.
- *Golf Digest* named Tiger Amateur Player of the Year when he was 15.

## MARGINS OF VICTORY

- Woods won his first Masters victory by 12 strokes, the widest margin of victory the tournament has ever seen. He was the youngest Masters winner in history.
- Woods won the U.S. Open at Pebble Beach by 15 strokes, the largest margin of victory ever recorded at a major tournament.
- Tiger Woods has broken or tied nine records at the U.S. Open.
- Woods won the British Open by 8 strokes, shooting a 269, the best score ever at St. Andrews and the lowest score (in relation to par) at a major tournament.

- Four players other than Woods have won a career grand slam (Ben Hogan, Gene Sarazen, Gary Player, and Jack Nicklaus).
- Woods was the youngest of all career grand slam winners.
- Ben Hogan and Bobby Jones are the only players other than Woods to win three majors in a season.

## JUST A JOB

- Tiger surpassed $40 million in career earnings at the age of 28.

## TIGER ROARS

*"There is no comfort zone in golf. Nor is it a game of perfection…only once do I recall feeling nearly in control of my game, and that was when I shot a 13-under-par 59 at my home course in Orlando."*
—Tiger Woods

*"I won twelve times around the world in 2000, including three majors, and I remember hitting only one shot I would call perfect—a 3-wood on No. 14 at St. Andrews in the third round of the British Open."*
—Tiger Woods

*"A lot of what I've been able to accomplish in golf is the direct result of becoming physically stronger. I had to make my body complement my mind to make the most of my natural ability. In this game you need every edge, and physical strength has definitely become one of mine."*
—Tiger Woods

"I think when Tiger…gets married and starts to have a family, he will be a better golfer than he is today. And he certainly isn't too bad today."—Jack Nicklaus

*"Fun is the real reason we play the game.
Sometimes we forget that. I did once."*—Tiger Woods

*"He can take his game to Europe, Africa, Asia,
or wherever he wants and the world will follow."*
—Earl Woods, Tiger's dad

---

### Short Putts

PUTTS BETWEEN 4 AND 6 FEET are ones we should expect to make most of the time. To insure that you do, use this drill. Take 10 balls and line up a straight putt of about 4 feet. It is important to practice a straight putt, because then you need only to focus on the stroke and not on the break. Now, start putting, making sure the putter head is going straight back and straight through and that your putter face is square to your line at all times. Set yourself a goal for the number of putts that you can sink in a row.

---

**19**

# Women in Golf

The first woman golfer on record is perhaps an unlikely suspect. It was Mary, Queen of Scots, who was publicly chastised for going out on the links too soon after the death of her husband, Lord Darnley, in 1567. She was later falsely convicted of his murder and beheaded, an inauspicious fate for the first queen of golf.

Other early references to women playing golf are rare, but in 1792 a letter circulated around the Musselburgh Golf Club, giving mention of the rules and duties of the club in relation to women. It wasn't until the end of the Victorian era that women really began to take their place on the golf course.

A women's course had existed at St. Andrews in Scotland since about 1867, but it was little more than a glorified putting green. In 1894, when members of the Shinnecock Hills Golf Club in Southampton, New York, no longer wanted to share their club with their wives, the women simply went out on their own. They organized the first all-women golf club in Morristown, New Jersey, building their own seven-hole golf course.

In 1895, they managed to organize the first Women's Amateur Championship at the Meadow Brook Club in Hempstead, New York, despite being suddenly denied the right to play at their own clubs, especially once Morris County was taken over by a group of gentleman golfers.

## On Their Own

The following years would see women's golf expand, however, most notably in Philadelphia where it played a vital role in prewar social circles. It was a way for society ladies to socialize and engage in respectable activities. It was from these circles that some of the greatest early players emerged, including Scot Dorothy Campbell, who is said to have won nearly 750 tournaments during her lifetime.

Following World War I, however, a new era in women's golf would begin with the appearance of Alexa Stirling, a childhood golfing companion of the great Bobby Jones. It was not Stirling, however, who would prove to be a golfing great, but rather a fan of hers who was inspired to play after having watched Stirling in action in the summer of 1918.

That fan was Glenna Collett, a fifteen-year-old girl from Providence, who would soon bedazzle the ladies' golf scene by winning six Amateur Championships beginning in 1922, earning her the affectionate nickname of "the female Bobby Jones."

Collett's reign came to an end when seventeen-year-old Patty Berg beat her in a championship in 1935. Berg's enthusiasm for the game would lead her, along with ten other women, to found the Ladies Professional Golf Association in 1950, which began the era of professional golf for women. Today it exists as the locus for women's professional golf.

## Arrival of the Babe

Among the other founders was Babe Zaharias, whose participation in the game would mark its second era. During a time when women's golf was still struggling, the game needed a flamboyant personality to give it an extra boost and Babe was it. She had been a genuine sports celebrity since the 1932 Olympics where she won two golds and a silver. Suddenly, ladies' professional golf had crowds—Zaharias loved crowds and they loved her back. For an industry still struggling to gain sound financial footing, Babe was instrumental in putting women's golf in the public's consciousness.

## A New Era

The 1980s and '90s would see the beginning of a third and modern era for women's golf, with the rise of Nancy Lopez on the scene. A daughter of Mexican American parents, she rose to stardom breaking previous records, and became the first golfer, male or female, to earn a $1 million. It was a period of enormous growth for women's professional golf. The LPGA expanded through corporate sponsorships, bringing women's tournaments in line with male-dominated tours, and television networks have made it even more popular.

By 2000, Annika Sorenstam was on the scene in women's golf, a scene that she dominates today. Having set or tied 30 LPGA records in 2001, and another 20 records in 2002, and with total career earnings of $13.2 million, making her the highest earning female professional golfer, she has only further solidified women's golf as a premiere sporting event. On May 22, 2003 she was the first woman since Babe Zaharias to compete against men in a PGA event.

## Babe Zaharias

Mildred "Babe" Didrikson was aptly named after the other famous Babe, after she is said to have hit five home runs in a single baseball game. Home runs were not the Babe's only specialty, though—she was a walking sports machine. In the 1932 U.S. National Track and Field Championships, she entered seven events, winning them all.

Although we know her as a golf legend, she didn't really take up the game seriously until she had already won two Olympic gold medals (she would have had three except one was taken back because of her unorthodox method in the high jump). In the other two events, the javelin and the hurdles, she set new world records. After the Olympics, she toured the country, showing off her skills in track, swimming, tennis, and baseball.

When Zaharias turned her attention to golf, America—and soon the world—paid attention. In a little less than three years after winning Olympic gold, Zaharias won the Texas Open. It announced her to the golf world all right, but she was also told she would be banned from all future amateur events and be considered a professional.

In 1938, Babe Didrikson married a professional wrestler, becoming, in the process, Babe Zaharias. In 1943, Zaharias applied for and was granted the right to be an amateur. Three years later, she captured the U.S. Amateur.

## ⧹ *Playing with the Boys* ⧹

For anyone who witnessed the tremendous crush of pressure facing Annika Sorenstam when she played in the men's professional tournament—the Colonial in 2003—imagine what the pressure must have been like for Zaharias in 1945 when she became the first woman to play in a PGA Tour event at the Los Angeles Open.

In 1947, Zaharias captured the British Ladies championship and decided to return to professional status. In 1948, she won the first of three U.S. Women's Open championships.

Zaharias attracted attention wherever she traveled. In England, she was asked to change out of her red and white checkered shorts, which she did—and then, of course, proceeded to win the tournament. Zaharias also put on exhibitions in America and England with British golfing legend Joyce Wethered.

In 1951, Zaharias traveled to Britain to be part of a team of women to take on a team of top-notch male golfers. The contest was a slam dunk, with the women winning all of their matches.

## ⧹ *One Last Fight* ⧹

There were few obstacles that Babe Zaharias could not overcome. She was not prepared, however, for what would come in 1953.

She was diagnosed with cancer and had surgery to try and control the dreadful disease. All looked good as she went on to claim her third U.S. Open title in 1954 by an incredible 12 strokes. In 1955, she won two more tournaments. In 1956, the American public mourned as 42-year-old Babe Zaharias passed away.

There simply is no quibble about it: Zaharias was a legend—made even more so by her premature death. She won an incredible 82 tournaments in a relatively short career. In a 1950 Associated Press poll she was voted the outstanding woman athlete of the century—who could argue?

## Long Putts

PRACTICE LENGTH PUTTS with emphasis placed on keeping the entire body perfectly still except for the hands, arms, and shoulders. It sounds easy, but you'll be surprised at how much concentration is needed at first to keep the body still during a purely hand, arms, and shoulder putting stroke.

## Women in Golf Today

- 6.1 million women in the U.S. play golf, according to the National Golf Foundation.
- 24 percent of all U.S. golfers are women.
- 2 out of 3 new golfers are women.
- 63 percent of female golfers are 40 or older, according to *Golf Magazine*.
- 56 percent of female golfers work full-time.
- 16 percent work part-time.
- 14 percent are retired.

# A Course for Women

- 80 yards were given for driving on the first women's golf course at St. Andrew's in 1867.

## In the U.S. Today

- 18 percent of all golf rounds are played by women.
- 3.3 million female golfers play just 1 to 7 rounds of golf a year.
- 1.5 million female golfers play 8 to 24 rounds a year.
- 1.4 million play 25 or more rounds a year.

## Pet Peeves

In a survey of women golfers in Washington State by GMA Research and GolfMarketingTeam.com, the two most oft-mentioned pet peeves for women when on the golf course:
1. Being accused of playing slow by course marshals when they are actually keeping up or waiting for those in front of them.
2. Being ignored or given a backseat to men when checking in for a tee time.

In the same survey, the factors that women say are the most important to them when choosing a golf course to play:
1. Dedicated tee times for women.
2. Multiple restrooms on the golf course.
3. Friendly greeting when checking in.

## You Spent How Much?

- 21 percent of all spending on golf is spent by women, according to a report by Nancy Berkley at the Golf 20/20 conference.
- Women golfers actually use only 38 percent of the golf apparel they purchase.
- $750 is the average amount female golfers spend on golf each year.
- $874 is the average amount spent by male golfers.

## The TV Age

- 260 hours of television coverage of ladies golf aired in 2002, making it the most-watched women's sport on television, according to the LPGA.

## *Professional Women*

The founding of the Women's Professional Golf Association in 1944 by Hope Seignious, Betty Hicks, and Ellen Griffin marked the beginning of professional golf for women. With little funding, the WPGA soon closed its doors.

In a 1949 meeting at the Venetian Hotel in Miami, Florida, between Fred Corcoran, a well-known sports agent, Patty Berg, and Babe and George Zaharias, the Ladies Professional Golf Association was conceived, this time with a legitimate sponsor—Wilson Sporting Goods—agreeing to fund the first tour. When the WPGA finally closed in 1950, the LPGA was born.

## Growth Industry

- 14 events were sponsored by the LPGA in its first year.
- 33 events were sponsored by the LPGA in 2004.
- Total prize money available in 2004 was $42 million.
- $1.3 million is the average purse size for an LPGA Tournament.
- Attendance at the LPGA has increased 14 percent since 2002.
- Network viewing of the LPGA has increased 26 percent since 2002.

## LAPPING THE FIELD

Louise Suggs won the 1949 U.S. Women's Open by 14 strokes—a record margin.

## Driver's License

Laura Baugh won the 1971 U.S. Amateur at the age of 16 years and 2 months.

##  Hundred G-Notes

In 1976, Judy Rankin became the first LPGA professional to earn more than $100,000 in a season.

## PIZZA, ANYONE?

Lori Garbacz ordered a pizza between holes at the 1989 U.S. Women's Open to protest slow play.

## Trans-Game

Australian Mianne Bagger became the first transsexual to play in a professional golf tournament when she played in the Women's Australian Open in 2004.

## From the Cradle

Did you know that the LPGA Tour, U.S. Golf Association, and the Ladies European Tour now have policies that players must be female at birth? They enacted the policy after transsexual Charlotte Wood placed third in the 1987 U.S. Senior Women's Amateur, and reached the semifinals of the U.S. Women's Mid-Amateur. All entry forms of the USGA and the LPGA now carry the "female at birth" clause.

## FIRSTS

- 88 is the most official tournament wins by a professional woman golfer, Kathy Whitworth (1962–85), according to the LPGA Hall of Fame.
- The youngest Women's U.S. Open qualifier, Beverly Klass, was 10 years old when she qualified for the event in 1967.
- In 2005, women golfers will have their own system for determining world rankings, giving tours a way to choose teams for international competitions in such events as the Olympics.
- The men's system for world rankings was developed in 1968.

## Breadwinners

- Mildred "Babe" Zaharias earned $14,800 in 1950 as the leading LPGA money winner that year.
- PGA money leader Sam Snead earned $35,758 that same year.
- Annika Sorenstam earned $2.03 million in 2003.
- Sorenstam has earned $13.2 million so far in her career, making her the richest player ever on the women's tour.
- Nancy Lopez has earned $5.3 million and is fourteenth on the list of female money winners.
- In 1981, Kathy Whitworth reached $1 million in career prize money, making her the first woman golfer to do so.
- In 1986, Pat Bradley reached $2 million in career prize money, making her the first woman golfer to do so.

## Battle for Augusta

In 2002, Martha Burk, head of the National Council of Women's Organizations, criticized the Augusta National Golf Club for its "men only" membership policy. It sparked a fierce debate at the highest levels in professional golf about private and exclusive golf clubs.

## THE LAW

- In 1994, the U.S. Senate passed a law prohibiting private golf clubs from favoring men on the links.
- 65 percent of men surveyed supported Augusta's decision to limit its membership to men only, according to a survey by the Polling Company.
- 60 percent of women also supported Augusta's decision.
- 72 percent felt Augusta should consider and review its own policies on its own time, and in its own way.

## We're Private

- 23 percent of the 129 golf courses on the PGA, LPGA, or Champions tour (all private, semiprivate, and resort golf clubs) responded to a survey by *USA Today* about the number of women memberships in their clubs.
- 32 percent of the members of the DuPont Country Club in Wilmington, Delaware, are women, one of the leading private clubs in terms of women's memberships.

## Treatment

- 47 percent of women golfers say they have at some point been mistreated or offended as a woman golfer, according to a survey by GMA Research and GolfMarketingTeam.com.

---

### LOW-LOFT CLUBS

FOR A GOLFER TO BENEFIT from a low-lofted driver (less than 10 degrees), you must have a very high clubhead speed to achieve the necessary launch angle or trajectory to maximize distance.

---

## A Woman's Game
### Women Are From Venus, Men Are From Mars

Women are willing to travel 88 miles round trip to play at a top golf course, according to *Golf Magazine's* "Report on the American Golfer," a survey of 2,000 golf enthusiasts, each of whom plays at least 25 rounds a year.

# Sex

- 70 percent of women golfers would give up sex for golf, according to the "Report on the American Golfer."
- 44 percent of male golfers said the same.
- 4 percent of female golfers report having had sexual relations on a golf course.
- 9 percent of male golfers reported the same.

## FAMILY TIME

- 11 percent of women golfers say they give up time with their families for the sake of golf, according to the National Golf Foundation and the "Report on the American Golfer."
- 31 percent of men golfers say they sacrifice family time for golf.

## The Gambling Itch

- 50 percent of women say they have wagered on the golf course, according to *Golf Magazine's* "Report on the American Golfer."
- 77 percent of men say they have.

## Anger Management

- 49 percent of men have thrown a club in anger, according to a survey by the National Golf Foundation.
- 14 percent of women have thrown a club in anger.

## IN THE BOARDROOM

- 16 percent of male executives say they hate playing golf with women, according to a survey by Starwood Choice Hotels and Resorts.
- 63 percent of women executives surveyed say their biggest business or sales deals have been made while playing golf.

- 75 percent believe that how a person plays golf is very similar to how he or she conducts their business affairs.
- 88 percent of women executives admit to cheating at golf.
- The average handicap of a female executive golfer is 17.
- A female executive plays an average of 30 rounds of golf each year.

## *Did You Know?*

- Did you know that in 1900, women who competed in the first modern Olympic Games in Paris, France, played in just three sports: tennis, golf, and croquet? Margaret I. Abbott was the first American woman to win an Olympic gold medal. An art student in Paris, she won the 9-hole golf tournament by shooting a 47.
- Did you know that golfing great Glenna Collett Vare won her last championship in 1935, defeating the teenage Patty Berg before an estimated crowd of 15,000, who had come to watch the grande dame of golf? Vare dominated the sport in the 1920s, winning 59 of 60 consecutive matches. Women golfers of the day competed for the fun of it since there were no money prizes for women. The Vare Trophy for the lowest scoring average was named in her honor in 1922.
- Did you know that in the romantic comedy *Pat and Mike* (1952) Katherine Hepburn plays an all-around athlete who competes against real-life athletes Babe Zaharias and Betty Hickes from women's golf?
- Did you know that in 1990 Juli Inkster of Los Altos, California, became the first woman to win the only professional golf tournament in the world in which women and men competed head to head? She won the Invitational Pro-Am at Pebble Beach in a one-stroke victory.
- Did you know that in 2000, 14-year-old ninth grader Michelle Wie became the youngest player in a PGA Tour event, missing

the cut by one stroke at the Sony Open in Hawaii? After two days of play, she finished at even-par 140 for the tournament, tied for 80th in the 144-player field and finishing ahead of more than a dozen tour event winners.

- Did you know that Nancy Lopez's father, Domingo, dug a hole in his backyard and filled it with sand so his 9-year-old daughter could practice hitting balls out of this makeshift sand trap?
- Did you know that one of Annika Sorenstam's teammates at the University of Arizona was U.S. Open winner Jim Furyk?

## Maximizing Distance

MAXIMUM DISTANCE is a function of many variables, including the spin rate of the golf ball. To maximize distance, the clubhead speed at impact must complement the spin rate of the golf ball, which provides the necessary lift on the golf ball to maintain its flight.

## Annika Sorenstam

Born in Stockholm, Sweden, to a sport-crazy family, Annika Sorenstam only took up golf after she began to get beat more frequently on the tennis court. Although she rose to twelfth in the junior tennis rankings in Sweden, that wasn't quite good enough, and young Annika was encouraged to take up golf.

She was soon taking lessons from one of Stockholm's top instructors (who plays a role in Sorenstam's development to this day). Another important person in Sorenstam's life was Swedish golf legend Pia Nilsson, who had gone to university in the U.S. before going on to the professional tour there. Sorenstam would follow in Nilsson's footsteps at the University of Arizona and later the LPGA tour.

Sorenstam took the college golf world in the U.S. by storm. In her first year, she led the University of Arizona Wildcats to the 1991 NCAA Championship, was named an All-American, and was named College Player of the Year. She was named All-American again in 1992 and helped lead the Wildcats to the '92 World Amateur Team Championship in Vancouver.

Sorenstam's college record qualified her for the U.S. Open in 1992. Although she finished 24 strokes behind the champion, she had arrived. When she turned professional, she did so on the European Tour. In ten starts there, she finished second four times and was voted the tour's Rookie of the Year. In the following year, she decided to play in the LPGA, and with a second place finish in the Women's British Open, fans were quickly put on notice that there was a new talent to watch.

In 1995, she atoned for her initial showing at the U.S. Women's Open, capturing the most prestigious title in women's golf. Sorenstam's rise has been one of steady and impressive achievement. She dominated the Ladies Professional Golf Tour in the late 1990s and early 2000s.

After winning the U.S. Women's Open in 1995, she turned around and did it again in 1996. Sorenstam was named the Rolex Player of the Year in 1995, 1997, 1998, 2001, and 2002. In 2002, she had an amazing eleven tour victories, bringing her career total to forty-two. She also won two international tournaments that year, making thirteen victories in twenty-five starts.

In May of 2003, she did something not done since Babe Zaharias at the LA Open in 1945; she entered a men's PGA event, the Colonial. Even cynical male golfers everywhere could not help but be impressed. With all the pressure and huge galleries, she had an opening round of 71, a score that easily could have been a 67 if putts had dropped for her.

Sorenstam's other accomplishments include being the first person to shoot under 60 in an LPGA event. In 2003, she took the Women's British Open, completing a career grand slam. Her dominance of the women's tour has often been compared to Tiger Woods's dominance of the PGA in the same era.

20

## Golf and Fitness

Golf hasn't always been a sport. Up until the twentieth century, it was merely a game for elite British and American society. But as the elite became more enthusiastic about the game, and the mass production of golf equipment became possible, everyone got involved. Soon it was a sport—a competitive sport—and everyone wanted to win. And to win at a sport, you've got to be good.

---

### Improving Clubhead Speed

A GOOD GRIP AND AN ATHLETIC POSTURE will improve clubhead speed. Once you have a good setup, it's easier for your body motion to move freely behind the ball in the backswing, and into the ball on the way through. A good drill is to swing a golf club three feet off the ground (sort of a baseball-type swing, but using your golf grip and posture). This will help you feel the right swing plane and release through impact.

---

# ≋ *A Passion for Practice* ≋

Enter Ben Hogan. Rising from Texas poverty, and having caddied for 65 cents an hour in his hometown of Fort Worth, he was on the verge of becoming one of the greatest golfers of all time. To make it in golf he would have to be good, and he knew the only way he could do it was through hard work. He became a compulsive practicer: the first golfer to really practice. Legend has it that he spent so much time practicing that his hands bled. Even his companions on tour would complain that they could hear golf balls bouncing off the walls inside his hotel room as he practiced his chipping and putting.

Until Hogan and his meticulous and dedicated approach to the game, fitness as a component of winning golf had largely been ignored or dismissed. In preparation for the British Open in 1953, Hogan, never having used the smaller British-size golf ball, practiced for two weeks to get used to the different feel of the ball. Perhaps not a remarkable feat today, but in an era when golfers were more concerned about the social activities surrounding golf, Hogan's determination stood out.

It was Hogan's passion for the game that gave rise to the professional golfer we know today. Up until Hogan's time, though, golfers simply chose to imitate the golfing greats they saw on the golf course, from Walter Hagen's straight-line putting to Gene Sarazen's sand-wedging techniques. But Hogan showed them that to be good at the game, you had to practice. His followers, however, took it another step, and made it their job not only to practice, but also to make their own personal fitness an essential part of the game.

# ≋ *The Player* ≋

Golfer Gary Player perhaps took Hogan's advice most to heart. During a round they played together, Hogan offered his younger colleague some advice. "Do you practice a lot?" he asked. When Player responded that he did, Hogan reportedly responded, "Well, practice even more." Player did, and set the standard for most golfing professionals by being one of the first to visit the gym regularly for aerobic and weight training.

Today, of course, almost every golf professional has followed suit, with a few very notable exceptions. Television viewers today would be shocked to see a player like Arnold Palmer, known in his early years always to have a cigarette dangling from his lips.

As golf professionals retired, they began to teach their successors what they learned on the course, whether through books or personal training. And as colleges and universities began opening up golf schools in the 1980s and 1990s, golf became an increasingly specialized field.

The latest golfing greats—Tiger Woods and Annika Sorenstam—rely on personal trainers. Teenage golf sensation Ty Tryon—who qualified for the PGA Tour at 17 in 2001, making him the youngest player ever to do so—has worked with a professional fitness trainer since age 12, and he attributes much of his success to a fitness regimen that's kept him in top shape.

## ⩵ *Many Advantages* ⩵

Most folks don't think of golf for its superior fitness results, but you'd be surprised!

- A golfer walks 5 miles per 18 holes.
- Fifty-five sedentary, middle-aged men lost an average of 5 pounds by playing golf two or three times per week over a five-month period.
- They shrank their waistlines by an average of 1 inch.

- They decreased their abdominal fat by 8 percent.
- They lowered their "bad" LDL cholesterol and triglycerides by 49 percent.
- A golfer's heart rate rises 25 beats per minute, on average, during a game of golf.
- A golfer must play 13 holes before his muscles begin to fatigue and tighten, according to sports doctors at some of the most exclusive golf clubs in Philadelphia.

## BURN IT OFF

According to the President's Council on Fitness:
- A golfer can burn an average of 1,750 calories per 18-holes by forgoing the golf cart.
- 324 calories are burned per hour of golf when playing without the cart.
- 168 calories are burned per hour when playing with a golf cart.
- 246 calories are burned per hour of housecleaning.
- 440 are burned in an hour of scrubbing floors.
- 198 are burned in an hour's walk.

## Hazards Everywhere

While every game has it advantages, there are also some downfalls. While most golfing injuries don't end up being serious, care should be taken. Herewith, some of the most common hot spots.
- For every 100,000 golfers, 104 are hurt on the course.

## Wrists and Yips

Just when you think you're getting good and the hours of practicing are paying off, this little ailment can strike with a vengeance. They're called "yips," when your hand starts to twitch and jerk just as you're about to hit the ball, throwing off your putts, especially. General Solution: Change your grip or stance, or use a putter with a longer or thicker handle.

- Half of all golfers suffer from yips, according to a study of 1,000 avid golfers by the Mayo Clinic.
- 21.2 percent of men are affected by hand or wrist injuries.
- 14.5 percent of women are affected by hand or wrist injuries.
- 20 percent of golfers admit to imbibing before a game in an attempt to prevent "yips."
- The average number of rounds of golf per year played by yipping golfers is 75.

## Lower Back

During a golf swing, the spine has to bend and contort in ways that sometimes aren't the most comfortable!

- The lower back is the most common site of injury for 36 percent of male amateur and professional golfers, according to the *Journal of Physicians and Sports Medicine*.
- For 27.4 percent of women, lower back injuries are the most common.
- 80 to 90 percent of muscle activity occurs for amateurs and professionals during a golf swing.
- An amateur golfer's back bends 80 percent more than a professional's during a golf swing.

## Elbows

- One of the most common injuries is Golfer's Elbow, similar to Tennis Elbow, which is simply an irritation in one's elbow joint caused by too much swinging.
- 32.5 percent of men's most common injury affects their elbows.
- 35.5 percent of female golfers' most common injury affects their elbows.

## Shoulders

- During the swing, one's shoulders can get overextended if you're not careful. So watch out!
- 11 percent of men say that their shoulders are the most common site of their golf injuries.
- 16.1 percent of women say shoulders are the most common site of their golf injuries.
- 97 percent of competitive golfers surveyed said that they had pain in the leading shoulder from golf.

## Head Down While Putting

To TRAIN YOURSELF to keep your head down when you putt, listen for the ball to enter the hole, rather than looking for it to do so. The main reason golfers lift their heads is because they focus too much on results rather than keeping their eye on the ball.

## Seniors

It's perhaps no surprise that golf is a popular sport for seniors—it's not too hard on those aches and pains, and it's a good balance of social activity while you're getting some exercise. Not to mention some good, clean fun! Ten percent of Americans over age 60 regularly golf for recreation, according to American Demographics.

The top five fitness activities for seniors, according to the Sporting Goods Manufacturing Association, are:

- Fitness walking
- Stretching
- Treadmill exercise
- Golf
- Freshwater fishing

## MAGNETIC PERSONALITY

- Senior PGA golfer Jim Colbert discovered the pain-relieving qualities of magnets in 1994.
- 70 percent of golfers on the Senior PGA tour wear magnet amulets to relieve their aches and pains.
- Pain-relieving magnetic products cost $31 to $500.

## What Annika and Tiger Say

Nearly every golfing professional touts the importance of aerobic, cardiovascular, and weight training to improve personal fitness as key to a good game of golf. Above all, it's a struggle to maximize distance, control, and accuracy, which requires strength and flexibility on the part of players.

While most professionals closely guard their workout regimens, they do drop some hints. And who better to give us advice than the winners?

---

### Sorenstam

*"I would not have tried to play in a PGA event two or three years ago. The reason why I am working out is to get better: play better golf, hit it farther, and be more consistent." —Annika Sorenstam*

---

- Annika Sorenstam's average driving distance is 271.6 yards.
- She's added 20 yards, which she attributes to her rigorous workout sessions.
- She can lift her chin up to the bar when working out 12 times.
- She generally bench-presses 150 pounds.

## Tiger

*"My mom always says that you can't fool Mother Nature.
However, with the right fitness regimen and modern
technology, you can sure fake her out longer than you used to."*
*—Tiger Woods*

- Tiger says he usually spends 90 minutes working out each day.
- He typically does a combination of aerobic and weight-training exercises for at least an hour or two, three to five times per week.

---

### SHAFT SIZE

A LONGER-SHAFTED DRIVER offers an opportunity for distance. Hitting the ball in the center of the clubface or sweet spot, however, is greatly influenced by the length of the shaft. The longer the shaft, the more difficult it becomes to hit your shots solidly and consistently.

---

**2 1**

## Golf...Rules

The first established rule regarding golf was one modern golfers wouldn't much like: it was a Scottish parliamentary ban on playing golf in 1457. It seems the locals were so keen on the game that they weren't showing up for military training. In

232

1491, the ban was finally lifted, with the signing of the Treaty of Glasgow, and by 1552 the Archbishop of St. Andrews issued a decree giving churchgoers the right to play golf (after attending church, of course).

As golf courses sprang up around the Scottish countryside, there seemed to be little need to lay down any specific rules or standards for the game. What rules there were existed in the heads of the members, and even then they differed from course to course.

In 1744, however, the Gentlemen Golfers of Leith (later the Honourable Company of Edinburgh Golfers) asked Duncan Forbes to draw up the first set of rules, written for their first Annual Challenge for the Silver Club. This tournament was to also involve golfers from Blackheath, Glasgow, Musselburgh, and St. Andrews, so they needed a standard set of rules to make it fair.

## Arrival of St. Andrews

The gentlemen of Leith soon found their course was too small to accommodate their growing numbers, and in the period between looking and establishing a new course, the golf club at St. Andrews was substituted as the rule-making body. It has been there ever since.

As the demand for golf grew, and more and more tournaments were being held, a need for a uniform set of rules became apparent. Golfers again turned to St. Andrews—now the Royal and Ancient (R&A) of St. Andrews Golf Club—to fill that need. In 1897, they set up the first Rules of Golf Committee and in 1899 they published their first official code.

Around the same time (in 1894) the United States Golf Association (USGA) was also forming, but they began to issue rules for U.S. golfers that diverged from the rules the R&A was producing. In 1921, the R&A and USGA got together and decided on a standard size for the golf ball. Ten years later the USGA broke rank and went for a smaller ball, and then, a year later, for a heavier ball.

## The Stymie

In 1951, the two groups again got together to settle differences, and also to debate the thorny issue of the stymie—whether players were required to move their ball from the green when it rested between the hole and their opponent's ball, thus preventing him or her from playing a direct shot. They managed to come to agreement on every issue except the weight of the golf ball. Although the differences on the ball continued, in 1956 the two organizations agreed to revisit the rules every four years.

In 1970, the R&A met for the first time with golfing bodies around the world to discuss the governance of the game, so that today every country, except the U.S. and Mexico, are governed by the rules set down by the R&A.

In 1988, the R&A adopted the heavier golf ball that the U.S. had been using since 1932, thereby bringing to a close the last debate between the two groups. The rules of the game were the same all over the world for the first time in fifty-six years.

## The Thirteen Commandments

The first known *Rules of Golf* were written by Duncan Forbes for the First Annual Edinburgh Silver Club Tournament, hosted by the Gentlemen Golfers of Leith. They were adopted ten years later with some minor adjustments by the Royal and Ancient St. Andrews Club when it hosted its first official Silver Club tournament. Here they are, complete with original spellings.

1. You must Tee your Ball within a Club length of the Hole.
2. Your Tee must be upon the ground.

3. You are not to change the Ball which you strike off the Tee.

4. You are not to remove Stones, Bones, or any Break-club for the sake of playing your Ball, except upon the fair Green, and that only within a Club length of your Ball.

5. If your Ball come among Water, or any watery filth, you are at liberty to take out your Ball, and bringing it behind the hazard, and teeing it, you may play it with any club and allow your Adversary a stroke for so getting out your Ball.

6. If your Balls be found anywhere touching one another, you are to lift the first Ball till you play the last.

7. At holing, you are to play your Ball honestly for the Hole, and not play upon your Adversary's Ball, not lying in your way to the Hole.

8. If you should lose your Ball by its being taken up, or in any other way, you are to go back to the spot where you struck last, and drop another Ball, and allow your Adversary a stroke for your misfortune.

9. No man, at Holing his Ball, is to be allowed to mark to the Hole with his Club or anything else.

10. If a Ball be stop'd by any person, Horse, Dog, or anything else, the Ball so stop'd must be played where it lyes.

11. If you draw your Club in order to strike, and proceed as far in the stroke as to be bringing down your Club—if then your Club shall break in any way, it is to be accounted a stroke.

12. He whose Ball lyes farthest from the Hole is obliged to play first.

13. Neither Trench, Ditch, nor Dyke made for the preservation of the Links, nor the Scholars' holes, nor the Soldiers' lines, shall be accounted a Hazard, but the Ball is to be taken out, Teed, and played with any iron Club.

## Reducing Sand on Bunker Shots

WHEN SETTING UP for your bunker shot, open the club-face of the sand wedge first, and then take your grip. This will help you take shallow divots, which will help your consistency in the sand.

## Milestones

**1759** Stroke play was introduced to the game, in which each player adds up the number of strokes it took for the round, and then deducts his or her handicap, so that the lowest score wins.

**1764** The Royal and Ancient Golf Club of St. Andrews decided that the first four and the last four holes of their 22-hole golf course were too small. They combined each of the four into two holes, thus making 18 holes on the course, creating the standard number of holes for a round of golf, which was later adopted by most other clubs.

**1850** A new rule allowed a player to drop a new ball without penalty where the largest piece of his previous ball fell, if the player's guttie or feathery ball broke up in mid-flight—which was not uncommon.

**1857** The first book on golf instruction, *The Golfer's Manual*, authored by "A Keen Hand" (H. B. Farnie) was published.

**1888** The Royal and Ancient issued its first code of *Golf Rules*, with a more comprehensive set following in 1897.

**1894** The United States Golf Association was founded and began to influence standards for American golfers.

**1897** The first *Rules of Golf* Committee was established by the R&A.

**1899** The first standard *Rules of Golf* were published by the R&A.

The Western Golf Association was formed in the U.S. By the 1930s it fell away as a governing body for golf, as the USGA, an eastern U.S. association, solidified its status as the governing body for golf in America.

**1909** The first rule limiting the form and make of golf clubs was made. It banned any clubs that incorporated any kind of mechanical devices on the clubhead and shaft.

**1922** Golf balls were first required to be a certain weight and size.

**1939** A rule allowing players to carry only 14 clubs was made. It was the first time players were limited in the number of clubs they could carry.

**1952** Stymieing was abolished—players no longer had to chip over an opponent's ball if it was between their own ball and the hole.

Stableford scoring was included in *The Rules* as a form of play long recognized in amateur play. In this method, players acquired points depending upon the number of strokes it took them to complete the hole. The fewer strokes, the more points. The player with the most points at the end, after adding handicaps, was the winner.

*1960* Distance-measuring devices were banned.

## RULE BOOKS

- There are 34 rules in golf today.
- The written rules today encompass 40,000 words, 132 pages, and 3 appendices.
- *The Decisions on the Rules of Golf*, published as a companion to *The Rules of Golf*, is 600 pages long.
- By 1812, the number of rules in the code posted by the St. Andrews Society of Golfers had grown to 17.
- The original set of rules consisted of 338 words.
- The 1812 set of rules was 541 words.
- The rules the USGA and the R&A were issuing by 1970 took 75 pages and 18,000 words.

### Eliminating Fat or Thin Pitch Shots

ELIMINATING FAT OR THIN PITCH SHOTS means hitting your pitch shots solidly, thereby getting the ball to travel the right distance. Your clubface and body alignment need to be open, while the ball should be in the middle of your stance. Make sure your weight is on your left side, and that during the swing your legs stay still, moving only with the momentum of the swing.

# Golf Etiquette

On or off the golf course, manners are an essential part of human interaction. On the golf course, however, they're about more than just trying to moderate human exchanges. Good golf etiquette is essential for the safety of golfers, the maintenance of the golf course, and the overall enjoyment of the game. Without proper etiquette on the golf course, a good game can go south.

Golf is one of the few sports played without a referee or umpire, and therefore requires players to show consideration for one another. Most newcomers have to watch and learn. They learn proper golf etiquette as they go, being coached by more experienced golfers. And in many clubs, slightly different etiquette rules can develop, depending upon with whom you're playing.

While there are hundreds of golfing etiquette suggestions, the basic principle is the same across the board: show honor and respect for the game and your fellow players, be patient, and don't do anything that would distract others from focusing on their game. Use your brain, and conduct yourself in a disciplined manner, with courtesy and sportsmanship at all times, no matter how competitive you are.

And just to be clear: if there is a serious breach of player etiquette on the course, a player can be disqualified from play under rule 33–7.

# Not by the Book

There is no specific book of written rules of golf etiquette that must be followed. The United States Golf Association, however, provides some simple guidelines for clubs to adopt that can help make the game go more smoothly.

## Safety

Make sure no one is standing close by or in a position to be hit by your ball or club. That includes players, greens staff, and even people you don't like. Make sure the players in front of you are out of range, and if you do play a ball in their direction, use the old familiar warning: "Fore."

## Consideration of Other Players

Try not to distract others from their game, whether it's by moving, talking, or making any unnecessary noise while others are trying to make a shot. This is perhaps most important when you're on the green: don't stand or cast a shadow in another player's line of putt; and make sure your own ball isn't in their way.

## Pace of Play

Perhaps one of the biggest frustrations for golfers is players who go too slowly on the course. Sometimes it may be necessary for you to let the team behind you play through while you're looking for that lost ball. In general, keep up the pace and be ready to play.

## Care of the Course

Keep in mind how much you hate it when your ball lands in a divot and you've got to get it out of there. Smooth over holes and footprints after you've been in the bunker, repair ball marks and divots, and any other damage, whether it be from putting down your club bag, moving the flagstick, or any other activity that may cause damage to the course. Want to really prevent damage to the course? Follow the signs that tell you where and where not to drive your golf cart.

## Bad Boys and Girls

You might think that you're getting away with it, but golf-course superintendents know what you're up to, and so do your fellow players.

- 60 percent of golf-course superintendents surveyed say that the worst breach of etiquette on the golf course is failure to repair ball marks on the putting green.
- 18 percent say failing to rake bunkers is the worst breach.
- 8 percent cite failing to replace divots.
- 40 percent say driving a golf cart on or too close to greens is the most common violation of golf course etiquette that they see, making it the number one violation.
- 33 percent say that ignoring daily postings of golf-cart restrictions is the second most common violation.

## Slow Play

It is often called a "leisurely" game, but let the draw of the 19th hole back at the clubhouse keep you moving forward.

- 37 percent of golfers surveyed say that the main thing they would like to ban from the golf course is slow players, according to *Golf Magazine's* "Report on the American Golfer."
- 23 percent of golf-course superintendents say that the decline in golfer etiquette is the primary cause of slow play on the golf course.
- On average, it takes about 70 percent of foursomes 4.5 hours to play 18 holes.
- 30 percent of golfers surveyed say it takes them closer to 5.5 hours.

## Gambling Away

Since the beginning of the game, golfers have often placed bets on their game. It's certainly given rise to playing for prize money in national tournaments, the purpose of which is to allow players to have resources with which to improve their game. But to preserve the game as a source of enjoyment, rather than turning it into a money-making industry, the USGA discourages players from placing bets or holding public golf competitions which involve gambling.

• Nonetheless, 72 percent of golfers have gambled on the course.
• The average amount of money lost in a single day is $31.92.

## No Respect

In a survey of golf-course superintendents, 67 percent feel that a lack of knowledge and respect for the game of golf is the biggest factor leading to poor player etiquette.

### Balance through the Finish of the Swing

SWINGING TOO HARD and having too narrow a stance are reasons for losing your balance during your swing. For a balanced swing, keep a good rhythm. Swing within yourself and, remember, the longer the club, the wider your stance should be.

# Golf Handicaps

## *What the Heck Are They, Anyway?*

he purpose of the system of golf handicaps is to allow golfers of differing abilities to play and compete together. By taking into account your score on the golf course, which tee you are playing from, and combining it with the difficulty rating of the course you're playing on, you can get your handicap. It is meant to demonstrate what you would shoot on your best day.

A handicap reflects your potential ability as a golfer. If you're playing on a more difficult course, it awards you extra strokes (i.e., you can deduct them from your score), while if you are playing on an easier course, it takes strokes away.

At the end of your game, you take your gross score and use your handicap to determine your net score. And because golfers each have their own handicap, based on their own abilities, they can play together competitively on the same course, on a level playing field (so to speak).

## *How'd We Get Them?*

The first reference to a system of handicapping is by Thomas Kincaid, a medical student at the University of Edinburgh in the 1680s, who wondered whether it would be better to give a player a two-hole start every three holes, or play even, paying three-to-one odds per hole. Often referred to as "assigning the odds," done by the "adjustor of the odds," generally the use of handicaps in golf was for a single purpose. It was a way for players to establish a level playing field, which in turn would then allow them to place bets on the game.

Since the mid-nineteenth century, there was an explosion in the number of ways golfers would calculate their handicaps. In 1904, Leighton Calkins, a member of the USGA Executive Committee, proposed a system of calculating golf handicaps, which was officially adopted by the USGA in 1911. Under this system, handicaps were calculated by averaging a player's three best scores for the season.

As the USGA began to develop a system of course ratings (at first basing the par ratings for each course on the play of U.S. Amateur Champion Jerome Travers), it became necessary to incorporate that into the system of calculating golf handicaps. Hence, over the years, the USGA has modified the handicap system numerous times, until the complex system we have today was settled upon.

## Get Out Your Calculator

Anyone can have a handicap, but if you want one that you can use in official tournaments, it has to be one issued by the United States Golf Association. It is normally done through your local golf club, but only golf clubs that are licensed by the USGA to assign handicaps may do so.

- And there's a reason the USGA makes it their business to calculate golfer's handicaps: it's simply too difficult and complicated for most folks to do on their own! But here's the basic idea:
- (Your Adjusted Gross Score – USGA Course Rating) x 113 ÷ USGA Slope Rating
- That'll give you a number that is your differential for your round of golf.
- Do that for every round you play, and average them out.
- Take that average number and multiply it by 96 percent (or 0.96).

- Round it to the nearest tenth, and you've got your Handicap Index.

Once you have your Handicap Index, you can use that number to determine your Course Handicap, which is what tells you how many strokes you can deduct from your score on a particular course. Usually, golf courses will post charts which golfers can consult to determine their course handicap. And once you've done that, you've got your score!

- The USGA requires a minimum of 5 scores in order to calculate your USGA Handicap Index.
- They suggest you provide 20, in order to get a truer value.
- Of those twenty, they use the 10 best to calculate your Handicap Index.

## So Who's Got One?

Not everyone maintains a handicap, but many clubs recommend that players do so. It allows players to get a better sense of their true golfing ability, and allows your peers on the course to have a better sense of what kind of player you are, especially when you play against them!

- 20 percent of golfers maintain a handicap, according to the National Golf Foundation.
- The average handicap is 19–20.
- 4.5 million golfers have an official USGA handicap issued to them by their golf club.
- 37 percent of golfers who don't have an official USGA handicap say it's because they don't belong to a club that offers the service, according to a survey by golfserv.com.
- 22 percent say they simply don't know how to get one.
- 19 percent don't want to pay the fee to get one.
- 16 percent say they have no use for one.
- 6 percent simply don't care to have one.

## BATTLE OF THE SEXES

In the UK, the establishment of a handicap system is attributed to the women of golf there. While different clubs experimented with a system for years, there wasn't a standardized national system in the UK until it was introduced by the Ladies Golf Union of Great Britain and Ireland around 1900, under the leadership of Issette Pearson. While it has been modified a number of times since it was introduced, it is still considered one of the great achievements of the Ladies Golf Union.

- 16 is the average golf handicap for men, according to *Golf Digest*.
- 31 is the average golf handicap for women.

## Don't Sweat It

The purpose of your handicap isn't to make you nervous. It's simply to give you a better idea of how well you can play. But don't worry, everyone has their off-days, and the USGA expects you'll have a lot of those.

- 25 percent of the time the USGA suggests players should be expected to play their course handicap, or better.
- The USGA suggests players should average 3 strokes higher than their course handicap over the course of their playing.
- Players post an average of 21 scores each year so their club can have their handicap calculated.

## Play Nice

A big reason for having a handicap is to give your fellow golfers an idea of how you play. But some people don't quite take that to heart.

- 1–2 percent of golfers are "sandbaggers," posting very few scores (usually only their worst rounds), adding strokes to their score, or intentionally playing a few bad holes near the end of a round, but then end up playing better than their handicaps in tournaments, according to *Golf Digest*.

- 10 percent are vanity handicappers, posting only their very best scores, or scores better than what they actually shot.

## SCORE BETTER WITH A LOW HANDICAP

- 8 percent of golfers have had sex on a golf course, according to "The Report on the American Golfer."
- 18 percent of low handicap golfers have had sex on a golf course.

---

### Back-Nine Collapses

FALLING APART on the back nine after you've played a great front nine is common among many golfers. When you are playing well, the key is to keep your mind off the score. Some golfers find that keeping their scores to themselves is a good tactic, the belief being that that the more you verbalize your round, the harder it is to keep focusing on the process. Focus on playing one shot at a time and on your preshot routine.

---

## Patty Berg

A fiery redhead from Minnesota, Patricia Berg became one of the driving forces behind the establishment of professional women's golf in North America. Although Berg did not take up golf until she was 13, in just three years she won the Minneapolis City Championship.

She caught the attention of the golf world as a 17-year-old when she was a finalist at the U.S. Amateur, losing to Glenna Collett Vare in Vare's sixth and final amateur victory. Three years later she announced her arrival to the golfing world with a win at the U.S. Amateur.

In 1940, she turned professional, but a little over a year later she was involved in a serious accident, keeping her away from golf for a year and a half. When she returned in 1943, there was no indication of any rust. In 1943, she won the Western Open and the All-American at Tam O'Shanter. These were the war years, however, and she went on to join the Marines.

After the war, she helped found and set up the LPGA; in 1948 she became its first president. She won the 1946 U.S. Women's Open and in the next eleven years she won 39 LPGA tournaments and was the leading money winner in 1954, 1955, and 1957. She won the Vare Trophy for the lowest average round in 1953, 1955, and 1956 and the Associated Press named her woman athlete of the year three times. In total, Berg won 57 tournaments on the LPGA tour.

Berg was playing and giving golf clinics well into her seventies. Despite cancer and back and hip problems, she managed to continue golfing and teaching. For her perseverance and dedication, she was awarded the Ben Hogan Award. Earlier, she had received the Bobby Jones Award for outstanding sportsmanship and the LPGA honored her by establishing the Patty Berg Award in 1978, given to the woman golfer who has made the greatest contribution to women's golf during the year.

Berg was a tireless goodwill ambassador for golf, giving thousands of exhibitions and clinics and training young professionals who signed contracts with Wilson. She was given the 1976 Humanitarian Sports Award by the United Cerebral Palsy Foundation, the first woman to be so honored.

## Gary Player

When South African Gary Player traveled to England as a 20-year-old, the professionals there told him to think about another profession. Were they ever wrong. One year later, he returned to England to win the Dunlop Masters and to begin a career that would span three decades.

Player was the first player of any era to take fitness seriously. Other golfers had routines and practiced, but not with the ferocity or to such good effect as Player. Player read everything ever written by or about Ben Hogan and he set about practicing with Hogan-like diligence. The difference with Player was that he also added a strict fitness regimen to a Hogan practice routine.

Player was the first African to win the U.S. Open, the first non-American to win the Masters, and one of only five players to ever win all of the majors. In total, he would win ten majors before his career was finished. In addition to the U.S. Open, he won the British Open three times in three different decades, the U.S. PGA twice, and the Masters three times.

Together with Nicklaus and Palmer, he became part of the modern triumvirate, or "Big Three," and endorsement and money-making opportunities began to flow in. In addition to that, as early as 1961, Player was the leading money winner on the U.S. tour. In total, he won twenty-one times on the PGA tour.

Wherever Player has gone, he has won. He won thirteen South African Opens and seven Australian Opens. From his base in South Africa, he estimates he has traveled more than 12 million miles while competing in tournaments all over the world. In South Africa he has been named Sportsman of the Century, was inducted into the PGA Hall of Fame in 1974, and was named an Honorary Member of the Royal and Ancient at St. Andrews in 1994.

Player is the spokesperson for a number of global companies, including Gary Player Golf Equipment, the Gary Player Golf Academy, and Gary Player Enterprises, which handles licensing, publishing, apparel, and memorabilia. He is also a highly acclaimed golf-course architect. He established the Gary Player Foundation to provide education for disadvantaged children in South Africa, as well.

## Soft Lob Shots

FOR THE LOB SHOT, you have to trust the design of your lob or sand wedge. That is, you must trust that by swinging through the grass, the club will lift the ball into the air and land it softly on the green. Don't try to help the ball into the air (hitting up on the ball). This only causes you to lose your body angles and creates inconsistent shots around the green.

# World Golf Hall of Fame

The World Golf Hall of Fame opened its doors in St. Augustine, Florida, in 1998. So far only 100 members have been inducted into the Hall of Fame. Its mandate is to celebrate and recognize golf's greatest players and contributors and serve as an inspiration to golfers and fans throughout the world.

After years of negotiations, the Hall of Fame is now supported by all of the world's leading golf organizations, including Augusta National Golf Club, European PGA Tour, LPGA, PGA Tour, PGA of America, the Royal and Ancient Golf Club of St. Andrews, and the USGA.

The heart and soul of the World Golf Hall of Fame are its members. Four new members, Asao Ioki, Tom Kite, Charlie Sifford, and Marlene Stewart Streit, were inducted at the 2004 Induction Ceremony to bring the total to 104.

Members of the Hall of Fame are honored throughout the museum by means of personal and professional memorabilia, artifacts, photographs, and videos. The Hall of Fame's exhibit program includes the opening of special exhibits devoted to its members throughout the year.

Traditionally each spring the Hall of Fame opens a marquee exhibit. In March 2004, "Byron Nelson: A Champion...A Gentleman" was unveiled and before that, in March 2003, "Ben Hogan's Historic Season: 1953—A Golden Anniversary Tribute" opened. Exhibits representing the personal lives and professional achievements of each inductee also are unveiled at each year's induction ceremony.

At the World Golf Hall of Fame you can also trace the history of golf through stories, artifacts, and distinct memorabilia, including a life-size reconstruction of the famous Swilcan Burn Bridge from the Old Course at St. Andrews; a replica 1880s-style putting green that allows visitors to use hickory-shafted putters and gutta-percha balls; and a state-of-the-art golf simulator, which allows guests to experience any one of more than forty famous courses found around the world.

## Induction Process

Each year, the World Golf Hall of Fame adds to its membership by inducting the greatest players and contributors in the game of golf. The "balloting season" begins in January when the PGA Tour and International ballots are distributed to their respective voting bodies, and it concludes in late spring with a press announcement on the latest class.

There are five avenues for a player or contributor to enter the World Golf Hall of Fame: PGA Tour/Champions Tour ballot, International ballot, LPGA Point System, Lifetime Achievement category, and Veteran's category.

Various criteria are set up for players to be eligible for the PGA Tour/Champions Tour and International ballots, including an age requirement of at least 40 years of age and, in the case of players, a substantial amount of regular tournament victories and majors.

The LPGA Point System requires a player to be an active member of the LPGA Tour for ten years and to have won either an LPGA major tournament, Vare Trophy, or Rolex Player of the Year honors, plus a number of other tournament victories.

Nominations for the Lifetime Achievement category are made by the international voting body members. The category is designed for any male or female supporter of the sport whose primary role in the game has come outside the playing arena. The

World Golf Foundation Board of Directors' Selection Committee decides this category each year.

Any male or female professional or amateur who played the bulk of his/her career before 1974 and may not have received proper recognition is eligible for selection through the Veteran's category. The World Golf Foundation Board of Directors' Selection Committee also decides this category each year.

## World Golf Hall of Fame Members

| MEMBER | YEAR | MEMBER | YEAR |
|---|---|---|---|
| Amy Alcott | 1999 | Fred Corcoran | 1975 |
| Willie Anderson | 1975 | Henry Cotton | 1980 |
| Isao Aoki* | 2004 | Ben Crenshaw | 2002 |
| Tommy Armour | 1976 | Bing Crosby | 1978 |
| John Ball | 1977 | Beth Daniel | 1999 |
| Seve Ballesteros | 1997 | Jimmy Demaret | 1983 |
| Jim Barnes | 1989 | Roberto De Vicenzo | 1989 |
| Judy Bell | 2001 | Joseph C. Dey | 1975 |
| Patty Berg | 1974 | Leo Diegel | 2003 |
| Deane Beman | 2000 | Chick Evans | 1975 |
| Tommy Bolt | 2002 | Nick Faldo | 1997 |
| Sir Michael Bonallack | 2000 | Raymond Floyd | 1989 |
| Julius Boros | 1982 | Herb Graffis | 1977 |
| Pat Bradley | 1991 | Ralph Guldahl | 1981 |
| James Braid | 1976 | Walter Hagen | 1974 |
| Jack Burke Jr. | 2000 | Marlene Hagge | 2002 |
| William Campbell | 1990 | Bob Harlow | 1988 |
| Donna Caponi | 2001 | Sandra Haynie | 1977 |
| JoAnne Carner | 1985 | Hisako "Chako" Higuchi | 2003 |
| Billy Casper | 1978 | Harold Hilton | 1978 |
| Neil Coles | 2000 | Ben Hogan | 1974 |
| Harry Cooper | 1992 | Bob Hope | 1983 |

| | | | |
|---|---|---|---|
| Dorothy Campbell | | Betsy Rawls | 1987 |
| Hurd Howe | 1978 | Clifford Roberts | 1978 |
| Juli Inkster | 2000 | Allan Robertson | 2001 |
| Hale Irwin | 1992 | Chi Chi Rodriguez | 1992 |
| Tony Jacklin | 2002 | Donald Ross | 1977 |
| John Jacobs | 2000 | Paul Runyan | 1990 |
| Betty Jameson | 1951 | Gene Sarazen | 1974 |
| Robert Trent Jones Sr. | 1987 | Patty Sheehan | 1993 |
| Robert Tyre Jones Jr. | 1974 | Charles Sifford* | 2004 |
| Betsy King | 1995 | Dinah Shore | 1994 |
| Tom Kite* | 2004 | Horton Smith | 1990 |
| Bernhard Langer | 2002 | Sam Snead | 1974 |
| Lawson Little | 1980 | Karsten Solheim | 2001 |
| Gene Littler | 1990 | Annika Sorenstam | 2003 |
| Bobby Locke | 1977 | Payne Stewart | 2001 |
| Nancy Lopez | 1989 | Marlene Stewart Streit* | 2004 |
| Lloyd Mangrum | 1998 | Louise Suggs | 1979 |
| Carol Mann | 1977 | J. H. Taylor | 1975 |
| Cary Middlecoff | 1986 | Peter Thomson | 1988 |
| Johnny Miller | 1996 | Jerome Travers | 1976 |
| Tom Morris Jr. | 1975 | Walter Travis | 1979 |
| Tom Morris Sr. | 1976 | Lee Trevino | 1981 |
| Byron Nelson | 1974 | Richard Tufts | 1992 |
| Jack Nicklaus | 1974 | Harry Vardon | 1974 |
| Greg Norman | 2001 | Glenna Collett Vare | 1975 |
| Francis Ouimet | 1974 | Tom Watson | 1988 |
| Arnold Palmer | 1974 | Joyce Wethered | 1975 |
| Harvey Penick | 2002 | Kathy Whitworth | 1982 |
| Gary Player | 1974 | Mickey Wright | 1976 |
| Nick Price | 2003 | Mildred "Babe" Zaharias | 1974 |
| Judy Rankin | 2000 | | |

* Indicates inducted November 15, 2004.

## Sam Snead

There are many legends about the poor hillbilly from Virginia, one of them being that he fashioned his first clubs from branches of trees on the family farm. Whatever the veracity of early stories about Sam Snead, he entered the game of golf like so many poor kids of his era: through the caddyshack.

He got his first caddying job at the Homestead Club, inevitably getting that most famous of caddy benefits: the cast-off set of clubs. Legend has it that at the Greenbriar Club and White Sulphur Springs club where Snead also caddied, he had the opportunity to play with Lawson Little, a former British and U.S. amateur champion and with U.S. Open champions John Goodman and Billy Burke. Snead shot a 61.

They convinced him he had a shot on the pro circuit, so Snead loaded up the car and went to California for the start of the 1937 season. He had the sum total of $300 in his pocket. In his third tournament on the circuit he won the Oakland Open and had five more victories to go along with a runner-up status at the U.S.

Open that year. It was the beginning of one of the greatest careers in golf.

He quickly became known as "Slammin' Sam" Snead because of the distance he could drive the ball. His homespun charm gave galleries their first real star since Bobby Jones had retired from competitive golf. His swing is still considered one of the sweetest in the game and served him so well that he played competitively well into his late sixties. With one exception, he won at least one tournament each year of his first twenty-three years on tour. In 1950, he won eleven times, a feat that has not been duplicated.

The swing brought him more victories (84) on the PGA Tour than any golfer in the history of the game. He also won a further 80 tournaments worldwide. He won seven majors (Masters in 1949, 1952, and 1954, U.S. PGA titles in 1942, 1949, and 1951, and the British Open in 1946) and was four-time runner-up at the U.S. Open.

Snead was the only player to have won sanctioned tournaments in six decades, from the 1936 West Virginia Closed Pro to the 1982 Legends of Golf. He was the oldest player to win on the PGA Tour, at age 52 at the Greater Greensboro Open. He tied for third in the 1974 PGA Championship at age 62, finishing just three strokes behind winner Lee Trevino.

In 1979, he became the first player to score at or below his age, when he shot a 67 and 66 in the Quad Cities Open at the age of 67. He was an eight-time member of the Ryder Cup team, once as non-playing captain. He is remembered for the sweetness of his swing, but just as importantly for the sweetness he brought to the game.

> ## Getting a Higher Trajectory of Shots
>
> A SHUT OR CLOSED CLUBFACE will cause the trajectory of a shot to be low. To play a high fade, place the ball forward in your stance and open the clubface slightly. Take a long follow-through and make sure the finish is high.

**2 5**

# The PGA Tour Record Book
## ≣ *Most Money* ≣
### All-Time PGA Tour Money List

| PLAYER | MONEY | PLAYER | MONEY |
|---|---|---|---|
| Tiger Woods | $39,777,265 | David Duval | $16,235,385 |
| Davis Love III | $26,132,746 | Justin Leonard | $16,108,759 |
| Vijay Singh | $25,854,923 | Mark Calcavecchia | $15,694,587 |
| Phil Mickelson | $23,773,106 | Fred Couples | $15,148,465 |
| Jim Furyk | $19,039,707 | Hal Sutton | $15,145,667 |
| Nick Price | $18,919,447 | Jeff Sluman | $14,494,507 |
| Ernie Els | $18,679,767 | Brad Faxon | $14,310,795 |
| Scott Hoch | $17,216,624 | Tom Lehman | $14,130,264 |
| David Toms | $16,585,384 | Kenny Perry | $13,957,135 |

| | | | |
|---|---|---|---|
| Greg Norman | $13,931,929 | David Frost | $ 8,584,414 |
| Mark O'Meara | $13,143,679 | Mark Brooks | $ 8,123,182 |
| Loren Roberts I | $13,083,271 | Steve Flesch | $ 8,024,835 |
| Fred Funk | $12,915,575 | Tim Herron | $ 7,961,913 |
| Mike Weir | $12,845,208 | Andrew Magee | $ 7,959,025 |
| Paul Azinger | $12,680,533 | Sergio Garcia | $ 7,806,269 |
| Bob Estes | $12,240,269 | Steve Pate | $ 7,806,237 |
| Bob Tway | $12,150,383 | Dan Forsman | $ 7,686,555 |
| John Huston | $12,131,701 | Scott McCarron | $ 7,656,128 |
| Payne Stewart | $11,737,000 | Curtis Strange | $ 7,599,951 |
| Jay Haas | $11,720,183 | Joey Sindelar | $ 7,451,769 |
| Scott Verplank | $11,281,259 | Steve Stricker | $ 7,392,146 |
| Lee Janzen | $11,263,976 | Peter Jacobsen | $ 7,340,119 |
| Rocco Mediate | $11,104,130 | Retief Goosen | $ 7,233,886 |
| John Cook | $11,084,705 | Dudley Hart | $ 7,221,318 |
| Tom Kite | $10,920,309 | Ben Crenshaw | $ 7,091,166 |
| Jeff Maggert | $10,753,185 | Charles Howell III | $ 7,055,867 |
| Chris DiMarco | $10,637,535 | Larry Mize | $ 6,967,713 |
| Stuart Appleby | $10,284,272 | Chris Perry | $ 6,866,671 |
| Kirk Triplett | $10,284,090 | Shigeki Maruyama | $ 6,852,705 |
| Corey Pavin | $10,257,093 | Frank Lickliter II | $ 6,745,125 |
| Steve Elkington | $10,018,932 | Kevin Sutherland | $ 6,625,693 |
| Billy Mayfair | $ 9,980,493 | Jose Maria Olazabal | $ 6,583,445 |
| Tom Watson | $ 9,881,778 | Scott Simpson | $ 6,551,731 |
| Jesper Parnevik | $ 9,846,860 | Glen Day | $ 6,479,938 |
| Stewart Cink | $ 9,654,318 | Jonathan Kaye | $ 6,476,174 |
| Craig Stadler | $ 9,593,493 | Bruce Lietzke | $ 6,474,794 |
| Steve Lowery | $ 9,350,137 | Chris Riley | $ 6,437,849 |
| Robert A. Henry | $ 9,253,571 | Lanny Wadkins | $ 6,355,681 |
| Jerry Kelly | $ 8,831,176 | Bernhard Langer | $ 6,353,515 |
| Billy Andrade | $ 8,808,559 | Bill Glasson | $ 6,330,231 |
| Duffy Waldorf | $ 8,695,756 | Len Mattiace | $ 6,222,248 |

| Chip Beck | $ 6,199,550 | Jay Don Blake | $ 5,513,915 |
| Craig Parry | $ 6,173,390 | Russ Cochran | $ 5,344,387 |
| Steve Jones | $ 5,052,026 | Raymond Floyd | $ 5,323,075 |
| Hale Irwin | $ 5,966,031 | Carlos Franco | $ 5,322,039 |
| Jim Gallagher Jr. | $ 5,860,720 | K. J. Choi | $ 5,310,642 |
| Fuzzy Zoeller | $ 5,803,343 | Mark McCumber | $ 5,309,688 |
| Jack Nicklaus | $ 5,722,901 | Rich Beem | $ 5,273,317 |
| Skip Kendall | $ 5,681,383 | Gil Morgan | $ 5,259,164 |
| Joe Durant | $ 5,624,641 | Robert Gamez | $ 5,246,201 |

## GETTING LOWER TRAJECTORY OF SHOTS

HAVING THE BALL TOO FAR forward in your stance and having a backswing and follow-through that are too long will cause a ball to go high. To produce a lower ball flight, put the ball farther back in your stance, remembering that the shorter the follow-through, the lower the flight of the ball.

## Annual Money Leaders on the PGA Tour

| YEAR | PLAYER | AMOUNT |
| --- | --- | --- |
| 2003 | Vijay Singh | $7,573,907 |
| 2002 | Tiger Woods | $6,912,625 |
| 2001 | Tiger Woods | $5,687,777 |
| 2000 | Tiger Woods | $9,188,321 |
| 1999 | Tiger Woods | $6,616,585 |
| 1998 | David Duval | $2,591,031 |
| 1997 | Tiger Woods | $2,066,833 |
| 1996 | Tom Lehman | $1,780,159 |

| 1995 | Greg Norman | $1,654,959 |
| 1994 | Nick Price | $1,499,927 |
| 1993 | Nick Price | $1,478,557 |
| 1992 | Fred Couples | $1,344,188 |
| 1991 | Corey Pavin | $ 979,430 |
| 1990 | Greg Norman | $1,165,477 |
| 1989 | Tom Kite | $1,395,278 |
| 1988 | Curtis Strange | $1,147,644 |
| 1987 | Curtis Strange | $ 925,941 |
| 1986 | Greg Norman | $ 653,296 |
| 1985 | Curtis Strange | $ 542,321 |
| 1984 | Tom Watson | $ 476,260 |
| 1983 | Hal Sutton | $ 426,668 |
| 1982 | Craig Stadler | $ 446,462 |
| 1981 | Tom Kite | $ 375,698 |
| 1980 | Tom Watson | $ 530,808 |
| 1979 | Tom Watson | $ 462,636 |
| 1978 | Tom Watson | $ 362,428 |
| 1977 | Tom Watson | $ 310,653 |
| 1976 | Jack Nicklaus | $ 266,498 |
| 1975 | Jack Nicklaus | $ 298,149 |
| 1974 | Johnny Miller | $ 353,021 |
| 1973 | Jack Nicklaus | $ 308,362 |
| 1972 | Jack Nicklaus | $ 320,542 |
| 1971 | Jack Nicklaus | $ 244,490 |
| 1970 | Lee Trevino | $ 157,037 |
| 1969 | Frank Beard | $ 164,707 |
| 1968 | Billy Casper | $ 205,168 |
| 1967 | Jack Nicklaus | $ 188,998 |
| 1966 | Billy Casper | $ 121,944 |
| 1965 | Jack Nicklaus | $ 140,752 |
| 1964 | Jack Nicklaus | $ 113,284 |

| 1963 | Arnold Palmer | $ 128,230 |
| 1962 | Arnold Palmer | $ 81,448 |
| 1961 | Gary Player | $ 64,540 |
| 1960 | Arnold Palmer | $ 75,262 |
| 1959 | Art Wall | $ 58,167 |
| 1958 | Arnold Palmer | $ 42,607 |
| 1957 | Dick Mayer | $ 65,835 |
| 1956 | Ted Kroll | $ 72,835 |
| 1955 | Julius Boros | $ 63,121 |
| 1954 | Bob Toski | $ 65,819 |
| 1953 | Lew Worsham | $ 34,002 |
| 1952 | Julius Boros | $ 37,032 |
| 1951 | Lloyd Mangrum | $ 26,068 |
| 1950 | Sam Snead | $ 35,758 |
| 1949 | Sam Snead | $ 31,598 |
| 1948 | Ben Hogan | $ 32,112 |
| 1947 | Jimmy Demaret | $ 27,936 |
| 1946 | Ben Hogan | $ 42,556 |
| 1945 | Byron Nelson | $ 63,335 (war bonds) |
| 1944 | Byron Nelson | $ 37,967 (war bonds) |
| 1943 | No stats compiled | |
| 1942 | Ben Hogan | $ 13,143 |
| 1941 | Ben Hogan | $ 18,358 |
| 1940 | Ben Hogan | $ 10,655 |
| 1939 | Henry Picard | $ 10,303 |
| 1938 | Sam Snead | $ 19,534 |
| 1937 | Harry Cooper | $ 14,138 |
| 1936 | Horton Smith | $ 7,682 |
| 1935 | Johnny Revolta | $ 9,543 |
| 1934 | Paul Runyan | $ 6,767 |

## Improving Club Selection on Approach Shot

MOST GOLFERS HAVE NO IDEA how far they actually hit the ball. Improving club selection requires that golfers take the time to prepare for every shot. It is important to have yardages written down. Confidence comes from knowing abilities and limitations, so take the time to figure out the distances you hit with your clubs.

## MOST MONEY WON IN A SINGLE SEASON

| $9,188,321 | Tiger Woods | (2000) |
| $7,573,907 | Vijay Singh | (2003) |
| $6,912,625 | Tiger Woods | (2002) |
| $6,673,413 | Tiger Woods | (2003) |
| $6,616,585 | Tiger Woods | (1999) |
| $6,081,865 | Davis Love III | (2003) |

## Most Money Won by a Rookie

| $1,864,584 | Carlos Franco | (1999) |
| $1,520,632 | Charles Howell III | (2001) |
| $1,502,888 | Jose Coceres | (2001) |
| $1,462,713 | Jonathan Byrd | (2002) |
| $1,451,726 | Pat Perez | (2002) |
| $1,434,911 | Ben Curtis | (2003) |

## Most Money Won by a Second-Year Player

| $3,912,064 | Chad Campbell | (2003) |
| $2,702,747 | Charles Howell III | (2002) |
| $2,617,004 | Retief Goosen | (2002) |
| $2,066,833 | Tiger Woods | (1997) |

| $1,968,685 | Robert Allenby | (2000) |
| $1,956,565 | John Rollins | (2002) |

## MOST MONEY WON IN FIRST TWO SEASONS

| $4,727,538 | Chad Campbell | (2002–2003) |
| $4,223,379 | Charles Howell III | (2001–2002) |
| $3,743,989 | Retief Goosen | (2001–2002) |
| $3,415,176 | Carlos Franco | (1999–2000) |
| $3,074,637 | Notah Begay III | (1999–2000) |
| $2,893,251 | Jonathan Byrd | (2002–2003) |
| $2,857,427 | Tiger Woods | (1996–1997) |

## Most Consecutive Years with $100,000 or More in Earnings

| 27: Tom Watson | (1974–2000) |
| 25: Jay Haas | (1979–2003) |
| 24: Craig Stadler | (1980–2003) |
| 23: Tom Kite | (1976–1998) |

## Most Consecutive Years with $200,000 or More in Earnings

20: Mark O'Meara (1984–2003)

18: Nick Price (1986–2003)

17: Mark Calcavecchia (1987–2003); Fred Couples (1987–2003)

## MOST CONSECUTIVE YEARS WITH $500,000 OR MORE IN EARNINGS

11: Mark Calcavecchia (1993–2003); Jeff Maggert (1993–2003); Phil Mickelson (1993–2003)

10: Ernie Els (1994–2003); Scott Hoch (1994–2003); Tom Lehman (1994–2003)

# Most Consecutive Years with $1,000,000 or More in Earnings

9: Davis Love III (1995–2003)
8: Scott Hoch (1996–2003); Phil Mickelson (1996–2003)
7: Jim Furyk (1997–2003); Vijay Singh (1997–2003); Justin
   Leonard (1997–2003); Tiger Woods (1997–2003); Nick Price
   (1997–2003)

# Most Years with $1,000,000 or More in Earnings

10: Davis Love III; Nick Price
8: Scott Hoch; Vijay Singh; Phil Mickelson

# Most Consecutive Years on Top 10 Money List

17: Jack Nicklaus (1962–78)
11: Arnold Palmer (1957–67)

# MOST YEARS TOTAL ON TOP 10 MONEY LIST

18: Jack Nicklaus
15: Sam Snead
13: Arnold Palmer

# Most Years Leading Money List

8: Jack Nicklaus

# Most Consecutive Years Leading Money List

4: Tom Watson (1977–80); Tiger Woods (1999–2002)

# Youngest to Win $1 Million in a Season

Tiger Woods (1997), 21 years, 5 months, 21 days years old

# Quickest to $1 Million in Career

5 Events: Retief Goosen

# QUICKEST TO $2 MILLION IN CAREER

16 Events: Tiger Woods

## Number of Players to Win $2 Million or More in a Season

| | |
|---|---|
| 2002: 23 | 1999: 9 |
| 2001: 16 | 1998: 3 |
| 2000: 15 | 1997: 1 |

## Number of Players to Win $1 Million or More in a Season

| | |
|---|---|
| 2003: 29 | 1997: 18 |
| 2002: 61 | 1995, 1996: 9 |
| 2001: 56 | 1994: 6 |
| 2000: 45 | 1993: 5 |
| 1999: 36 | 1992: 4 |
| 1998: 26 | 1989, 1990: 2 |

## FIRST-YEAR PLAYERS TO WIN $1 MILLION OR MORE

| | | |
|---|---|---|
| $1,864,584 | Carlos Franco | (1999) |
| $1,520,632 | Charles Howell III | (2001) |
| $1,502,888 | Jose Coceres | (2001) |
| $1,462,713 | Jonathan Byrd | (2002) |
| $1,451,726 | Pat Perez | (2002) |

| | | |
|---|---|---|
| $1,434,911 | Ben Curtis | (2003) |
| $1,413,113 | Peter Lonard | (2002) |
| $1,255,314 | Notah Begay III | (1999) |
| $1,238,736 | Adam Scott | (2003) |
| $1,207,104 | Shigeki Maruyama | (2000) |
| $1,182,883 | Alex Cejka | (2003) |
| $1,126,985 | Retief Goosen | (2001) |
| $1,088,205 | Luke Donald | (2002) |
| $1,073,847 | J. J. Henry | (2001) |

## Growth of PGA Tour Purses

| YEAR | # OF EVENTS | TOTAL PURSE | YEAR | # OF EVENTS | TOTAL PURSE |
|---|---|---|---|---|---|
| 1938 | 38 | $158,000 | 1959 | 43 | $1,225,205 |
| 1939 | 28 | $121,000 | 1960 | 41 | $1,335,242 |
| 1940 | 27 | $117,000 | 1961 | 45 | $1,461,830 |
| 1941 | 30 | $169,200 | 1962 | 49 | $1,790,320 |
| 1942 | 21 | $116,650 | 1963 | 43 | $2,044,900 |
| 1943 | 3 | $ 17,000 | 1964 | 41 | $2,301,063 |
| 1944 | 22 | $150,500 | 1965 | 36 | $2,848,515 |
| 1945 | 36 | $435,380 | 1966 | 36 | $3,704,445 |
| 1946 | 37 | $411,533 | 1967 | 37 | $3,979,162 |
| 1947 | 31 | $352,500 | 1968 | 45 | $5,077,600 |
| 1948 | 34 | $427,000 | 1969 | 47 | $5,465,875 |
| 1949 | 25 | $338,200 | 1970 | 55 | $6,751,523 |
| 1950 | 33 | $459,950 | 1971 | 63 | $7,116,000 |
| 1951 | 30 | $460,200 | 1972 | 71 | $7,596,749 |
| 1952 | 32 | $498,016 | 1973 | 75 | $8,657,225 |
| 1953 | 32 | $562,704 | 1974 | 57 | $8,165,941 |
| 1954 | 26 | $600,819 | 1975 | 51 | $7,895,450 |
| 1955 | 36 | $782,010 | 1976 | 49 | $9,157,522 |
| 1956 | 36 | $847,070 | 1977 | 48 | $9,688,977 |
| 1957 | 32 | $820,360 | 1978 | 48 | $10,337,332 |
| 1958 | 39 | $1,005,800 | 1979 | 46 | $12,801,200 |

| YEAR | # OF EVENTS | TOTAL PURSE | YEAR | # OF EVENTS | TOTAL PURSE |
|------|------------|-------------|------|------------|-------------|
| 1980 | 45 | $13,371,786 | 1993 | 43 | $ 53,203,611 |
| 1981 | 45 | $14,175,393 | 1994 | 43 | $ 56,416,080 |
| 1982 | 46 | $15,089,576 | 1995 | 44 | $ 61,650,000 |
| 1983 | 45 | $17,588,242 | 1996 | 45 | $ 70,700,000 |
| 1984 | 46 | $21,251,382 | 1997 | 45 | $ 80,550,000 |
| 1985 | 47 | $25,290,526 | 1998 | 45 | $ 96,150,000 |
| 1986 | 46 | $25,442,242 | 1999 | 47 | $135,808,500 |
| 1987 | 46 | $32,106,093 | 2000 | 49 | $164,025,325 |
| 1988 | 47 | $36,959,307 | 2001 | 49 | $185,350,000 |
| 1989 | 44 | $41,288,787 | 2002 | 49 | $198,650,000 |
| 1990 | 44 | $46,251,831 | 2003 | 48 | $228,700,000 |
| 1991 | 44 | $49,628,203 | 2004 | 48 | $240,000,000 |
| 1992 | 44 | $49,386,906 | | | |

## Alignment

ALIGNMENT IS EXTREMELY important for golfers. When lining up a golf shot, there are two main things to consider—first and foremost is the target line (the line that the golf club is actually on) and secondly, the stance line, also known as the body line, which is determined first by the target line. Let your mind's eye swing to your target, which is the fairway or the green, and your stance line will come.

## Lee Trevino

The son of Mexican immigrants who came to the U.S. to escape poverty, Lee Trevino grew up in a ramshackle house on the outskirts of Dallas, his mother eking out a living cleaning houses and his grandfather (his father had left) helping out by working as a grave digger. The humble house may not have had electricity or running water, but it did have one benefit: it was located next to the Glen Lakes Country Club. Before long, young Lee was finding and selling balls he found in the roughs.

By the time he was eight, he started caddying, practicing in between gigs on the three holes behind the caddyshack. There was no talk or speculation about a career in the pros, but by grade seven Trevino had dropped out of school and by 17 had enlisted in the U.S. Marine Corps. What the Marine Corps provided was some much-needed discipline and, ironically, a chance to play golf.

Although much has been made about Trevino's skill as a hustler—"Pressure," he once said, "is playing for ten dollars when you've got three in your pocket"—he knew he was good, he just didn't know how good. To his credit, he was willing to find out.

After his discharge in 1961, Trevino hooked up with Dallas driving-range owner Hardy Greenwood, working with him, and at the same time working his tail off to get a Class A card and a ticket to the big leagues. In 1967, he attained that dream. He placed 45th on the money list and was named Rookie of the Year.

Still there were plenty of naysayers. Critics thought he just couldn't win with the way he struck the ball. He lined up his body to the left of his target and on his downswing he looked incredibly off-balance. Imagine, then, the reaction when he won the U.S. Open in 1968, defeating the greatest player in the game, Jack Nicklaus, by four strokes. Mr. Trevino had arrived on center stage.

In 1971, Trevino had one of those years that professional golfers dream about. In a four-week period, he captured the U.S., Canadian, and British Opens, establishing himself as one of the legends of the game. In total, he would win three U.S. PGA Championships, two British Opens, and two U.S. Opens, and he was deserving of the name "Supermex" that the media pinned on him.

He was named PGA Player of the Year and the Associated Press and *Sports Illustrated's* Athlete of the Year in 1971. When he retired from the pro tour in 1985, he was second on the total career earnings list at the time.

This father of four sons and two daughters has also given a lot back. Media reports indicate that Trevino's total dollar contributions to charity are very significant. How significant is going to remain a secret as long as Trevino has anything to do with it. He demands complete confidentiality in all of his charitable works, believing that if you tell people about it, it's not charity.

## ≣ *Most Wins* ≣
### CAREER WINS ON THE PGA TOUR

82: Sam Snead
73: Jack Nicklaus
64: Ben Hogan
62: Arnold Palmer
52: Byron Nelson
51: Billy Casper
44: Walter Hagen

40: Cary Middlecoff; Tiger Woods
39: Gene Sarazen; Tom Watson
36: Lloyd Mangrum
32: Horton Smith
30: Leo Diegel
29: Gene Littler; Paul Runyan; Lee Trevino
26: Henry Picard
25: Tommy Armour; Johnny Miller
24: Gary Player; Macdonald Smith
23: Phil Mickelson
22: Johnny Farrell; Raymond Floyd
21: Willie Macfarlane; Lanny Wadkins; Craig Wood
20: Jim Barnes; Hale Irwin; Bill Mehlhorn; Greg Norman; Doug Sanders
19: Ben Crenshaw; Doug Ford; Green; Tom Kite
18: Nick Price; Julius Boros; Jim Ferrier; Davis Love III

## Most Consecutive Victories

11: Byron Nelson
6: Ben Hogan; Tiger Woods
4: Byron Nelson; Jack Burke, Jr.; Ben Hogan

## Most Victories in a Calendar Year

| | |
|---|---|
| 18: Byron Nelson | (1945) |
| 13: Ben Hogan | (1946) |
| 11: Sam Snead | (1950) |
| 10: Ben Hogan | (1948) |

9: Paul Runyan (1933); Tiger Woods (2000)
8: Horton Smith (1929); Gene Sarazen (1930); Sam Snead (1938); Byron Nelson (1944); Arnold Palmer (1960, 1962); Johnny Miller (1974); Tiger Woods (1999)

## MOST WINS BY PLAYERS IN THEIR 20S

34: Tiger Woods
30: Jack Nicklaus

## Most Wins by Players in Their 30s

42: Arnold Palmer
40: Ben Hogan

## Most Wins by Players after Age 40

17: Sam Snead

## YOUNGEST WINNERS ON PGA TOUR

Johnny McDermott, 19 years, 10 months old (1911 U.S. Open)
Gene Sarazen, 20 years, 5 days old (1922 Southern Open)
Charles Evans, Jr. (amateur), 20 years, 1 month, 15 days old
    (1910 Western Open)
Francis Ouimet (amateur), 20 years, 4 months, 12 days old
    (1913 U.S. Open)
Gene Sarazen, 20 years, 4 months, 18 days old (1922 U.S.
    Open)
Horton Smith, 20 years, 5 months, 13 days old (1928 Oklahoma
    City Open)
Gene Sarazen, 20 years, 5 months, 22 days old (1922 PGA)
Raymond Floyd, 20 years, 6 months, 13 days old (1963 St.
    Petersburg Open)
Phil Mickelson (amateur), 20 years, 6 months, 28 days old (1991
    Northern Telecom Open)
Horton Smith, 20 years, 7 months, 1 day old (1928 Catalina
    Island Open)
Tom Creavy, 20 years, 7 months, 16 days (1931 PGA
    Championship)

# Most Consecutive Years Winning

| YEAR | WINS | PLAYER |
|------|------|--------|
| 2003 | 8 | Tiger Woods (1996–2003) |
| 2002 | 7 | Tiger Woods (1996–2002) |
| 2001 | 6 | Tiger Woods (1996–2001) |
| 2000 | 7 | Ernie Els (1994–2000) |
| 1999 | 6 | Ernie Els (1994–99) |
| 1998 | 6 | Phil Mickelson (1993–98) |
| 1997 | 6 | Greg Norman (1992–97) |
| 1996 | 5 | Greg Norman (199296) |
| 1995 | 4 | Ben Crenshaw, Lee Janzen, Greg Norman (1992–95) |
| 1994 | 5 | Fred Couples (1990–94) |
| 1993 | 7 | Paul Azinger (198793) |
| 1992 | 6 | Paul Azinger (198792) |
| 1991 | 5 | Paul Azinger (1987–91) |
| 1990 | 4 | Paul Azinger (1987–90) |
| 1989 | 7 | Curtis Strange (1983–89) |
| 1988 | 6 | Curtis Strange (1983–88) |
| 1987 | 7 | Tom Kite (1981–87) |
| 1986 | 6 | Tom Kite (1981–86) |
| 1985 | 5 | Hale Irwin, Tom Kite (1981–85) |
| 1984 | 4 | Hale Irwin, Tom Kite (1981–84) |
| 1983 | 4 | Johnny Miller (1980–83) |
| 1982 | 6 | Bruce Lietzke, Tom Watson (1977–82) |
| 1981 | 14 | Lee Trevino (1968–81) |
| 1980 | 13 | Lee Trevino (1968–80) |
| 1979 | 12 | Lee Trevino (1968–79) |
| 1978 | 17 | Jack Nicklaus (1962–78) |
| 1977 | 16 | Jack Nicklaus (1962–77) |
| 1976 | 15 | Jack Nicklaus (1962–76) |
| 1975 | 14 | Jack Nicklaus (1962–75) |
| 1974 | 13 | Jack Nicklaus (1962–74) |

| 1973 | 12 | Jack Nicklaus (1962–73) |
| 1972 | 11 | Jack Nicklaus (1962–72) |
| 1971 | 17 | Arnold Palmer (1955–71) |
| 1970 | 16 | Arnold Palmer (1955–70) |

## Long Bunker Shots

INSTEAD OF TRYING to hit a hard sand wedge an inch or so behind the ball, use an 8-iron and enter the sand a safer two inches behind using a full swing, but without trying to hit it as hard as you can. In using this approach, if a mistake is made you won't be as likely to hit the ball over the green where there may be even more trouble.

## Severiano Ballesteros

One of four golfing brothers, all of whom turned professional, Severiano Ballesteros grew up on golf. His uncle was the local pro and Ballesteros began caddying at a young age.

Young Severiano was good enough that by the age of sixteen, he turned professional. As a 19-year-old, two important events sent a signal to the golf world that they had a new contender ready to step onto the world stage. He claimed his first tournament win at the Dutch Open and followed that up by winning the Lancome Trophy. Ballesteros also gave a brilliant performance at the British Open at Birkdale, tying with Jack Nicklaus for second, behind Johnny Miller.

Ballesteros would continue his winning ways, staying on top of the money lists for the next two years. In 1979 he broke through, capturing the first of three British Open titles at Royal Lytham and St. Anne's, and beating golfing greats Jack Nicklaus and Ben Crenshaw by three strokes. Ballesteros would follow his major win in Britain with two Masters titles, giving him a total of five majors in his career.

Although the major victories will forever mark him as a champion, they fail to underscore the excitement he brought to the game. Like Arnold Palmer, Ballesteros became famous for being able to extricate himself from trouble he found himself in. Wherever the handsome Ballesteros went, the galleries followed to find out what would come next from the brilliant Spaniard.

He single-handedly elevated the European tour to its current status. In addition to his five majors (British Open in 1979, 1984, and 1988, and Masters in 1980 and 1983), he won 48 tournaments on the European tour and captured five World Match Play titles. He played on eight European Ryder Cup teams and captained the victorious European team in 1997 in his native Spain. He was also three-time European Golfer of Year and is a certainty for the Hall of Fame.

## ≋ *PGA Tour Trivia* ≋
### WIDEST WINNING MARGINS

16: J. D. Edgar (1919 Canadian Open); Joe Kirkwood Sr. (1924 Corpus Christi Open); Bobby Locke (1948 Chicago Victory National Championship)

15: Tiger Woods (2000 U.S. Open)

14: Ben Hogan (1945 Portland Invitational); Johnny Miller (1975 Phoenix Open)

13: Byron Nelson (1945 Seattle Open); Gene Littler (1955 Tournament of Champions)

12: Byron Nelson (1939 Phoenix Open); Arnold Palmer (1962 Phoenix Open); Jose Maria Olazabal (1990 NEC World Series of Golf); Tiger Woods (1997 Masters Tournament)

## Best Come-from-Behind in Final Round to Win (Strokes)

10: Paul Lawrie (1999 British Open)
8: Jack Burke Jr. (1956 Masters Tournament); Ken Venturi (1959 Los Angeles Open); Mark Lye (1983 Bank of Boston Classic); Hal Sutton (1985 St. Jude Memphis Classic); Chip Beck (1990 Buick Open); Scott Simpson (1998 Buick Invitational)

## Largest Lead with 18 Holes to Play (Strokes)

13: Bobby Locke, won by 16 (1948 Chicago Victory National Championship)
11: Gene Sarazen, won by 11 (1927 Long Island Open)
10: Walter Hagen, won by 12 (1920 Florida West Coast Open); Ben Hogan, won by 14 (1945 Portland Invitational); Gene Littler, won by 13 (1955 Tournament of Champions); Tiger Woods, won by 15 (2000 U.S. Open)

## Largest Lead with 18 Holes to Play and Lost (Strokes)

6: Bobby Cruickshank (1928 Florida Open); Gay Brewer (1969 Danny Thomas–Diplomat Classic); Hal Sutton (1983 Anheuser-Busch Golf Classic); Greg Norman (1986 Masters Tournament)

## Most Consecutive Events without Missing Cut

128: Tiger Woods, as of August, 2004; from Buick Invitational, February 1998

113: Byron Nelson, during the 1940s

105: Jack Nicklaus, from Sahara Open, November 1970, through World Series of Golf, September 1976 (missed cut in 1976 World Open)

86: Hale Irwin, from Tucson Open, February 1975, through conclusion of 1978 season (missed cut in first start of 1979 season at Bing Crosby)

72: Dow Finsterwald, from Carling Golf Classic, September 1955, through Houston Invitational, February 1958

53: Tom Kite, from Western Open, July 1980, through Manufacturers Hanover Westchester Classic, June 1982; Vijay Singh, from NEC World Series of Golf, August 1995, through The Players Championship, March 1998

## Best Playoff Records
## (Six or More Playoff Victories)

| PLAYER | WINS | LOSSES |
| --- | --- | --- |
| Arnold Palmer | 14 | 10 |
| Jack Nicklaus | 14 | 11 |
| Sam Snead | 12 | 5 |
| Tom Watson | 9 | 4 |
| Billy Casper | 8 | 8 |
| Ben Hogan | 8 | 12 |
| Cary Middlecoff | 7 | 6(+1 tie) |
| Tiger Woods | 6 | 1 |
| Curtis Strange | 6 | 3 |
| Tom Kite | 6 | 3 |
| Bruce Lietzke | 6 | 6 |
| Byron Nelson | 6 | 6 |

| Year | HIO | Year | HIO |
|------|-----|------|-----|
| 2003 | 32 | 1993 | 25 |
| 2002 | 40 | 1992 | 33 |
| 2001 | 27 | 1991 | 29 |
| 2000 | 31 | 1990 | 34 |
| 1999 | 27 | 1989 | 32 |
| 1998 | 27 | 1988 | 22 |
| 1997 | 31 | 1987 | 30 |
| 1996 | 39 | 1986 | 21 |
| 1995 | 35 | 1985 | 35 |
| 1994 | 44 | | |

## Positioning Your Head

JUST BEFORE YOU PREPARE to make a backswing, focus your left eye on or slightly behind the clubhead. Position your chin so that it is pointing toward your right knee. This movement will "set" your head in the position and will keep it steady during the swing. Since the head is the center of the swing axis, it must be kept perfectly still throughout the backswing. The "setting" of the head just before you commence your swing will minimize any tendency you may have to move your head.

## PGA Vardon Trophy Winners

The Vardon Trophy is awarded annually by the PGA of America to the PGA Tour's leader in scoring average. When the award was first given in 1937, it was awarded on the basis of a points system. But in 1947, the PGA began awarding it for low scoring average. In 1988, the trophy began going to the golfer with the lowest adjusted scoring average over a minimum of 60 rounds.

# Year-by-Year Scoring Average Leaders

| YEAR | PLAYER | AVERAGE |
|------|--------|---------|
| 2003 | Tiger Woods | 68.41 |
| 2002 | Tiger Woods | 68.56 |
| 2001 | Tiger Woods | 68.81 |
| 2000 | Tiger Woods | 67.79 |
| 1999 | Tiger Woods | 68.43 |
| 1998 | David Duval | 69.13 |
| 1997 | Nick Price | 68.98 |
| 1996 | Tom Lehman | 69.32 |
| 1995 | Steve Elkington | 69.92 |
| 1994 | Greg Norman | 68.81 |
| 1993 | Nick Price | 69.11 |
| 1992 | Fred Couples | 69.38 |
| 1991 | Fred Couples | 69.59 |
| 1990 | Greg Norman | 69.10 |
| 1989 | Greg Norman | 69.49 |
| 1988 | Chip Beck | 69.46 |
| 1987 | Dan Pohl | 70.25 |
| 1986 | Scott Hoch | 70.08 |
| 1985 | Don Pooley | 70.36 |
| 1984 | Calvin Peete | 70.56 |
| 1983 | Raymond Floyd | 70.61 |
| 1982 | Tom Kite | 70.21 |
| 1981 | Tom Kite | 69.80 |
| 1980 | Lee Trevino | 69.73 |
| 1979 | Tom Watson | 70.27 |
| 1978 | Tom Watson | 70.16 |
| 1977 | Tom Watson | 70.32 |
| 1976 | Don January | 70.56 |
| 1975 | Bruce Crampton | 70.51 |
| 1974 | Lee Trevino | 70.53 |

| 1973 | Bruce Crampton | 70.57 |
| 1972 | Lee Trevino | 70.89 |
| 1971 | Lee Trevino | 70.27 |
| 1970 | Lee Trevino | 70.64 |
| 1969 | Dave Hill | 70.34 |
| 1968 | Billy Casper | 69.82 |
| 1967 | Arnold Palmer | 70.18 |
| 1966 | Billy Casper | 70.27 |
| 1965 | Billy Casper | 70.85 |
| 1964 | Arnold Palmer | 70.01 |
| 1963 | Billy Casper | 70.58 |
| 1962 | Arnold Palmer | 70.27 |
| 1961 | Arnold Palmer | 69.85 |
| 1960 | Billy Casper | 69.95 |
| 1959 | Art Wall | 70.35 |
| 1958 | Bob Rosburg | 70.11 |
| 1957 | Dow Finsterwald | 70.30 |
| 1956 | Cary Middlecoff | 70.35 |
| 1955 | Sam Snead | 69.86 |

# Best Vardon Trophy Scoring Average
## NON-ADJUSTED

68.17: Tiger Woods, 5,181 strokes, 76 rounds (2000)
68.87: Tiger Woods, 5,234 strokes, 76 rounds (2001)
69.00: Tiger Woods, 4,692 strokes, 68 rounds (2002)
69.03: Davis Love III, 5,177 strokes, 75 rounds (2001)
69.16: Phil Mickelson, 5,671 strokes, 82 rounds (2001)
69.23: Sam Snead, 6,646 strokes, 96 rounds (1950)
69.30: Ben Hogan, 5,267 strokes, 76 rounds (1948)
69.33: Greg Norman, 4,368 strokes, 63 rounds (1994)
69.34: Vijay Singh, 6,379 strokes, 92 rounds (2001)
69.37: Sam Snead, 5,064 strokes, 73 rounds (1949)

67.79: Tiger Woods (2000)
68.43: Tiger Woods (1999)
68.56: Tiger Woods (2002)
68.81: Greg Norman (1994)
68.81: Tiger Woods (2001)
68.90: Greg Norman (1993)

## HAND PRESSURE

HAND PRESSURE is one of the most crucial parts of your golf game. Without proper hand pressure, you'll be unable to develop your fullest potential. An essential part of that power comes from the pressure exerted on the tips of the first three fingers of the left hand. These three fingers not only control the line of the back-swing, they bring power to the swing through the ball. Without constant left-hand pressure, your game will lack consistency.

# PGA Player of the Year

The award is given by the PGA of America and has been based on a points system since 1982. Points awarded for accomplishments throughout the year (wins, top ten finishes, bonus for wins in majors, plus the player's standing on the money list and scoring average).

| | | | |
|---|---|---|---|
| 2003 | Tiger Woods | 1999 | Tiger Woods |
| 2002 | Tiger Woods | 1998 | Mark O'Meara |
| 2001 | Tiger Woods | 1997 | Tiger Woods |
| 2000 | Tiger Woods | 1996 | Tom Lehman |

| | | | |
|---|---|---|---|
| 1995 | Greg Norman | 1971 | Lee Trevino |
| 1994 | Nick Price | 1970 | Billy Casper |
| 1993 | Nick Price | 1969 | Orville Moody |
| 1992 | Fred Couples | 1968 | Not awarded |
| 1991 | Corey Pavin | 1967 | Jack Nicklaus |
| 1990 | Nick Faldo | 1966 | Billy Casper |
| 1989 | Tom Kite | 1965 | Dave Marr |
| 1988 | Curtis Strange | 1964 | Ken Venturi |
| 1987 | Paul Azinger | 1963 | Julius Boros |
| 1986 | Bob Tway | 1962 | Arnold Palmer |
| 1985 | Lanny Wadkins | 1961 | Jerry Barber |
| 1984 | Tom Watson | 1960 | Arnold Palmer |
| 1983 | Hal Sutton | 1959 | Art Wall |
| 1982 | Tom Watson | 1958 | Dow Finsterwald |
| 1981 | Bill Rogers | 1957 | Dick Mayer |
| 1980 | Tom Watson | 1956 | Jack Burke |
| 1979 | Tom Watson | 1955 | Doug Ford |
| 1978 | Tom Watson | 1954 | Ed Furgol |
| 1977 | Tom Watson | 1953 | Ben Hogan |
| 1976 | Jack Nicklaus | 1952 | Julius Boros |
| 1975 | Jack Nicklaus | 1951 | Ben Hogan |
| 1974 | Johnny Miller | 1950 | Ben Hogan |
| 1973 | Jack Nicklaus | 1949 | Sam Snead |
| 1972 | Jack Nicklaus | 1948 | Ben Hogan |

## PGA Tour Player of the Year (Jack Nicklaus Award)

Beginning in 1990, the PGA Tour began handing out its own award. The award is voted on by the players.

| | | | |
|---|---|---|---|
| 2003 | Tiger Woods | 2001 | Tiger Woods |
| 2002 | Tiger Woods | 2000 | Tiger Woods |

| 1999 | Tiger Woods  | 1994 | Nick Price    |
|------|--------------|------|---------------|
| 1998 | Mark O'Meara | 1993 | Nick Price    |
| 1997 | Tiger Woods  | 1992 | Fred Couples  |
| 1996 | Tom Lehman   | 1991 | Fred Couples  |
| 1995 | Greg Norman  |      |               |

## Right Hand

THE PRIMARY ROLE of the right hand in golf is to help you hold the club in a stable position at the start of the swing and to steady the club during the execution of the entire swing. There should be little or no pressure exerted by the right hand at any time during the swing. The right hand simply acts as a brace to the left, and should not dominate it. Try to minimize the dominance of your right hand as much as possible. It will automatically get into play without your help.

## PGA Tour Rookie of the Year

The award is based on balloting by PGA Tour players.

| 1990 | Robert Gamez   | 1997 | Stewart Cink      |
|------|----------------|------|-------------------|
| 1991 | John Daly      | 1998 | Steve Flesch      |
| 1992 | Mark Carnevale | 1999 | Carlos Franco     |
| 1993 | Vijay Singh    | 2000 | Michael Clark II  |
| 1994 | Ernie Els      | 2001 | Charles Howell III|
| 1995 | Woody Austin   | 2002 | Jonathan Byrd     |
| 1996 | Tiger Woods    | 2003 | Ben Curtis        |

## Byron Nelson Award

The Byron Nelson Award is based on each player's adjusted scoring average. The adjusted score is computed from the average score of the field at each tournament. As a result, a player's score may be higher or lower than his actual score. Actual scoring average was used to determine the scoring leader prior to 1988.

In order to qualify for the Byron Nelson Award, a player must compete in a minimum of fifty official rounds on the PGA Tour.

| YEAR | PLAYER | AVERAGE |
|------|--------|---------|
| 1980 | Lee Trevino | 69.73 |
| 1981 | Tom Kite | 69.80 |
| 1982 | Tom Kite | 70.21 |
| 1983 | Raymond Floyd | 70.61 |
| 1984 | Calvin Peete | 70.56 |
| 1985 | Don Pooley | 70.36 |
| 1986 | Scott Hoch | 70.08 |
| 1987 | David Frost | 70.09 |
| 1988 | Greg Norman | 69.38 |
| 1989 | Payne Stewart | 69.485 |
| 1990 | Greg Norman | 69.10 |
| 1991 | Fred Couples | 69.59 |
| 1992 | Fred Couples | 69.38 |
| 1993 | Greg Norman | 68.90 |
| 1994 | Greg Norman | 68.81 |
| 1995 | Greg Norman | 69.06 |
| 1996 | Tom Lehman | 69.32 |
| 1997 | Nick Price | 68.98 |
| 1998 | David Duval | 69.13 |
| 1999 | Tiger Woods | 68.43 |
| 2000 | Tiger Woods | 67.79 |
| 2001 | Tiger Woods | 68.81 |
| 2002 | Tiger Woods | 68.56 |
| 2003 | Tiger Woods | 68.41 |

# PGA Tour Comeback Player of the Year

| | | | |
|---|---|---|---|
| 1991 | Bruce Fleisher, D. A. Weibring | 1997 | Bill Glasson |
| 1992 | John Cook | 1998 | Scott Verplank |
| 1993 | Howard Twitty | 1999 | Steve Pate |
| 1994 | Hal Sutton | 2000 | Paul Azinger |
| 1995 | Bob Tway | 2001 | Joe Durant |
| 1996 | Steve Jones | 2002 | Gene Sauers |
| | | 2003 | Peter Jacobsen |

*Source: Records supplied by PGA TOUR.*

## Good Ball Position

A RULE OF THUMB regarding where to place your ball is that a low-handicap player who tends to use his lower body more aggressively should place the ball opposite the left heel when hitting a wood; and up to a couple of ball widths behind that point for an iron. A higher handicapper should put the ball in the middle of his stance when hitting an iron, a little forward of that for a wood.

## Nick Faldo

Born in Hertfordshire, England, Faldo was one of the world's top golfers for almost 20 years. According to Faldo, his passion for the game took a significant turn one day in 1972. Faldo was watching television and saw Jack Nicklaus in action at the U.S. Masters and he says it was all the inspiration he needed.

With a set of clubs borrowed from the next-door neighbors, Faldo started learning golf at his local club. Within four years he was the best amateur player in Europe, winning the English Amateur Championship and the British Youth Championships in 1975. The following year, at the tender age of 19, he turned professional.

In 1977, Faldo became the youngest ever Ryder Cup team member and more important, went on to win all his matches. In the years since, he has represented Europe a record eleven times and holds the record for the number of points and matches won in the competition.

Throughout the 1980s, Faldo quickly became one of Europe's top golfers. At the height of his success, Faldo worked with golf instructor David Leadbetter to radically alter his swing. It was a two-year journey, but it paid huge dividends. Critics doubted whether he could regain his form, but he emerged from the process as one of the best golfers in the world.

In 1990, Faldo became the first international player to win the PGA Tour's Player of the Year award. He won thirty European Tour titles, including three Volvo PGA Championships and three successive Irish Opens. He also won four regular tournaments in USA. He went on to win six majors, including three Open Championships and three U.S. Masters. Faldo's Masters victory in 1996 is the one most remembered by fans. Trailing Greg Norman by six strokes after 54 holes, Faldo shot a final round 67 to win by five strokes.

In 1992 Faldo became the first European player to win over £1 million in prize money during a single season. He was alone at the top of the Sony World Rankings for 81 weeks. He is a member of the World Golf Hall of Fame and one of the greatest golfers Europe has ever produced.

# Ryder Cup

Any professional golfer will tell you that one of the biggest honors is being named to the Ryder Cup team. It is a competition that dates back seventy-eight years and its prestige has only been enhanced over time.

There had been early matches between Great Britain and U.S. teams, and promoters on both sides of the Atlantic were anxious to see it continue. The first of those informal matches happened in 1921 in Gleneagles, Scotland, where the British team trounced the Americans.

The next meeting came in 1926 and again the British team

pummeled the American squad. This time, however, one of the onlookers was a wealthy English seed merchant and entrepreneur named Samuel Ryder.

Ryder had made a fortune selling penny seed packets; unfortunately the hard work had made him ill. Doctors advised him to get fresh air and exercise. They recommended golf and, despite some initial resistance, before long Ryder was one of the game's biggest enthusiasts.

Ryder hired a local professional and began practicing six days a week. Soon, Ryder felt he had outgrown the local professional and hired Abe Mitchell, a British Open winner, as his personal instructor. It was no surprise, then, that Ryder was in the gallery to watch the match between America's and Britain's best.

After the matches, and over champagne and sandwiches, Ryder was asked by players on both squads if perhaps he could provide a trophy for matches that would happen on a regular basis. Ryder agreed, and the Ryder Cup was born. The first official match took place in the Worcester, Massachusetts, country club in 1927. Led by golf legend Walter Hagen, this time the United States team defeated the team from Great Britain.

By 1977, and with matches increasingly being decided in America's favor, Jack Nicklaus approached the British PGA to urge them to widen the selection process to include Europeans. The British PGA agreed and the luster and interest was again restored to one of the great sporting exchanges.

Over the last twenty years, the competition has been a virtual dead heat. Europe has won five times, the United States has won four times, and they have tied once. In eight of the ten matches, less than two points have separated the teams.

# Rules

The 2000 *Rules of Golf* issued by the Royal and Ancient Golf Club of St. Andrews apply, and, where applicable, local rules. Play consists of match play, including foursomes (two-man teams in alternate shot), four-ball (two-man teams in better ball), and singles (18 holes at match play). There are a total of 28 matches.

## Match Play

Match play is decided hole by hole instead of cumulatively, like stroke play, over 18 holes.

A hole is won by the team, which holes its ball in the fewer strokes. Score is kept by the number of holes up (won) and the number of holes to play. When a team is up (winning) by more holes than there are holes remaining, then the match is closed out and a point is awarded. One point is awarded for each match won. If the match is tied or "halved" through 18 holes of play, each team receives one half of a point. A total of 28 points are awarded in Ryder Cup competition.

A match is considered "dormie" when one side is up by the exact number of holes that remain. A player/twosome is said to be 3-up through 11 after winning three more holes than their opponent(s) through 11 holes. A player/twosome is said to win the match 2-up after winning two more holes than their opponent through 18 holes. A player/twosome is said to win 3 and 2 after winning three holes more than their opponent(s) with only two holes left to play.

## CONCESSIONS

A stroke, hole, or an entire match can be conceded at any time prior to the conclusion of the hole or the match. Concession of a stroke, hole, or match may not be declined or withdrawn.

## Points to Win

There are a total of 28 matches. One point is awarded for each match won. The side with the most points at the conclusion of the Ryder Cup Matches wins the Ryder Cup.

## A Tie

If, at the conclusion of the Ryder Cup Matches, the teams are tied at 14 points each, the team who last won the Ryder Cup retains the Cup. To win the Matches, either team will need 14 1/2 or more points.

## FOURSOMES (FOUR GROUPS OF TWO-MAN TEAMS)

"Foursome" play is a match where two golfers compete on a team against two other golfers and each side plays one ball. The golfers play alternate shots (player 1 hits tee shot, player 2 hits second shot, etc.) until the hole is played out. Team members alternate playing the tee shots, with one golfer hitting the tee shot on odd-numbered holes, and the other hitting the tee shot from the even-numbered holes. The team with the better score wins the hole. Should the two teams tie for best score, the hole is halved.

## Four-Ball (four groups of two-man teams)

"Four-ball" play is a match in which each member of the two-man teams play their own ball. Four balls are in play per hole with each of the four players recording a score on the hole. The team whose player posts the best score on that hole wins the hole. Should players from each team tie for the best score, the hole is halved.

## Singles (twelve groups of one-man teams)

"Singles" is a match in which one player competes against another player. A player wins the match when he is up by more holes than there are holes remaining to play.

### PAIRINGS

Each team captain submits the order of play for his team to the appointed tournament official. The lists from each captain are matched, resulting in the pairings. The pairings can be modified by the team captains at any time prior to the beginning of a match.

---

### Tempo

ONE OF THE MOST IMPORTANT aspects of any swing—and nearly impossible to teach—is tempo. Personality has a lot to do with tempo. Whatever your tempo, slow, fast, or somewhere in between, the secret is to make it the same day-in and day-out. This will take the inconsistency out of your game.

---

## Ryder Cup Results

2002: Europe 15.5, U.S. 12.5
1999: U.S. 14.5, Europe 13.5
1997: Europe 14.5, U.S. 13.5
1995: Europe 14.5, U.S. 13.5
1993: U.S. 15, Europe 13
1991: U.S. 14.5, Europe 13.5
1989: Europe 14, U.S. 14 (Europe retains cup)
1987: Europe 15, U.S. 13
1985: Europe 16.5, U.S. 11.5

1983: U.S. 14.5, Europe 13.5
1981: U.S. 18.5, Europe 9.5
1979: U.S. 17, Europe 11
1977: U.S. 12.5, Great Britain and Ireland 7.5
1975: U.S. 21, Great Britain and Ireland 11
1973: U.S. 19, Great Britain and Ireland 13
1971: U.S. 18.5, Great Britain 13.5
1969: U.S. 16, Great Britain 16 (U.S. retains cup)
1967: U.S. 23.5, Great Britain 8.5
1965: U.S. 19.5, Great Britain 12.5
1963: U.S. 23, Great Britain 9
1961: U.S. 14.5, Great Britain 9.5
1959: U.S. 8.5, Great Britain 3.5
1957: Great Britain 7.5, U.S. 4.5
1955: U.S. 8, Great Britain 4
1953: U.S. 6.5, Great Britain 5.5
1951: U.S. 9.5, Great Britain 2.5
1949: U.S. 7, Great Britain 5
1947: U.S. 11, Great Britain 1
*1939–1945: No matches held (World War II)*
1937: U.S. 8, Great Britain 4
1935: U.S. 9, Great Britain 3
1933: Great Britain 6.5, U.S. 5.5
1931: U.S. 9, Great Britain 3
1929: Great Britain 7, U.S. 5
1927: U.S. 9.5, Great Britain 2.5

---

## Mickey Wright

Mary "Mickey" Wright is one of the greatest golfers America has ever produced. Although she only began playing at the age of 12, within five years she won the U.S. Girls Junior, followed two years later with the 1954 World Amateur title, as well as being low amateur at the 1954 U.S. Women's Open. While still studying at Stanford in 1954, she turned professional.

In the second year of turning pro, Wright embarked on a fourteen-year winning streak that lasted from 1956 to 1969. The streak has been bettered only by Kathy Whitworth.

In the 10-year span from 1959–1968, Wright captured 79 of her 82 victories, averaging 7.9 victories per year over that span. Wright won the 1958, 1959, 1961, and 1964 U.S. Women's Open Championships. In 1961, Wright won three of the four LPGA majors, the U.S. Women's Open, LPGA Championship, and the Titleholders Championship. She is the only woman in LPGA history to have won the LPGA Championship four times (1958, 1960, 1961, 1963) and her 13 victories in 1963 (of 32 Tour events held at that time) is a record that has never been approached since.

Wright stopped playing regularly on the professional circuit in 1969. In 1979, however, as a 44-year-old, she participated in the Coca-Cola Classic and was good enough to be part of a five-way play-off that was eventually won by Nancy Lopez. Despite topping the money list between 1961 and 1964, her 1994 second-place finish in the Sprint Senior Challenge earned her $30,000—the biggest paycheck of her career.

She was voted the Associated Press Woman Athlete of the Year in 1963 and 1964. She was made the 1994 Honoree of the Memorial Tournament, a PGA Tour event founded by Jack Nicklaus. She was inducted into the LPGA Hall of Fame in 1964 and the World Golf Hall of Fame in 1976. Perhaps the greatest player in LPGA history, Wright had a total of 82 victories in a brilliant twenty-six-year career.

## YOUR BACKSWING TEMPO

TO DETERMINE THE SPEED of the backswing best suited for you, stand in front of a mirror, club in hand, assuming a full address position. With a deliberate slow-motion swing, reach low and back. Turn your upper body to complete a full backswing. Check your position in the mirror. Is your left arm straight? Is your left wrist cocked? Are your hip and right knee firm? Is your right elbow pointing downward? Soon you will establish the tempo that will give you maximum control over your swing without losing your balance.

**2 7**

# LPGA Record Book

## Most Wins
### Career Money Leaders

| RANK | PLAYER | TOTAL |
|------|--------|-------|
| 1 | Annika Sorenstam | $13,199,874 |
| 2 | Karrie Webb | $9,488,298 |
| 3 | Juli Inkster | $8,695,041 |
| 4 | Beth Daniel | $7,831,273 |
| 5 | Betsy King | $7,505,838 |
| 6 | Se Ri Pak | $7,336,690 |
| 7 | Rosie Jones | $7,215,131 |
| 8 | Meg Mallon | $7,194,084 |

| 9 | Dottie Pepper | $6,764,220 |
| 10 | Laura Davies | $6,565,659 |
| 11 | Pat Bradley | $5,746,685 |
| 12 | Patty Sheehan | $5,513,409 |
| 13 | Kelly Robbins | $5,401,896 |
| 14 | Nancy Lopez | $5,320,876 |
| 15 | Lorie Kane | $4,965,592 |
| 16 | Liselotte Neumann | $4,611,952 |
| 17 | Sherri Steinhauer | $3,974,074 |
| 18 | Tammie Green | $3,935,962 |
| 19 | Jane Geddes | $3,805,553 |
| 20 | Brandie Burton | $3,764,982 |
| 21 | Rachel Teske | $3,740,813 |
| 22 | Mi Hyun Kim | $3,753,510 |
| 23 | Chris Johnson | $3,538,265 |
| 24 | Danielle Ammaccapane | $3,512,176 |
| 25 | Michele Redman | $3,508,068 |
| 26 | Donna Andrews | $3,448,586 |
| 27 | Amy Alcott | $3,408,074 |
| 28 | Pat Hurst | $3,265,231 |
| 29 | Michelle McGann | $3,242,998 |
| 30 | Grace Park | $3,153,370 |
| 31 | Helen Alfredsson | $3,124,494 |
| 32 | Jan Stephenson | $3,045,552 |
| 33 | Dawn Coe-Jones | $2,965,421 |
| 34 | JoAnne Carner | $2,961,986 |
| 35 | Catriona Matthew | $2,923,936 |
| 36 | Emilee Klein | $2,815,150 |
| 37 | Ayako Okamoto | $2,749,508 |
| 38 | Colleen Walker | $2,747,278 |
| 39 | Deb Richard | $2,640,312 |
| 40 | Nancy Scranton | $2,622,281 |

| 41 | Tina Barrett | $2,611,878 |
| 42 | Cristie Kerr | $2,601,837 |
| 43 | Kris Tschetter | $2,599,198 |
| 44 | Hollis Stacy | $2,580,040 |
| 45 | Hiromi Kobayashi | $2,494,326 |
| 46 | Carin Koch | $2,488,827 |
| 47 | Val Skinner | $2,463,848 |
| 48 | Janice Moodie | $2,429,710 |
| 49 | Laura Diaz | $2,427,796 |
| 50 | Barb Mucha | $2,402,351 |
| 51 | Dale Eggeling | $2,339,526 |
| 52 | Wendy Ward | $2,272,843 |
| 53 | Sherri Turner | $2,218,402 |
| 54 | Maria Hjorth | $2,204,723 |
| 55 | Judy Dickinson | $2,179,744 |
| 56 | Sophie Gustafson | $2,125,897 |
| 57 | Kristi Albers | $2,050,811 |
| 58 | Cindy Rarick | $2,016,871 |
| 59 | Jane Crafter | $1,919,985 |
| 60 | Sally Little | $1,908,097 |
| 61 | Hee-Won Han | $1,856,276 |
| 62 | Cindy Figg-Currier | $1,837,839 |
| 63 | Kelli Kuehne | $1,770,630 |
| 64 | Jenny Lidback | $1,766,525 |
| 65 | Leta Lindley | $1,763,121 |
| 66 | Dorothy Delasin | $1,756,409 |
| 67 | Wendy Doolan | $1,753,970 |
| 68 | Kathy Whitworth | $1,731,770 |
| 69 | Penny Hammel | $1,703,724 |
| 70 | Vicki Fergon | $1,612,546 |
| 71 | Michelle Estill | $1,590,718 |
| 72 | Elaine Crosby | $1,543,985 |

| 73 | Alice Ritzman | $1,490,016 |
| 74 | Mhairi McKay | $1,473,039 |
| 75 | Cindy Schreyer | $1,471,698 |
| 76 | Alison Nicholas | $1,467,453 |
| 77 | Amy Benz | $1,457,028 |
| 78 | Kathy Postlewait | $1,445,723 |
| 79 | Dana Dormann | $1,441,390 |
| 80 | Charlotta Sorenstam | $1,403,822 |
| 81 | Martha Nause | $1,390,170 |
| 82 | Donna Caponi | $1,387,919 |
| 83 | Amy Fruhwirth | $1,382,879 |
| 84 | Missie McGeorge | $1,374,519 |
| 85 | Sandra Palmer | $1,354,001 |
| 86 | Kim Saiki | $1,344,778 |
| 87 | Becky Iverson | $1,327,745 |
| 88 | Debbie Massey | $1,296,507 |
| 89 | Joan Pitcock | $1,291,165 |
| 90 | Jane Blalock | $1,290,943 |
| 91 | Gail Graham | $1,285,769 |
| 92 | Vicki Goetze-Ackerman | $1,264,929 |
| 93 | Akiko Fukushima | $1,249,266 |
| 94 | Marta Figueras-Dotti | $1,247,905 |
| 95 | Tracy Hanson | $1,222,845 |
| 96 | Trish Johnson | $1,209,264 |
| 97 | Susie Parry | $1,208,677 |
| 98 | Candie Kung | $1,199,123 |
| 99 | Jill McGill | $1,189,445 |
| 100 | Lauri Merten | $1,187,317 |

## Topping It

PLAYERS MAY TOP THE BALL because their arms and body are not in sync. To work on this, extend a golf towel across your chest and hold it in place under your arms. Hit some balls with a 7-iron. Notice how the towel makes you turn your body more in sync with your arms. You will also notice that the balls you are hitting have a draw. Practice this to get your muscles used to the timing of the body and arms swinging closer together.

## ANNUAL LEADERS ON THE LPGA MONEY LIST

| YEAR | PLAYER | AMOUNT |
|------|--------|--------|
| 2003 | Annika Sorenstam | $1,914,506 |
| 2002 | Annika Sorenstam | $2,863,904 |
| 2001 | Annika Sorenstam | $2,105,868 |
| 2000 | Karrie Webb | $1,876,853 |
| 1999 | Karrie Webb | $1,591,959 |
| 1998 | Annika Sorenstam | $1,092,748 |
| 1997 | Annika Sorenstam | $1,236,789 |
| 1996 | Karrie Webb | $1,002,000 |
| 1995 | Annika Sorenstam | $ 666,533 |
| 1994 | Laura Davies | $ 687,201 |
| 1993 | Betsy King | $ 595,992 |
| 1992 | Dottie Pepper | $ 693,335 |
| 1991 | Pat Bradley | $ 763,118 |
| 1990 | Beth Daniel | $ 863,578 |
| 1989 | Betsy King | $ 654,132 |

| | | | |
|---|---|---|---|
| 1988 | Sherri Turner | $ | 350,851 |
| 1987 | Ayako Okamoto | $ | 466,034 |
| 1986 | Pat Bradley | $ | 492,021 |
| 1985 | Nancy Lopez | $ | 416,472 |
| 1984 | Betsy King | $ | 266,771 |
| 1983 | JoAnne Carner | $ | 291,404 |
| 1982 | JoAnne Carner | $ | 310,400 |
| 1981 | Beth Daniel | $ | 206,998 |
| 1980 | Beth Daniel | $ | 231,000 |
| 1979 | Nancy Lopez | $ | 197,489 |
| 1978 | Nancy Lopez | $ | 189,814 |
| 1977 | Judy Rankin | $ | 122,890 |
| 1976 | Judy Rankin | $ | 150,734 |
| 1975 | Sandra Palmer | $ | 76,374 |
| 1974 | JoAnne Carner | $ | 87,094 |
| 1973 | Kathy Whitworth | $ | 82,864 |
| 1972 | Kathy Whitworth | $ | 65,063 |
| 1971 | Kathy Whitworth | $ | 41,181 |
| 1970 | Kathy Whitworth | $ | 30,235 |
| 1969 | Carol Mann | $ | 49,152 |
| 1968 | Kathy Whitworth | $ | 48,379 |
| 1967 | Kathy Whitworth | $ | 32,937 |
| 1966 | Kathy Whitworth | $ | 33,517 |
| 1965 | Kathy Whitworth | $ | 28,658 |
| 1964 | Mickey Wright | $ | 29,800 |
| 1963 | Mickey Wright | $ | 31,269 |
| 1962 | Mickey Wright | $ | 21,641 |
| 1961 | Mickey Wright | $ | 22,236 |
| 1960 | Louise Suggs | $ | 16,892 |
| 1959 | Betsy Rawls | $ | 26,774 |
| 1958 | Beverly Hanson | $ | 12,639 |
| 1957 | Patty Berg | $ | 16,272 |

| 1956 | Marlene Hagg | $ | 20,235 |
| 1955 | Patty Berg | $ | 16,492 |
| 1954 | Patty Berg | $ | 16,011 |
| 1953 | Louise Suggs | $ | 19,816 |
| 1952 | Betsy Rawls | $ | 14,505 |
| 1951 | Babe Didrikson Zaharias | $ | 15,087 |
| 1950 | Babe Didrikson Zaharias | $ | 14,800 |

# Single-Season Earnings

## Most Official Single-Season Earnings

$2,863,904: Annika Sorenstam (2002)

## Most Times Finishing First on the Season-Ending Money List

8: Kathy Whitworth (1965–68, 1970–73)
6: Annika Sorenstam (1995, 1997–98, 2001–03)

## Most Official Single-Season Earnings by a Rookie

$1,002,000: Karrie Webb (1996)

## First to Reach $100,000 in Single-Season Earnings

Judy Rankin, July 11, 1976

## First to Reach $1 Million in Single-Season Earnings

Karrie Webb, November 24, 1996

## FIRST TO REACH $2 MILLION
## IN SINGLE-SEASON EARNINGS

Annika Sorenstam, November 19, 2001

---

### Uphill and Downhill Lies

THE MOST IMPORTANT THING to remember when playing an uphill lie is to square your shoulders to the angle of the hill. Think of it as if you were playing the ball from a flat lie—your shoulder angle should be the same in comparison to the ground. On the uphill lie, the hill adds loft to the ball, so if you are looking to hit it a certain distance, you may need to add more club. Downhill lies are treated the same, so you need to square your shoulders to the hill.

---

## Career Earnings Milestones

## Youngest to Reach $1 Million

Dorothy Delasin (2002), 21 years, 7 months, 12 days old
Brandie Burton (1993), 21 years, 7 Months. 21 days
Se Ri Pak (1999), 21 years, 8 months, 16 days

## FIRST TO REACH $1 MILLION
Kathy Whitworth, July 26, 1981

## First to Reach $2 Million
Pat Bradley, May 18, 1986

## First to Reach $3 Million
Pat Bradley, March 25, 1990

## FIRST TO REACH $4 MILLION
Pat Bradley, September 22, 1991

## First to Reach $5 Million
Betsy King, May 7, 1995

## First to Reach $6 Million
Betsy King, March 22, 1998

## FIRST TO REACH $7 MILLION
Annika Sorenstam, May 6, 2001

## First to Reach $8 Million
Annika Sorenstam, October 28, 2001

## First to Reach $9 Million
Annika Sorenstam. May 19, 2002

## FIRST TO REACH $10 MILLION
Annika Sorenstam, July 7, 2002

---

## Kathy Whitworth

Although she didn't take up golf until she was fifteen years old, Kathy Whitworth had the benefit of being taught by Harvey Penwick, one of the masters of the game. After she won the New Mexico State Amateur for two consecutive years, Whitworth thought there was nothing more to prove, and so turned professional in 1958.

She would have to wait four years for her first victory on the pro circuit—the Kelly Girl Open, in 1962—but it was the beginning of a record of achievement unmatched on the male or female professional tours.

In a career that spanned four decades, she was the leading money winner eight times (1965–1968 and 1970–1973), Player of the Year seven times (1966–1969 and 1971–1973) and winner of the Vare Trophy with the lowest stroke average seven times (1965–1967 and 1969–1972).

She was also named Associated Press Athlete of the Year in 1965 and 1967. Paired with Mickey Wright, together they made golf history as the first women's team to compete in the PGA sanctioned Legends of Golf.

When she placed third at the 1981 U.S. Women's Open, she became the first LPGA player to record $1 million in career earnings. Her last official victory came in 1985 and was the 88th of her career, more than any other golfer before or since.

She was captain of the U.S. team in both the inaugural Solheim Cup in 1990 and again in 1992. Whitworth was inducted into the LPGA's Hall of Fame in 1975 and has been inducted into the New Mexico Hall of Fame, Texas Sports and Golf Hall of Fame, World Golf Hall of Fame, and the Women's Sports Foundation Hall of Fame.

## Most Wins

### Most Career Wins on the LPGA Tour

| | |
|---|---|
| 88: Kathy Whitworth | 43: JoAnne Carner |
| 82: Mickey Wright | 42: Sandra Haynie |
| 60: Patty Berg | 41: Babe Zaharias |
| 58: Louise Suggs | 38: Carol Mann |
| 55: Betsy Rawls | 35: Patty Sheehan |
| 52: Annika Sorenstam | 34: Betsy King |
| 48: Nancy Lopez | 33: Beth Daniel |

| | |
|---|---|
| 31: Pat Bradley | 19: Sandra Palmer |
| 30: Juli Inkster; | 18: Hollis Stacy |
|     Karrie Webb | 17: Dottie Pepper; |
| 29: Amy Alcott |     Ayako Okamoto; |
| 27: Jane Blalock |     Beverly Hanson |
| 26: Judy Rankin; | 16: Jan Stephenson |
|     Marlene Hagge | 15: Sally Little; |
| 24: Donna Caponi |     Meg Mallon |
| 22: Se Ri Pak | 13: Betty Jameson; |
| 21: Marilynn Smith |     Rosie Jones |
| 20: Laura Davies | 12: Liselotte Neumann |

## Most Major Championship Titles

15: Patty Berg
13: Mickey Wright
11: Louise Suggs
10: Babe Zaharias
8: Betsy Rawls
7: Juli Inkster
6: Pat Bradley; Betsy King; Patty Sheehan; Annika Sorenstam;
    Karrie Webb; Kathy Whitworth
5: Amy Alcott
4: Donna Caponi; Laura Davies; Sandra Haynie; Se Ri Pak; Hollis
    Stacy
3: Beverly Hanson; Betty Jameson; Nancy Lopez; Meg Mallon;
    Jan Stephenson

## MOST OFFICIAL TOURNAMENT WINS IN ONE SEASON

13: Mickey Wright (1963)
11: Mickey Wright (1964); Annika Sorenstam (2002)

## Most Majors Won in Career

15: Patty Berg (one U.S. Women's Open, seven Titleholders, and seven Western Opens)

## Most Majors Won in a Season

3: Babe Zaharias (1950 U.S. Women's Open, Titleholders, Western Open)*; Mickey Wright (1961 LPGA Championship, U.S. Women's Open, Titleholders); Pat Bradley (1986 Nabisco Dinah Shore, LPGA Championship, du Maurier Ltd. Classic)

*Only three majors were held in 1950.

## Most Consecutive Seasons with a Victory

17: Kathy Whitworth (1962–78)

15: Betsy Rawls (1951–65)

14: Mickey Wright (1956–69); Sandra Haynie (1962–75)

13: Louise Suggs (1950–62)

12: JoAnne Carner (1974–85); Amy Alcott (1975–86)

11: Jane Blalock (1970–80)

10: Judy Rankin (1970–79); Betsy King (1984–93)

## Most Career Seasons with a Victory

22: Kathy Whitworth

18: Betsy Rawls

16: Sandra Haynie; Nancy Lopez

15: Mickey Wright; Amy Alcott; Patty Sheehan; Juli Inkster

14: JoAnne Carner; Betsy King

13: Louise Suggs; Pat Bradley; Marilynn Smith

12: Beth Daniel

11: Patty Berg; Marlene Hagge; Carol Mann; Judy Rankin; Jane Blalock; Laura Davies

10: Sandra Palmer; Hollis Stacy; Rosie Jones

## Fairway Putt

IF YOUR BALL is on the fairway but still short of the green, you can sometimes use your putter from that distance. This will depend on the speed of the green and the height of the fairway grass. Practice this shot and you will learn your limits on when to use it. This is a good stroke saver if you are not chipping well that day.

## ⟨ Vare Trophy ⟩

The Vare Trophy is awarded annually to the player with the lowest scoring average. To be eligible for the Vare Trophy, players must compete in at least 70 rounds.

| YEAR | PLAYER | AVERAGE |
|------|--------|---------|
| 1953 | Patty Berg | 75.00 |
| 1954 | Babe Zaharias | 75.48 |
| 1955 | Patty Berg | 74.47 |
| 1956 | Patty Berg | 74.57 |
| 1957 | Louise Suggs | 74.64 |
| 1958 | Beverly Hanson | 74.92 |
| 1959 | Betsy Rawls | 74.03 |
| 1960 | Mickey Wright | 73.25 |
| 1961 | Mickey Wright | 73.55 |
| 1962 | Mickey Wright | 73.67 |
| 1963 | Mickey Wright | 72.81 |
| 1964 | Mickey Wright | 72.46 |
| 1965 | Kathy Whitworth | 72.61 |
| 1966 | Kathy Whitworth | 72.60 |

| 1967 | Kathy Whitworth | 72.74 |
| 1968 | Carol Mann | 72.04 |
| 1969 | Kathy Whitworth | 72.38 |
| 1970 | Kathy Whitworth | 72.26 |
| 1971 | Kathy Whitworth | 72.88 |
| 1972 | Kathy Whitworth | 72.38 |
| 1973 | Judy Rankin | 73.08 |
| 1974 | JoAnne Carner | 72.87 |
| 1975 | JoAnne Carner | 72.40 |
| 1976 | Judy Rankin | 72.25 |
| 1977 | Judy Rankin | 72.16 |
| 1978 | Nancy Lopez | 71.76 |
| 1979 | Nancy Lopez | 71.20 |
| 1980 | Amy Alcott | 71.51 |
| 1981 | JoAnne Carner | 71.75 |
| 1982 | JoAnne Carner | 71.49 |
| 1983 | JoAnne Carner | 71.41 |
| 1984 | Patty Sheehan | 71.40 |
| 1985 | Nancy Lopez | 70.73 |
| 1986 | Pat Bradley | 71.10 |
| 1987 | Betsy King | 71.14 |
| 1988 | Colleen Walker | 71.26 |
| 1989 | Beth Daniel | 70.38 |
| 1990 | Beth Daniel | 70.54 |
| 1991 | Pat Bradley | 70.66 |
| 1992 | Dottie Pepper | 70.80 |
| 1993 | Betsy King | 70.85 |
| 1994 | Beth Daniel | 70.90 |
| 1995 | Annika Sorenstam | 71.00 |
| 1996 | Annika Sorenstam | 70.47 |
| 1997 | Karrie Webb | 70.00 |
| 1998 | Annika Sorenstam | 69.99 |

| 1999 | Karrie Webb | 69.43 |
|------|-------------|-------|
| 2000 | Karrie Webb | 70.05 |
| 2001 | Annika Sorenstam | 69.42 |
| 2002 | Annika Sorenstam | 68.70 |
| 2003 | Se Ri Pak | 70.03 |

## Louise Suggs
## Rolex Rookie of the Year

YEAR PLAYER

1962 Mary Mills
1963 Clifford Ann Creed
1964 Susie Berning
1965 Margie Masters
1966 Jan Ferraris
1967 Sharron Moran
1968 Sandra Post
1969 Jane Blalock
1970 JoAnne Carner
1971 Sally Little
1972 Jocelyne Bourassa
1973 Laura Baugh
1974 Jan Stephenson
1975 Amy Alcott
1976 Bonnie Lauer
1977 Debbie Massey
1978 Nancy Lopez
1979 Beth Daniel
1980 Myra Van Hoos
        (Blackwelder)
1981 Patty Sheehan
1982 Patti Rizzo

1983 Stephanie Farwig
1984 Juli Inkster
1985 Penny Hammel
1986 Jody Rosenthal (Anschutz)
1987 Tammie Green
1988 Liselotte Neumann
1989 Pamela Wright
1990 Hiromi Kobayashi
1991 Brandie Burton
1992 Helen Alfredsson
1993 Suzanne Strudwick
1994 Annika Sorenstam
1995 Pat Hurst
1996 Karrie Webb
1997 Lisa Hackney
1998 Se Ri Pak
1999 Mi Hyun Kim
2000 Dorothy Delasin
2001 Hee-Won Han
2002 Beth Bauer
2003 Lorena Ochoa

## CHUNKING

"CHUNKING" MEANS hitting the ball "fat." When this happens, the club often strikes the turf behind the ball and produces the shot you call "chunking." To change this, practice gripping the club properly with your left hand and lowering the club while flexing your knees. Keep your right hand off the club. Roll your ankles to cause the club to move back and forth along the intended path. This will allow you to swing the club with the large muscles of the lower body.

## Rolex Player of the Year

The Rolex Player of the Year is based on top-ten finishes.

| YEAR | PLAYER | POINTS |
|------|--------|--------|
| 1966 | Kathy Whitworth | 131 |
| 1967 | Kathy Whitworth | 116 |
| 1968 | Kathy Whitworth | 141 |
| 1969 | Kathy Whitworth | 102 |
| 1970 | Sandra Haynie | 41 |
| 1971 | Kathy Whitworth | 57 |
| 1972 | Kathy Whitworth | 91 |
| 1973 | Kathy Whitworth | 83 |
| 1974 | JoAnne Carner | 82 |
| 1975 | Sandra Palmer | 40 |
| 1976 | Judy Rankin | 79 |
| 1977 | Judy Rankin | 66 |
| 1978 | Nancy Lopez | 92 |
| 1979 | Nancy Lopez | 88 |
| 1980 | Beth Daniel | 78 |
| 1981 | JoAnne Carner | 60 |

| 1982 | JoAnne Carner | 75 |
| 1983 | Patty Sheehan | 61 |
| 1984 | Betsy King | 55 |
| 1985 | Nancy Lopez | 85 |
| 1986 | Pat Bradley | 78 |
| 1987 | Ayako Okamoto | 68 |
| 1988 | Nancy Lopez | 49 |
| 1989 | Betsy King | 76 |
| 1990 | Beth Daniel | 82 |
| 1991 | Pat Bradley | 59 |
| 1992 | Dottie (Pepper) Mochrie | 54 |
| 1993 | Betsy King | 40 |
| 1994 | Beth Daniel | 48 |
| 1995 | Annika Sorenstam | 43 |
| 1996 | Laura Davies | 250.50* |
| 1997 | Annika Sorenstam | 313.50 |
| 1998 | Annika Sorenstam | 225.89 |
| 1999 | Karrie Webb | 347.79 |
| 2000 | Karrie Webb | 339.75 |
| 2001 | Annika Sorenstam 3 | 84.25 |
| 2002 | Annika Sorenstam | 486.50 |
| 2003 | Annika Sorenstam | 340.19 |

*In 1996, the sponsor in conjunction with the LPGA changed the point system.*

## ≋ *Heather Farr Player Award* ≋

Heather Farr was an outstanding Junior golfer, and later an All-American player at Arizona State. She was clearly a star on the rise when she joined the LPGA Tour. That promise was cut short when on November 20, 1993, she lost an almost five-year battle with breast cancer at the age of 28.

In celebration of her life, the LPGA has established an annual award in Heather Farr's name. The Heather Farr Player Award recognizes an LPGA Tour player who, through her hard work, dedication, and love of the game of golf, has demonstrated determination, perseverance, and spirit in fulfilling her goals as a player, qualities for which Farr is so fondly remembered.

| YEAR | PLAYER | YEAR | PLAYER |
|------|--------|------|--------|
| 1994 | Heather Farr | 1999 | Nancy Scranton |
| 1995 | Shelley Hamlin | 2000 | Brandie Burton |
| 1996 | Martha Nause | 2001 | Kris Tschetter |
| 1997 | Terry-Jo Myers | 2002 | Kim Williams |
| 1998 | Lorie Kane | 2003 | Beth Daniel |

## The William and Mousie Powell Award

Screen legend William Powell and his wife Mousie, an actor in her own right, were early boosters of women's golf and the LPGA Tour. In 1986, Mousie Powell established an award to recognize the qualities of sportsmanship and to emphasize that sportsmanship transcends winning.

The William and Mousie Powell Award is an annual presentation that gives LPGA members an opportunity to acknowledge the performance and accomplishments of their colleagues. The award is given annually to a member who, in the opinion of her playing peers, by her behavior and deeds best exemplifies the spirit, ideals, and values of the LPGA. The William and Mousie Powell Award recognizes that, while every winner deserves the spoils, the qualities of sportsmanship are not reserved for the victors alone; true sportsmanship is the gift of all who take part.

| YEAR | PLAYER | YEAR | PLAYER |
|------|--------|------|--------|
| 1986 | Kathy Whitworth | 1995 | JoAnne Carner |
| 1987 | Nancy Lopez | 1996 | Betsy King |
| 1988 | Marlene Hagge | 1997 | Sherri Turner |
| 1989 | Heather Farr | 1998 | Judy Rankin |
| 1990 | Judy Dickinson | 1999 | Meg Mallon |
| 1991 | Pat Bradley | 2000 | Lorie Kane |
| 1992 | Shelley Hamlin | 2001 | Wendy Ward |
| 1993 | Alice Miller | 2002 | Gail Graham |
| 1994 | Jill Briles-Hinton | 2003 | Suzy Whaley |

## Safe or Sorry?

WHEN TO GO THOUGH the trees or chip out for a safe shot is a matter of good strategy. Good strategy calls for playing the shot most likely to set up the easiest next shot.

# Patty Berg Award

The LPGA's Board of Directors instituted the Patty Berg award in 1979 to reward outstanding contributions to women's golf, and to honor Patty Berg by recognizing her diplomacy, sportsmanship, goodwill, and contributions to the game. Any person may be nominated for the award.

| YEAR | PLAYER | YEAR | PLAYER |
|------|--------|------|--------|
| 1979 | Marilynn Smith | 1987 | Kathy Whitworth |
| 1980 | Betsy Rawls | 1988 | John D. Laupheimer |
| 1984 | Ray Volpe | 1990 | Patty Berg |
| 1985 | Dinah Shore | 1991 | Karsten Solheim |
| 1986 | David Foster | 1992 | Judy Dickinson |

| 1993 | Kerry Graham | 2000 | Louise Suggs |
|------|--------------|------|--------------|
| 1994 | Charles S. Mechem Jr. | 2001 | Pat Bradley |
| 1996 | Suzanne Jackson | 2002 | Patty Sheehan |
| 1997 | Judy Bell | 2003 | Annika Sorenstam |
| 1999 | Judy Rankin | | |

## Joyce Wethered

Many golf writers call Joyce Wethered the greatest woman golfer of all time. Born in Devon, England, she and her brother (Roger Wethered, who tied for the British Open title in 1921 but lost in a play-off) learned the game as children. After Bobby Jones saw her play, he called her the greatest golfer—man or woman—he had ever seen.

Her golf debut came in 1920, when she entered the English Ladies at Sheringham, Norfolk, where she shocked the golf world by defeating the leading golf figure in women's golf, Cecil Leitch, in the final.

It was a see-saw battle they would renew over the ensuing years, meeting again in the finals of the British and French Opens. In the 1924 British Open they fought a titanic battle until Wethered finally pulled away in the later holes.

Another rivalry was soon to present itself in the great American player Glenna Collett. In 1925 and 1929, they faced off at the British Ladies, which Wethered won. In the 1929 match, the American was up by 5 strokes after 11 holes, but Wethered came back to win on the 35th hole.

In 1935, she toured the U.S., competing against the best American and British golfers of the era. There she proved to American audiences her greatness, consistently scoring in the 70s, and often beating her male counterparts.

Her competitive playing career only spanned nine years. In that time period she won an incredible five consecutive English Amateur titles and four British Ladies titles. Records indicate that she was good enough to have made the men's Walker Cup team if women had been permitted to qualify.

In 1937 she married Sir John Heathcoat-Amory, and created a notable garden that was one of the leading British botanical collections at that time. For that achievement, she was awarded the Royal Horticultural Society's Victoria Medal of Honor.

In 1951, she became the first president of the English Ladi es' Golf Association and was inducted into the Professional Golfers' Association (PGA) of America World Golf Hall of Fame in 1975.

## The Rough Stuff

GETTING THE BALL out of green-side rough is difficult because if you hit the ball firmly enough to ensure getting out of the rough, the tendency is to go too far, often over the green. Use a highly lofted wedge (60 degrees or more) if you find yourself in this situation.

# The Solheim Cup

The Solheim Cup is named after Karsten Solheim, the founder of Karsten Manufacturing Corporation, maker of the Ping golfing equipment line. In association with the LPGA and the Women's Professional Golfers European Tour (now the Evian Ladies European Tour), she developed the concept of international match play that would pit the best European women golfers against the best American women golfers. Held every two years, the Solheim Cup has quickly established itself as one of the most prestigious golf prizes in women's golf.

## Golf Play

The first two days feature eight four-ball matches. The final day is 12 singles matches. The first two days include eight foursomes and eight four-ball matches.

### FOURSOMES
### (FOUR GROUPS OF TWO-MAN TEAMS)

"Foursome" play is a match where two golfers compete on a team against two other golfers and each side plays one ball. The golfers play alternate shots (player 1 hits tee shot, player 2 hits second shot, etc.) until the hole is played out. Team members alternate playing the tee shots, with one golfer hitting the tee shot on odd-numbered holes, and the other hitting the tee shot from the even-numbered holes. The team with the better score wins the hole. Should the two teams tie for best score, the hole is halved.

## Four-Ball
## (four groups of two-man teams)

"Four-ball" play is a match in which each member of the two-man teams play their own ball. Four balls are in play per hole with each of the four players recording a score on the hole. The team whose player posts the best score on that hole wins the hole. Should players from each team tie for the best score, the hole is halved.

## Singles (twelve groups of one-man teams)

"Singles" is a match in which one player competes against another player. A player wins the match when he is up by more holes than there are holes remaining to play.

### PAIRINGS

Each team captain submits the order of play for his team to the appointed tournament official. The lists from each captain are matched, resulting in the pairings. The pairings can be modified by the team captains at any time prior to the beginning of a match.

## Solheim Cup Match History

| YEAR | LOCATION | EUROPE | U.S. |
|------|----------|--------|------|
| 1990 | Lake Nona, Florida | 4.5 | 11.5 |
| 1992 | Dalmahoy, Edinburgh | 11.5 | 6.5 |
| 1994 | Greenbriar, West Virginia | 7.0 | 13.0 |
| 1996 | Marriott St. Pierre Hotel, Wales | 11.0 | 17.0 |
| 1998 | Muirfield Village Golf Club, Ohio | 12.0 | 16.0 |
| 2000 | Loch Lomond Golf Club, Scotland | 14.5 | 11.5 |

| 2002 | Interlachen Country Club, Minnesota | 12.5 | 15.5 |
| 2003* | Barseback Golf and CC, Sweden | 17.5 | 10.5 |
| 2005 | Crooked Stick Golf Club, Indiana | TBA | TBA |

*The Solheim Cup was held for two consecutive years so it could be played on opposite years from the men's.*

---

## Visualize

BEFORE YOU TAKE YOUR SHOT, visualize it. Visualize what can go wrong, but more important, what will go right if you strike your ball properly. Use all five of your senses, incorporating into your mind's eye all that's possible and impossible.

**2 9**

# Champions Tour Record Book
## *Most Money*

### CHAMPIONS TOUR MONEY LEADERS

| 2003 | Tom Watson | $1,853,108 |
| 2002 | Hale Irwin | $3,028,304 |
| 2001 | Allen Doyle | $2,553,582 |
| 2000 | Larry Nelson | $2,708,005 |
| 1999 | Bruce Fleisher | $2,515,705 |
| 1998 | Hale Irwin | $2,861,945 |
| 1997 | Hale Irwin | $2,343,364 |

| 1996 | Jim Colbert | $1,627,890 |
| 1995 | Jim Colbert | $1,444,386 |
| 1994 | Dave Stockton | $1,402,519 |
| 1993 | Dave Stockton | $1,175,944 |
| 1992 | Lee Trevino | $1,027,002 |
| 1991 | Mike Hill | $1,065,657 |
| 1990 | Lee Trevino | $1,190,518 |
| 1989 | Bob Charles | $ 725,887 |
| 1988 | Bob Charles | $ 533,929 |
| 1987 | Chi Chi Rodriguez | $ 509,145 |
| 1986 | Bruce Crampton | $ 454,299 |
| 1985 | Peter Thomson | $ 386,724 |
| 1984 | Don January | $ 328,597 |
| 1983 | Don January | $ 237,571 |
| 1982 | Miller Barber | $ 106,890 |
| 1981 | Miller Barber | $ 83,136 |
| 1980 | Don January | $ 44,100 |

## Career Money Leaders

| | | | |
|---|---|---|---|
| Hale Irwin | $18,557,568 | George Archer | $8,314,648 |
| Gil Morgan | $12,712,799 | Mike Hill | $8,119,490 |
| Jim Colbert | $11,184,384 | Jay Sigel | $7,988,376 |
| Larry Nelson | $10,595,595 | Jim Thorpe | $7,683,613 |
| Bruce Fleisher | $10,467,772 | Graham Marsh | $7,527,906 |
| Dave Stockton | $10,075,282 | Bruce Summerhays | $7,052,639 |
| Lee Trevino | $9,687,963 | John Jacobs | $7,000,707 |
| Dana Quigley | $9,072,584 | J. C. Snead | $6,936,110 |
| Bob Charles | $8,874,820 | Bob Murphy | $6,874,920 |
| Allen Doyle | $8,806,936 | Dale Douglass | $6,864,085 |
| Isao Aoki | $8,661,016 | Tom Wargo | $6,733,391 |
| Raymond Floyd | $8,636,897 | Tom Jenkins | $6,713,583 |
| Jim Dent | $8,520,456 | Chi Chi Rodriguez | $6,634,738 |

| | | | |
|---|---|---|---|
| Vicente Fernandez | $6,620,810 | Bob Eastwood | $3,336,078 |
| John Bland | $6,207,725 | DeWitt Weaver | $3,334,326 |
| Mike McCulloughn | $6,074,957 | Gary McCord | $3,321,208 |
| Doug Tewell | $6,006,364 | Jack Nicklaus | $3,264,598 |
| Jim Albus | $5,993,544 | Larry Gilbert | $3,238,187 |
| Jose Maria Canizares | $5,979,047 | Don January | $3,217,678 |
| Gary Player | $5,812,282 | Jerry McGee | $3,206,490 |
| Tom Kite | $5,780,209 | Jack Kiefer | $3,188,395 |
| Tom Watson | $5,716,693 | John Mahaffey | $3,148,424 |
| Dave Eichelberger | $5,335,795 | Walter Zembriski | $3,136,419 |
| Bob Gilder | $5,330,869 | Tom Shaw | $3,010,681 |
| Al Geiberger | $5,282,995 | Don Bies | $2,929,324 |
| Walter Hall | $5,260,685 | Stewart Ginn | $2,920,307 |
| Hubert Green | $5,255,611 | Jim Ahern | $2,908,382 |
| Ed Dougherty | $5,109,933 | Bobby Wadkins | $2,762,101 |
| Hugh Baiocchi | $4,854,731 | Tommy Aaron | $2,721,242 |
| Rocky Thompson | $4,816,251 | John Schroeder | $2,629,019 |
| Bruce Crampton | $4,652,684 | Larry Laoretti | $2,613,268 |
| Leonard Thompson | $4,536,263 | Butch Baird | $2,596,820 |
| Gibby Gilbert | $4,438,026 | Bob Dickson | $2,590,496 |
| Kermit Zarley | $4,343,456 | Larry Ziegler | $2,584,205 |
| Terry Dill | $4,292,988 | Jim Ferree | $2,551,671 |
| Bruce Lietzke | $4,258,075 | Morris Hatalsky | $2,541,627 |
| Walter Morgan | $4,188,133 | Frank Conner | $2,537,801 |
| Simon Hobday | $4,182,988 | Dave Hill | $2,378,112 |
| Miller Barber | $4,048,940 | Gene Littler | $2,317,234 |
| David Graham | $4,040,446 | Bob Duval | $2,243,264 |
| Charles Coody | $3,936,883 | Larry Mowry | $2,105,127 |
| Harold Henning | $3,921,332 | Fred Gibson | $2,067,228 |
| Jimmy Powell | $3,759,535 | Dick Hendrickson | $2,063,449 |
| Orville Moody | $3,541,789 | Bud Allin | $2,030,557 |
| Joe Inman | $3,514,990 | Ben Smith | $1,975,108 |

| Gay Brewer | $1,957,242 | John Paul Cain | $1,840,623 |
| Bobby Nichols | $1,956,263 | David Lundstrom | $1,825,494 |
| Sammy Rachels | $1,929,348 | Tom Purtzer | $1,804,033 |
| Brian Barnes | $1,923,001 | Tom Weiskopf | $1,775,785 |
| Don Pooley | $1,913,444 | Steven Veriato | $1,752,582 |

## Fear

MANY GOLFERS ARE AFRAID of hitting the ground with their club, but hitting the ground is a natural part of a good golf shot. If you are afraid of hitting the ground, take easy practice swings, coming in contact with the ground. In essence, make friends with the ground.

## MOST MONEY WON IN A SINGLE SEASON

| $3,028,304 | Hale Irwin | 2002 |
| $2,861,945 | Hale Irwin | 1998 |
| $2,708,005 | Larry Nelson | 2000 |
| $2,553,582 | Allen Doyle | 2001 |
| $2,515,705 | Bruce Fleisher | 1999 |
| $2,411,543 | Bruce Fleisher | 2001 |
| $2,373,977 | Bruce Fleisher | 2000 |
| $2,367,637 | Bob Gilder | 2002 |
| $2,343,364 | Hale Irwin | 1997 |
| $2,179,047 | Gil Morgan | 1998 |
| $2,160,562 | Gil Morgan | 1997 |

## Most Money Won by a Rookie

| $2,515,705 | Bruce Fleisher | 1999 |
| $2,160,562 | Gil Morgan | 1997 |

# Most Years Leading Money List

3: Don January (1980, 1983, 1984); Hale Irwin (1997, 1998, 2002)

2: Miller Barber (1981, 1982); Bob Charles (1988, 1989); Lee Trevino (1990, 1992); Dave Stockton (1993, 1994); Jim Colbert (1995, 1996)

## MOST CONSECUTIVE YEARS LEADING MONEY LIST

2: Miller Barber (1981–1982); Don January (1983–1984); Bob Charles (1988–1989); Dave Stockton (1993–1994); Jim Colbert (1995–1996); Hale Irwin (1997–1998)

## Most Years in Top 10 on Money List

9: Hale Irwin

8: Miller Barber; Bob Charles; Hale Irwin

7: Don January; Gene Littler; Dave Stockton; Jim Colbert

## Most Consecutive Years in Top 10 on Money List

9: Hale Irwin (1995–2003)

8: Miller Barber (1981–1988); Bob Charles (1986–1993); Hale Irwin (1995–2002)

7: Gene Littler (1981–1987); Dave Stockton (1992–1998)

## Most Consecutive $1 Million Seasons

8: Hale Irwin (1996–2003)

6: Gil Morgan (1997–2002)

## MOST CONSECUTIVE $2 MILLION SEASONS

6: Hale Irwin (1997–2002)

3: Bruce Fleisher (1999–2001)

## Bad Shot

EVERYBODY HITS BAD SHOTS; the thing is not to hit two or more bad shots in a row. To avoid this catastrophe, focus on what is at hand. The last shot was the last shot, so don't let negative feelings about yourself or your game get the best of you. Focus your energy positively.

# ≣ *Most Wins* ≣
## Most Champions Tour Career Victories

40: Hale Irwin
29: Lee Trevino
24: Miller Barber
23: Bob Charles; Gil Morgan
22: Don January; Chi Chi Rodriguez
20: Bruce Crampton; Jim Colbert
19: Gary Player; George Archer
18: Mike Hill
17: Larry Nelson; Bruce Fleisher
14: Dave Stockton; Raymond Floyd
12: Jim Dent
11: Dale Douglass; Orville Moody; Bob Murphy; Peter Thomson
10: Arnold Palmer; Al Geiberger; Jack Nicklaus

## MOST WINS BY SEASON

| 2003 | Craig Stadler, 3 | 2000 | Larry Nelson, 6 |
|------|------------------|------|-----------------|
| 2002 | Hale Irwin, 4    | 1999 | Bruce Fleisher, 7 |
|      | Bob Gilder, 4    | 1998 | Hale Irwin, 7   |
| 2001 | Larry Nelson, 5  | 1997 | Hale Irwin, 9   |

| 1996 | Jim Colbert, 5 | 1987 | Chi Chi Rodriguez, 7 |
|------|----------------|------|----------------------|
| 1995 | Jim Colbert, 4 | 1986 | Bruce Crampton, 7 |
|      | Bob Murphy, 4 | 1985 | Peter Thomson, 9 |
| 1994 | Lee Trevino, 6 | 1984 | Miller Barber, 4 |
| 1993 | Dave Stockton, 5 | 1983 | Don January, 6 |
| 1992 | Lee Trevino, 5 | 1982 | Miller Barber, 3 |
| 1991 | Mike Hill, 5 | 1981 | Miller Barber, 3 |
| 1990 | Lee Trevino, 7 | 1980 | Roberto De Vicenzo, |
| 1989 | Bob Charles, 5 |      | Don January |
| 1988 | Bob Charles, 5 |      | |
|      | Gary Player, 5 |      | |

## Most Consecutive Years Winning at Least One Tournament

9: Miller Barber (1981–1989)

8: Hale Irwin (1995–2002); Don January (1980–1987); Chi Chi Rodriguez (1986–1993)

7: Gary Player (1985–1991); Bruce Crampton (1986–1992); Mike Hill (1990–1996); Lee Trevino (1990–1996); Gil Morgan (1996–2002)

## Most Consecutive Years Winning Multiple Tournaments

8: Hale Irwin (1995–2002)

6: Don January (1981–1986); Lee Trevino (1990–1995); Jim Colbert (1991–1996)

## Players Winning Champions Tour Debut

Don January, 1980 Atlantic City International
Roberto De Vicenzo, 1980 U.S. Senior Open
Arnold Palmer, 1980 PGA Seniors Championship

Rod Funseth, 1983 Hall of Fame Tournament
Gary Player, 1985 Quadel Seniors Classic
George Archer, 1989 Gatlin Brothers Southwest Senior Classic
Jack Nicklaus, 1990 The Tradition
Bruce Fleisher, 1999 Royal Caribbean Classic
Lanny Wadkins, 2000 The ACE Group Classic
Bobby Wadkins, 2001 Lightpath Long Island Classic

## Players Winning First Two Career Starts on the Champions Tour

Bruce Fleisher, 1999 Royal Caribbean Classic, American Express
Invitational

## Most Victories in a Calendar Year

9: Peter Thomson, 1985; Hale Irwin, 1997

## Most Top-10 Finishes in a Season

26: Lee Trevino (1990)
25: Tom Wargo (1994); Allen Doyle (2001)

## Most Consecutive Top-5 Finishes

19: Hale Irwin (1997 Energizer Senior Tour Championship–1998
Comfort Classic)

## Most Consecutive Top-10 Finishes

36: Don January (1980 Atlantic City Seniors International–1984
MONY, Senior Tournament of Champions)

## Best Scores

| 1988 | Bob Charles | 70.05 |
| 1989 | Bob Charles | 69.78 |

| 1990 | Lee Trevino | 68.89 |
| 1991 | Lee Trevino | 69.50 |
| 1992 | Lee Trevino | 69.46 |
| 1993 | Bob Charles | 69.59 |
| 1994 | Raymond Floyd | 69.08 |
| 1995 | Raymond Floyd | 69.47 |
| 1996 | Hale Irwin | 69.47 |
| 1997 | Hale Irwin | 69.92 |
| 1998 | Hale Irwin | 68.59 |
| 1999 | Bruce Fleisher | 69.19 |
| 2000 | Gil Morgan | 68.83 |
| 2001 | Gil Morgan | 69.20 |
| 2002 | Hale Irwin | 68.93 |
| 2003 | Tom Watson | 68.81 |

## Math and Physics

TRUE ENOUGH, a golf swing can be broken down into math and physics, but that shouldn't scare you. Quite the opposite—it should inspire you, because now you have something to work from. Always ask and understand the whys of what you are doing, because in so doing you have a working base of knowledge upon which to build.

## Those Golden Years

## Wins by Age Group

| AGE | VICTORIES | PERCENT |
| --- | --- | --- |
| 50 | 133 | 18.14 |
| 51 | 142 | 19.37 |

| 52 | 108 | 14.73 |
| 53 | 109 | 14.87 |
| 54 | 76 | 10.37 |
| 55 | 68 | 9.28 |
| 56 | 34 | 4.64 |
| 57 | 29 | 3.96 |
| 58 | 15 | 2.05 |
| 59 | 7 | 0.95 |
| 60 | 6 | 0.82 |
| 61 | 4 | 0.55 |
| 62 | 1 | 0.14 |
| 63 | 1 | 0.14 |
| 64+ | 0 | 0.00 |

## OLDEST WINNERS

Mike Fetchick (63 years to the day), 1985 Hilton Head Seniors Invitational

Gary Player (62 years, 9 months, 22 days), 1998 Northville Long Island Classic

J. C. Snead (61 years, 8 months, 9 days), Greater Baltimore Classic

Jimmy Powell (61 years, 8 months, 5 days), 1996 Brickyard Crossing Championship

Bruce Crampton (61 years, 7 months, 20 days), 1997 Cadillac NFL Golf Classic

Roberto De Vicenzo (61 years, 3 months, 2 days), 1984 Merrill Lynch/*Golf Digest* Commemorative

Bob Charles (60 years, 7 months, 17 days), 1996 Hyatt Regency Maui Kaanapali Classic

Lee Trevino (60 years, 6 months, 25 days), 2000 Cadillac NFL Golf Classic

Jimmy Powell (60 years, 6 months, 9 days), 1995 First of America Classic

George Archer (60 years, 3 months, 23 days), 2000 MasterCard
    Championship
Dale Douglass (60 years, 3 months, 20 days), 1996 Bell Atlantic
    Classic
Jim Colbert (60 years, 2 days), 2001 SBC Senior Classic

## Youngest Winners

Bobby Wadkins (50 years, 10 days), 2001 Lightpath Long Island
    Classic
Gil Morgan (50 years, 11 days), 1996 Ralph's Senior Classic
George Archer (50 years, 14 days), 1989 Gatlin Brothers
    Southwest Classic
Tom Watson (50 years, 15 days), 1999 Bank One Championship
Ray Floyd (50 years, 16 days), 1992 GTE North Classic
Dale Douglass (50 years, 18 days), 1986 Vintage Invitational
Gary Player (50 years, 22 days), 1985 Quadel Seniors Classic
John Bland (50 years, 23 days), 1995 Ralphs Senior Classic
Bruce Lietzke (50 years, 25 days), 2001 3M Championship
Isao Aoki (50 years, 27 days), 1992 Nationwide Championship
Source: All data supplied by the Champions Tour.

## To Train or Not to Train

TRAINING IS THE MOST reliable way to improve a swing.
By training, you can work on core skills or changes
until they are ingrained and integrate themselves into
your swing. True success comes to those who are willing to put in the time.

# ABOUT THE AUTHOR

John MacIntyre is a prolific freelance writer and former magazine editor, whose work has appeared in magazines and journals across North America and Europe. His golf statistics column appears in *Travel and Leisure*, *Golf*, and *Tee to Green*. On good days, he shoots in the 90s.